ONE WEEK LOAN

palgrave
macmillan

D1387782

RACIAL STIGMA ON THE HOLLYWOOD SCREEN
Copyright © Brian Locke, 2009.

First published in hardcover in 2009 by PALGRAVE MACMILLAN® in the United States—a division of St. Martin's Press LLC, 175 Fifth Avenue, New York, NY 10010.

Where this book is distributed in the UK, Europe and the rest of the world, this is by Palgrave Macmillan, a division of Macmillan Publishers Limited, registered in England, company number 785998, of Houndmills, Basingstoke, Hampshire RG21 6XS.

Palgrave Macmillan is the global academic imprint of the above companies and has companies and representatives throughout the world.

Palgrave® and Macmillan® are registered trademarks in the United States, the United Kingdom, Europe and other countries.

ISBN: 978–1–137–02934–8

The Library of Congress has cataloged the hardcover edition as follows:

Locke, Brian.
   Racial stigma on the Hollywood screen from WWII to the present : the Orientalist buddy film / Brian Locke.
      p. cm.
   ISBN 978–0–230–61882–4 (alk. paper)
   1. Minorities in motion pictures. 2. Race relations in motion pictures. 3. African Americans in motion pictures. 4. Asians in motion pictures. 5. Male friendship in motion pictures. 6. Motion pictures—United States—History—20th century. I. Title.

PN1995.9.M56L63 2009
791.43′6529—dc22   2009010765

A catalogue record of the book is available from the British Library.

Design by Newgen Imaging Systems (P) Ltd., Chennai, India.

First PALGRAVE MACMILLAN paperback edition: September 2012

10 9 8 7 6 5 4 3 2 1

Printed and bound in Great Britain by
CPI Antony Rowe, Chippenham and Eastbourne

For

my parents, Diane Sumiye Locke and
James Han Locke (1942–2011),

my grandmothers, Bessie Kazuye Okada (1919–2004) and Wanda
Chin Locke (1921–2005), and

my great grandmother, Yayoi Inouye (1900–1988).

Contents

Figures

All reproductions courtesy of Photofest

Acknowledgments

This is going to be an embarrassingly long list. It's an embarrassment of riches, now that I think about it. First, I want to recognize a number of people who have been incredibly generous to me and have provided invaluable support during the writing of this book, which, aside from my personality, has been my longest-running project to date: Leslie Bow, the late Gillian Brown, Johnnella Butler, Lewis Gordon, Howard Horwitz, Christina Klein, Rudy Locke, Claude-R. Malary, Stacey Margolis, Ellen Rooney, and Carlo Rotella.

I am grateful to Nicole Aljoe, Chris Amirault, anonymous readers, Nancy Armstrong, Matthew Bacon, Michael Bacon, D'ana Baptiste, Holly Bays, Charles Berger, Rochelle Blanco, John Boylan, Laura Briggs, the late Bernard Bruce, Tyler Chin, Denise Davis, Thérèse De Raedt, Alex Des Forges, Maria D'Onofrio, Maran Elancheran and the rest of the team at Newgen Imaging Systems, Mary Ellerbe, Eric Espenhorst, Joan Fanning, Yvette Fields, Andy Franta, Lauren M. E. Goodlad, Diane Griffiths, Gema Guevara, Natalie Gummer, Carla Hansen, Corrinne Harol, Ed Hayslip, Renea Henry, Shannon Holt, Ni Hui, Jennifer Jang, Shawn L. Johnson, Sandra Katz, Stacey Katz, Tamara Ketabjian, Marie-Chantal Killeen, Helen Kjolby, Amanda Lashaw, Kim Lau, Bob Lee, Sharon Lee, Nettie Legters, Kristy Lilas at Palgrave Macmillan, Hubert Locke, Jason Locke, Wesley Locke, Joan Lusk, Kim Lynn, Ron Mallon, Martin Manalansan, Ron Mandelbaum at Photofest, Gina Marchetti, Cei Maslen, Alice Maurice, Barbara Maxwell, Sybil Mazor, Victor Mendoza, Erin Menut, Joe Metz, Elijah Millgram, Scott Moore, Haruko Moriyasu, James Morone, Fatima Mujcinovic, Ilia M. Rodriguez Nazario, Lee Norton at Palgrave Macmillan, Kent Ono, Yoon Pak, Crystal Parikh, Dana Patterson, Anna Pegler-Gordon, Patty Picha, John Reed, Todd Reeser, David Roediger, Monique Roelofs, Wilfred Samuels, Eleuterio Santiago-Díaz, David F. Schmitz, Brigitte Shull at Palgrave Macmillan, Susan Smulyan, Rachel Starbuck, Edward "Ted" Stein, Judy Stein, Kathryn Stockton, Stephen L. Thompson, Jennifer Ting,

Sasha Torres, Kim Warren, John Watrous, Shawn Wong, Yutian Wong, Mari Yoshihara, Daniel Youd, and Natasha Zaretsky for sharing with me one or some combination of the following: constructive criticism of my research or my teaching or both, food, friendship, love, professional advice, professional opportunities, research material, and yoga instruction.

I thank the Asian American Studies Program at the University of Illinois, Urbana-Champaign for granting me a year-long research fellowship and the American Civilization Department at Brown University for giving me the freedom to roam across the curriculum and design my own program of study.

Introduction

Three's a Crowd: *Crash* (2005)

It is always possible to bind together a considerable number of people in love, so long as there are other people left over to receive the manifestations of their aggressiveness.

—*Sigmund Freud*, Civilization and Its Discontents[1]

And the goat shall bear upon him all their iniquities unto a land not inhabited.

—*Leviticus 16:22*

Crash (2005), Paul Haggis's account of racial intolerance in Los Angeles, stages a seemingly intractable conflict between white and black. The tension starts with a scenario of white racism familiar to most contemporary American audiences: an incident at a traffic stop. John Ryan (Matt Dillon), a working-class LA policeman, pulls over a young professional black couple, Christine and Cameron Thayer (Thandie Newman and Terrence Howard), ostensibly for a moving violation. While the husband looks on helplessly, the cop submits the wife to a body search, which she will characterize later as a "finger fuck." Ryan pins the black woman against the couple's car, first putting his hand between her legs, and then running his fingers slowly toward her crotch. The white policeman's prurience aligns him with a common trope of the American slave narrative: the white plantation master who uses his black female slaves for sexual satisfaction.

The film establishes hostility between white and black only to resolve it by pitting them against a common threat. While on patrol, Officer Ryan finds Christine trapped in her vehicle, crumpled and upside down in the road, the result of a collision with another car. When he climbs into the cramped interior to free her, Christine rejects Ryan's help, a delay that endangers both of them. But when she sees gasoline splashing down the chassis and the other vehicle burning nearby, she stops fighting him. Working together, they extricate themselves just before the car explodes in a gigantic orange ball of flames. The scene leaves white and black, former antagonists, bonded. Forced to transcend their racial differences in the face of mutual destruction, they acknowledge their shared humanity with a loving embrace, her forehead to his cheek.

The intimate physical contact between these two figures who represent the dominant white and black binary of contemporary American racial discourse demonstrates the opening scene's meditation on what it means to be human. Driving to the scene of a crime, an African American homicide detective, Graham Waters (Don Cheadle), has a revelation that he connects to the city's car culture. "It's the sense of touch," he muses. "In LA nobody touches you.... We're always behind this metal and glass," he says. "We miss that touch so much that we crash into each other just so we can feel something." As we learn over the course of the film, the car is a metaphor for racial stereotyping.

Figure 0.1   Christine (Thandie Newman) and Officer Ryan (Matt Dillon) embrace in *Crash*.

Graham likens a racial stereotype to a car's exterior, the hard shell of metal and glass that both protects, but, like a prison, also isolates us from the rest of the world.

One can gloss the film as a series of interwoven vignettes, each addressing a different part of Los Angeles's vast racial and ethnic diversity. Each of these story lines, however, conveys the same message about why stereotypes are harmful. Ensconced in our beliefs that deny the salient differences that make us unique, we misidentify others, engendering distrust, fragmenting the human family. A white gun shop owner blames an innocent Iranian man (Shaun Toub) for 9/11 terrorism. Himself a shopkeeper, the Iranian wrongly accuses a Latino locksmith (Michael Peña) of cheating him, a charge that leads both of them to the brink of disaster. On the locksmith's next job, a white woman named Jean (Sandra Bullock) repeatedly refers to him as a "gangbanger," again incorrectly. Jean's white husband, the LA District Attorney (Brendan Fraser), assumes an Arab in the local news is black, misled by the Middle Easterner's dark skin. The African American Graham mistakes his own partner, a detective named Ria (Jennifer Esposito), as Mexican when, in fact, she is the issue of a Puerto Rican father and a Salvadoran mother. For her part, Ria thinks that all Asians are bad drivers.

Many of the vignettes replicate Officer Ryan's movement from the brutal to the benevolent by counterbalancing racism with its opposites, kindness and generosity, which shows that people are a mix of both bad and good. Graham may insult Ria's ancestry with a cruel remark, for example, but later we find that he is a loving son to his incapacitated mother. Another African American figure, a young car thief named Anthony (Chris "Ludacris" Bridges), refers to every Asian man as a "Chinaman," regardless of ethnicity. The film's ending, however, surprises us when Anthony frees a group of slaves smuggled into the country from Southeast Asia. Ryan's white partner, Officer Tom Hanson (Ryan Phillippe), undergoes a similar reversal of character. Though he goes in the other direction, moving from nonracist to racist action. At great risk to himself, Hanson saves the life of a black man while policing the streets, but on his way home from work, he shoots an African American hitchhiker (Larenz Tate), the murder triggered by the cop's fear of black men. As *New York Magazine*'s film reviewer David Edelstein remarks of Ryan and Hanson, "When you scratch a vicious racist you get a caring human, but when you push a caring human, you can get a vicious racist."[2]

Such multidimensional characterizations illustrate another of the film's iterations of what it means to be human. In *Crash*, psychological complexity marks us as human. Nearly all the film's principal characters reveal a broad range of emotions and desires, many of which are conflicting. The movie is "about the fact that we all embody great contradictions," the director Haggis explains. "You never know which way a character's going to turn."[3] These dramatic reversals of character lie at "the core of what's happening in *Crash*," according to Matt Dillon. "A lot of the characters," he explains, "have this arc where they come to this realization of who they are and there's some sort of epiphany or this change that comes over them."[4] The same car crash that prompts Ryan's humane and brave act makes Christine realize that she should stop blaming her husband, whom she had derided earlier as an "Uncle Tom," for failing to prevent Ryan from molesting her. In another example, Jean does not trust Latinos, but eventually she acknowledges that, in a time of need, her Latina maid (Yomi Perry) is more reliable than all of her rich white friends.

Experiencing an epiphany redeems the humanity of the central characters, most of whom are white or black. Unadulterated racism, however, does not disappear entirely from the film. *Crash*'s Asian figures, an elderly Korean couple (Alexis Rhee and Greg Joung Paik), are absolute racists. After rear-ending the detective Ria's car, the wife utters the movie's first stereotypical remark when she assumes that Ria is an illegal Mexican immigrant. The film's representation of the husband takes an even less favorable turn. As with Officer Ryan, the film associates the Korean man with an icon of American racism: the slave trader. In one scene, the husband arranges to sell his cargo, the aforementioned Southeast Asians, to another Korean man (Daniel Dae Kim). The mundane tone of their brief conversation makes us think that they discuss the disposition of things rather than of human beings. "It's good doing business with you," the husband smiles as he takes his payment. "How soon can I have them?" asks the buyer, impatient to get his goods. "I'm picking them up right now," the husband replies. The Korean men strike a deal, but the buyer never gets his slaves, who are chained together in the back of a van. While delivering the slaves, the husband has an accident, putting him in the hospital and the van in the possession of Anthony, the car thief. When the Korean slaver's wife finds her husband in intensive care, his immediate response to her shows his greed and callousness. Referring to the buyer's check, the husband urges his wife to "cash it right away," before the buyer realizes that something has gone wrong.

Unlike the white characters, such as Matt Dillon's Officer Ryan, whose dose of decent behavior goes a long way toward cleansing his stain of racial intolerance, none of *Crash*'s Asian figures undergoes the kind of change that would redeem or complicate their roles.[5] If a dramatic reversal of character signals humanity, the film reinforces its sense of what it means to be human by providing a foil whose one-dimensionality stands in stark contrast to the figures whose multidimensionality marks them as human. Ultimately, the film defines the Asian figures by the single attribute of racism. In effect, *Crash* vilifies the Asians as being more racist toward black people than are the white characters in the diegesis, transferring the stigma of American racism from white to yellow.

Achieving widespread acclaim as the Academy Award winner for best picture of 2005, *Crash* combines the lofty liberal intention of white and black reconciliation with the vilification of Asians. Thus, it serves as a good introduction to what I call the Orientalist buddy film.[6] The films of this wholly unexamined category present a narrative that revolves around the relationship between two figures, one white and the other black.[7] Initially, the two buddies hate each other because of racial difference. By the movie's end, however, white and black form a more perfect union by facing a mutual threat that the film codes as Asian.

The present study charts the evolution of the Orientalist buddy film from, roughly, the WWII era to the end of the millennium. It argues that movies of this type represent race relations in the United States in a triangulated form to create an illusory unity between former white master and former black slave, ameliorating the long-standing contradiction between the nation's democratic ideals and white America's persistent domination over black people. By portraying the Asian as an abject figure, a monstrously inhumane character (or an actual non-human, an extraterrestrial, in the case of some science fiction films) who lacks the core values that define personhood, the Orientalist buddy film dissolves the differences between white and black so that the two buddies may emphasize what they share and diffuse tensions between them.

My identification of a trope that bonds two rivals at the expense of a third, of course, has its precursors. René Girard calls it the "scapegoat effect...[the] strange process through which two or more people are reconciled at the expense of a third party...[who] appears guilty or responsible for whatever ails, disturbs, or frightens the scapegoaters." Once "relieved of their tensions," Girard continues, the other two "coalesce into a more harmonious group" united under "a single purpose, which is to prevent the scapegoat from harming them, by expelling and destroying him."[8] Eve Sedgwick's analysis of the scapegoat mirrors that of Girard, but pivots on the axis of gender, analyzing the representation of the woman who functions as a "solvent" between two male figures in a narrative. "In the presence of a woman who can be seen as pitiable or contemptible," she writes, "men are able to exchange power and confirm each other's value even in the context of the remaining inequalities in their power."[9]

Robyn Wiegman employs a similar triangle to analyze Hollywood's representation of race, showing how a third party serves as a catalyst for a false reconciliation between white and black. Her study of 1980s white and black buddy films, which she calls "interracial male bonding narratives," argues that portraying some third figure as more racist than the white buddy enables white America to disavow, rather than eradicate, its chronic mistreatment of black America. Such a film reproduces white supremacy by " 'proving' U.S. cultural equality [through] the displacement of U.S. racial history and politics" onto a foil to the white male lead who represents mainstream white America. "The representation of a seemingly more extreme racism and oppression," existing somewhere else or practiced by somebody else, Wiegman writes, produces "a disavowal of internal racial hierarchies" by implying that American racism exists solely "as part of an errant past" or at the extremes of white society.[10]

In addition to showing how easily the Asian fits into a racial representation that vilifies a third term, my analysis shows how such a narrative shapes the possibilities for the Asian subject with respect to American identity. Because the white and the black buddies bond on their common status as Americans, the Orientalist buddy film's degradation of the Asian must include an emphasis on the third party's status as a foreigner, a non-American. *Crash*'s Asian husband and wife, for example, speak to one another in Korean, a tidbit that indicates foreign birth. After rear-ending the Latina detective's car, the wife offers her diagnosis of what went wrong. "Mexicans no know how to drive," she yells, using the poor grammar of a rank newcomer, "she 'blake' too fast." She cannot distinguish between the spoken *l* and *r*, a common phonetic problem for native speakers of East Asian languages. Thus, her mispronunciation of *brake* underscores her status as both an Asian and an alien.

Historically, Asian American Studies scholarship has constructed the field in large part on this topic of Asian exclusion from representations of American identity. A good portion of both early and recent key works, for example, registers the persistence with which American mainstream culture represents citizens of Asian ancestry as foreigners.[11] "A national memory haunts the conception of the Asian American," Lisa Lowe writes in her 1996 *Immigrant Acts: On Asian American Cultural Politics*, "persisting beyond the repeal of actual laws prohibiting Asians from citizenship and sustained by the wars in Asia....The Asian is always seen as an immigrant, as 'the foreigner-within' even when born in the United States and the descendant of generations born here before."[12] Robert G. Lee's 1999 *Orientals: Asian Americans in Popular Culture* conveys the same idea with an anecdote of an encounter in which a "silver-haired Caucasian gentleman" refuses to believe that a group of Asian American scholars in a San Diego restaurant are not tourists from Asia.[13] "The label *Chinaman*," Karen Shimakawa writes in her 2002 *National Abjection: The Asian American Body Onstage*, "marked Chinese Americans as fundamentally different from (and inferior to) a 'norm,' as politically and biologically not-'American.'" The label persists, Shimakawa observes, "despite the fact that by the [start of the twentieth] century 118,000 Chinese Americans lived and worked in the United States, establishing businesses, communities, institutions, and families here, much like every other immigrant group before and since."[14]

These important texts focus to varying degrees on the status of the Asian or Asian American subject in relation to national identity. Lee places in historical context representations that equate "the Asian with alien" (ix) in American popular culture from the mid-nineteenth to the late-twentieth centuries. Lowe argues that the Asian acts as a foil for the generic national subject, which in turn produces the Asian as foreigner stereotype. "The American *citizen*," Lowe writes, "has been defined over against the Asian [as] immigrant, legally, economically, and culturally" (4; emphasis in the original). Shimakawa extends Lowe's insight through psychoanalysis, arguing that American identity relies on the degradation of the Asian American. "Asian Americanness," she writes, "functions as *abject* in relation to Americanness" (3; emphasis in original). Borrowing Julia Kristeva's formulation, Shimakawa tells us why dominant American culture tends to represent the Asian American as foreign. She reasons that the Asian abject "is simply a frontier," possessing "only one quality of the object—that of being opposed to" American identity (3). "Asian Americanness thus occupies a role both necessary to and mutually constitutive of national subject formation," Shimakawa continues, *"but it does not result in the formation of an Asian American subject or even an Asian American object"* (3; emphasis in original).

This significant scholarship identifies the problem that structures the field of Asian American Studies, but it never explains why American popular culture recruits the Asian so often to play the role of the foreigner in the first place. In the case of Lee, Lowe, and Shimakawa, the exclusion of the African American experience from the analysis may explain the inability to get at the root of the issue. Their three books focus on the relationship between the Asian American subject and a conception of America figured as white, thus restricting their analyses to the binary of white and yellow, despite the fact that the fraught history of European American exploitation of Africans or African Americans has framed racial discourse for the better part of the national past. Lee, for example, cites a 1997 *National Review* cartoon about the Democratic Party's Chinese fund-raising scandal as exemplifying the sort of representation that alienates the Asian. The depiction dresses Bill and Hillary Clinton and Al Gore in stereotypical Asian garb. "Yellowface," Lee observes, "sharply defines the Oriental in a racial opposition to whiteness" (2). "The project of imagining the nation as homogeneous," Lowe remarks, "requires the orientalist construction of cultures and geographies from which Asian immigrants come as fundamentally 'foreign' origins antipathetic to the modern American society that 'discovers,' 'welcomes,' and 'domesticates' them" (5). *Homogeneous* evokes the nation's numerous efforts to maintain white supremacy. *Orientalist* refers to Edward Said's critical term for the one-dimensional "Eastern," in this case Asian, figure that acts as a foil for the multidimensional "Western" or white figure. "*Asian American*," writes Shimakawa, "is a category both produced through and in reaction to abjection within and by dominant U.S. culture," by which she means white U.S. culture (2; emphasis in original).[15]

This scholarship correctly insists that Asian American abjection defines the generic American subject through contrast. But analysis that restricts itself to a white and Asian binary overlooks the relationship between the figure of the Asian and the dominant binary that structures the U.S. racial discourse, what Linda Williams calls the "black and white racial melodrama."[16] As a result, even though these books have made important contributions to Asian American Studies, they cannot address the question of why post-WWII American popular culture so often chooses an Asian figure to signify the foreigner, even though, as Shimakawa points out, significant numbers of Asians have lived in the United States for well over one hundred years.

The present study is not the first to claim that the question of Asian American subjectivity depends in part on where we are located in the dominant white-black schema.[17] A groundbreaking comparative study of race, Claire Jean Kim's 2000 *Bitter Fruit: The Politics of Black-Korean Conflict in New York City* analyzes an aspect of the 1990s Asian American experience in relation to the white and black binary. "Incoming immigrants and other groups," she writes, "get positioned relative to these two loci" of black and white.[18] "Blacks and whites," Kim writes, "constitute the major anchors (bottom and top, respectively) of" the U.S. racial hierarchy. Rather than envisioning the "racial order" as organized along a single "simple vertical hierarchy" of "A over B over C," her analysis explores the "two dimensions" of "superior/inferior" and "insider/foreigner" (16).[19] Thus, Kim describes "the racial triangulation of Asian Americans" as a process in which "White opinionmakers" simultaneously "valorize Asian Americans as superior to Blacks" through the model minority stereotype and "construct Asian Americans as permanently foreign and unassimilable" (45). But like the books by Lee, Lowe, and Shimakawa, Kim's *Bitter Fruit* takes as a given the Asian's position as foreign, thereby overlooking the question of why mainstream American culture has persisted in representing the Asian as foreign in the first instance, making the Asian American an impossible subject.

Another anecdote in Robert Lee's *Orientals* illustrates how this mutually exclusive relationship between "Asian" and "American" manifests itself on the capillary level. One of his Asian American students relates a story concerning the pervasive "assumption that Asians are indelibly alien" relative to American culture (ix). When called an "Oriental," a name that signifies exotic origin, the student's standard response registers resistance with sarcasm: "Orientals are rugs, not people" (ix). This book offers a historical account of why the connection between "Asian" and "alien" feels so permanent. It illustrates how and the extent to which the ruling white and black binary of U.S. racial discourse governs Hollywood's representation of the Asian and in turn how this representation governs the possibilities for an Asian subject.[20] The WWII era's racial politics create a need to project a narrative of unity between white America and black America, a fantasy that denies rather than resolves the long-running and ongoing practice of white supremacy. The Orientalist buddy film's depiction of bonding between white and black fulfills this longing.

Armed with this history of an obscure, at least until now, type of interracial buddy film, the reader will have a key to interpret the

wide variety of movies (and other cultural texts) that offer to dif-
fering degrees a white and black dyad confronting Asian perfidy.
Making a brief appearance during a futuristic blood-sport match in
Rollerball (Norman Jewison, 1975), for example, a robotic Japanese
team skates in precise formation against a salt-and-pepper American
one led by James Caan. In *Platoon* (Oliver Stone, 1986), white and
black soldiers vow to take revenge on the Vietnamese communists
who have lynched one of their African American brothers-in-arms.
In *Forrest Gump* (Robert Zemeckis, 1994), Tom Hanks and a mor-
tally wounded Mykelti Williamson pledge eternal brotherhood in a
Vietnamese jungle. In *Star Wars: Episode I: The Phantom Menace*
(George Lucas, 1999), several white Jedi knights and a token Samuel
L. Jackson deploy "the Force" against alien rulers with unmistak-
able "Oriental" accents. In *The Family Man* (Brett Ratner, 2000),
Nicholas Cage and Don Cheadle begin their eternal friendship over
an argument with an immigrant Asian grocery clerk. In *Die Another
Day* (Lee Tamahori, 2002), Pierce Brosnan and a well-armed Halle
Berry battle Korean communists who build a doomsday machine that
harnesses the power of the sun.

   This book has six chapters. Chapter 1 analyzes Tay Garnett's 1943
WWII combat film, *Bataan*, an important precursor to the Orientalist
buddy film that pits white and black Americans against Japanese
forces who have invaded the Philippines. *Bataan* exhibits two distinct tropes that subsequent movies will fuse into the white and black
buddy portion of the Orientalist buddy film. Two white men begin
the film as enemies, but eventually they bond in the face of the common foe. This standard version of the buddy dyad—what Ed Guerrero
calls the "white male" buddy movie—covers nearly the entire history
of film from, for example, *What Price Glory?* (Raoul Walsh, 1926) to
Mississippi Burning (Alan Parker, 1988) and beyond.[21] In addition to
the buddy dyad that drives the narrative, the film includes, for the first
time in Hollywood history, a sympathetic black American character
as part of its combat unit. Even though the American military did not
desegregate until well after WWII, *Bataan*'s black soldier appears in
a few key scenes in response to the era's emphasis on building a façade
of national racial unity.

   Chapter 2 addresses the Cold War era, showing how three more
combat movies—*China Gate* (Samuel Fuller, 1957), *Pork Chop Hill*
(Lewis Milestone, 1959), and *All the Young Men* (Hall Bartlett,
1960)—repeat *Bataan*'s triangulation of race in response to the same
need to mend, at least cinematically, the gap between American

democratic theory and practice as it relates to race. Like the WWII war movie of the previous chapter, these films include a lone black figure as part of a mostly white combat team, which they set against an Asian communist enemy. The chapter focuses on the relationship between the black figure and the buddy dyad that propels the narrative. In *Bataan*, two white male characters constitute the buddy dyad. With a change that reflects the American military's desegregation of 1948, however, these three war movies incorporate the black soldier into the buddy dyad, putting racial tension, and eventually the transcendence of that tension, at the center of the story. By promoting blackness from a token to a central role, the movies depict the reconciliation of two men, one white and the other black, in the face of an Asian threat, making them three of Hollywood's earliest Orientalist buddy films.

Chapter 3 sharpens my profile of the Orientalist buddy film by analyzing what I call the Blaxploitation buddy film, a derivative of the standard Blaxploitation genre that surfaced in the wake of the civil rights movement and Hollywood's financial crisis of the early 1970s. Al Adamson's *The Dynamite Brothers* (1974), Chuck Bail's *Cleopatra Jones and the Casino of Gold* (1975), Cirio Santiago's *TNT Jackson* (1975), and Chih Chen's *Way of the Black Dragon* (1978) repeat the triangle of an interracial buddy dyad set against a common enemy. Instead of the formula of white and black buddies fighting an Asian threat, however, the political and cultural solidarity between African American and various Asian and Asian American groups generated by black America's push for equality at home and an unpopular war in Southeast Asia forces a reconfiguration of the Orientalist buddy film's racial assignments, such that black and yellow buddies bond in the face of a racist white villain. Thus, in the Blaxploitation buddy film, the racist villain who functions as the scapegoat, the one who bears the stigma of America's racism toward black people, is white instead of Asian.

Chapter 4 focuses on *Flash Gordon* (Mike Hodges, 1980), the *Lethal Weapon* series (Richard Donner, 1987–1998), and *Rising Sun* (Philip Kaufman, 1993) to illustrate how the Orientalist buddy film evolves near the end of the century. *Rising Sun* repeats several key aspects of the previous chapters' movies. Like the Cold War era combat films in chapter 2, it features a white and black dyad, two men who distrust each other initially but eventually bond in the face of a common Asian threat. Like *All the Young Men* and the WWII era *Bataan*, *Rising Sun* represents that enemy as even more racist against

African Americans than the white characters in the diegesis, thereby transferring onto the Asian the stigma of white America's history of racism toward African Americans. In other words, the common Asian foe to both white and black functions as a scapegoat. The film registers the historical particularities of its time by changing its representation of the Asian enemy to reflect the widespread paranoia in the United States during the 1980s and 1990s of a Japanese industrial conquest. *Rising Sun* resurrects *Bataan*'s WWII enemy by depicting the mutual threat to white and black Americans as yet another invading samurai force. But rather than a military peril of sword-wielding soldiers, the film represents its villain as an economic one, an army of model minority businessmen who work for a wealthy Nipponese multinational corporation.

Chapter 5 argues that Sir Ridley Scott's science fiction classic *Blade Runner* (initially released in 1982 and rereleased in 1992 and 2007) fits the Orientalist buddy film formula as I have characterized it, even though the film contains no black bodies. The film depicts a bonding between two men against the backdrop of an Asian cultural and economic invasion of Los Angeles. The movie's absence of black actors, however, seems to disqualify it as an example of the trope as I have defined it. The chapter shows that, instead of using actual black bodies, the film codes one of its two white male leads, the rogue replicant Roy Batty, as black by making him a slave. In the post–civil-rights era, more often than not Hollywood films disguise their use of race, signifying it indirectly through metaphor rather than directly through bodies that conform to our traditional notions of biological race. Important critics such as Toni Morrison ("race as metaphor"), Michael Omi and Howard Winant (race as "code words" or "race in disguise"), Stuart Hall ("inferential racism"), Tali Mendelberg ("implicit racial appeals"), Claire Jean Kim ("color blind talk"), and John Fiske ("nonracist racism") exhort us to pay particular attention to the metaphorical deployment of race.[22] In the post–civil-rights period of "equality," white supremacy persists largely by means of racial metaphor despite the disappearance of older forms of de jure racism.

Chapter 6 argues that, like *Blade Runner*, Andy and Larry Wachowski's popular science fiction film *The Matrix* (1999) advances the project of the Orientalist buddy film by signaling race, in particular the Asian, indirectly through metaphor. The movie's computer-generated villains are racially ambiguous signs. White actors fill the villain roles, but, in a form of rhetorical recycling, the film represents them according to the formulas of the WWII yellow peril Japanese enemy and the 1960s Asian model minority. This multivalence enables the film tacitly to scapegoat Asians for white mistreatment of black Americans, in particular, the 1991 Rodney King beating and the subsequent acquittal of his LA police assailants in 1992.

As I outline above and explain in greater detail in the pages that follow, the Orientalist buddy film dictates the evacuation of the yellow image from national identity and scapegoats the Asian for white America's mistreatment of black people. At the very least, the Orientalist buddy film's production of a racist Asian subject rings an ironic tone for an Asian American Studies scholar. As other books emphasize, based on our nonwhite status, we share with other racial groups a legacy of mistreatment, both individual and institutional, at the hands of whites. White America has, among other things, barred Asians from naturalization and from immigration, exploited us as cheap labor, forced us to live in segregated areas, and interned some of us during WWII. Because Asian Americans comprise only 3.6 percent of the total population of the United States, according to the 2000 census,[23] as a group, neither Asians nor Asian Americans have ever held institutional power in this country. Thus, we can claim no record of institutional discrimination against African Americans. To quote Muhammad Ali, one black man reviled in the 1960s but beloved in the 1990s, "No Vietcong ever called me nigger."[24] As this book demonstrates, post-WWII Hollywood does its part to reverse the charge of Ali's civil-rights era claim by repeatedly blaming Asians for the racism that white America disavows.

Strange Fruit: *Bataan* (1943)

A young Negro, about to be inducted into the Army, said, "Just carve on my tomb-stone, 'Here lies a black man killed fighting a yellow man for the protection of a white man.'"

—*Gunnar Myrdal*, An American Dilemma: The Negro Problem and Modern Democracy[1]

Tay Garnett's 1943 WWII combat film *Bataan* cites the 1942 Japanese surprise invasion of the Philippines with its opening shot: an image of the enemy's flag ascending high atop a flagpole while the sound-track trumpets an ominous refrain. A dramatization of the United States' ill-fated struggle to repel the invasion, the film tells the story of how a hastily formed patrol of thirteen soldiers who, as the film tells us, have "never served together before" bond into a coherent fighting unit under enemy fire. Each of the men has volunteered for a rearguard suicide mission to delay what the crawl calls "the wave of barbaric conquest" while the combined American and Filipino main body retreats down the Bataan peninsula to the southern island of Corregidor. "General MacArthur," says one soldier, "needs time to organize and consolidate down below." Eventually, the larger and better-equipped Japanese force surrounds the isolated patrol, killing the men one by one in a grim decimation of the ranks.

The film quickly establishes the Japanese invaders as an especially formidable foe. Captain Lassiter (Lee Bowman), the leader of the unit, falls first when a sniper's bullet hits him in the head. As the second in command, the tough Sergeant Bill Dane (Robert Taylor), attends to the fallen leader, another bullet narrowly misses his head.

The hidden killer's lethal accuracy prompts Dane to characterize the Japanese as an especially formidable foe, a strange mix of the sub- and superhuman whom they underestimate at their own peril. "Listen you guys," warns Dane, the captain's death "was no accident!" "Those no-tailed baboons out there are *ichiban jozu*," he bellows, "number one skillful." "They climb trees better than monkeys," he continues, "got the best trees marked on their maps."

Dane stresses the difference between themselves and the invaders. "They can live and fight for a month," he says, "on what wouldn't last one of you guys two days." Dane's description of the foreign force mirrors much older instances of what we would call the yellow peril, which Gina Marchetti defines as "the belief that the West will be overpowered and enveloped by the irresistible, dark, occult forces of the East."[2] In a 1275 description, for example, the Venetian Marco Polo characterizes Genghis Khan's Mongol soldiers as simultaneously subhuman and superhuman. "Their disposition is cruel," he writes. "They are capable of supporting every kind of privation....Perfectly obedient to their chiefs...[and] maintained at small expense." He continues, they are "fitted to subdue the world."[3] Many years after WWII, at least one critic of Vietnam combat films would coin the template as "the Asian super-soldier stereotype," describing Hollywood's representation of the North Vietnamese communist army as a "yellow horde" exhibiting "extraordinary endurance and power."[4]

This chapter considers the role that the white and black binary of American racial discourse plays in the WWII era's cinematic degradation of the Asian. Adjusting to a wartime context that forced white Americans to reassess their stance toward black people, *Bataan* rewrote the respective relationships of the black and the Asian to the white norm. For the first time in Hollywood history and five years before President Harry Truman integrated the military, the film features a black American soldier who stands as a moral equal to the white ones in the diegesis. The film's white and black characters, in turn, bond through the common trait of "American," defined by the yellow peril's un-American essence. Adding a new layer of meaning to the yellow peril stereotype to tailor it to the racial politics of the time, *Bataan* presents the Asian as the true culprit of bigotry, displacing the stigma of American racism from white onto yellow.

Predictably, after America's declaration of war, the sense of the Japanese as a yellow peril prompted many prominent Americans to represent the United States as a unified front. Shortly after the start of the war, for example, the Republican National Committee (RNC) chair delivered a radio address entitled "130,000,000 Free People Working in Unison and without Partisan Lines." "When the Japanese so treacherously and savagely struck at Pearl Harbor," declared the congressman, they created "a strong unity [that] binds the men and women of this nation of every race, color, religious and political belief into one resistless onsweeping determination [to protect] the ideals which make life in America beautiful and worthwhile."[5] In a 1942 speech, President Franklin Roosevelt echoed the RNC chair's sentiment that antagonisms between individual Americans or between American groups ought to disappear when threatened by a formidable foreign foe. "The times do certainly render it incumbent on all good citizens," Roosevelt said, quoting a Thomas Jefferson speech delivered just before the War of 1812, "to bury in oblivion all internal differences and rally around the standard of their country."[6]

Responding to the wartime desire for domestic unity, *Bataan*'s patrol, which Captain Lassiter describes initially as "a mixed crew," stands as the film's trope for Roosevelt's "internal differences." The volunteers come from different branches of the armed forces: Army, Navy, Air Force, and National Guard. They have different military classifications: tank corps, engineering, medical, and the motor pool. One is a cynical veteran of many battles, another a naïve newcomer. They are international: American and Filipino. The Americans hail from different regions of the United States, including rural Kansas and urban California. They represent different economic classes. The lone officer graduated from West Point; another soldier worked as a mechanic prior to the war. They have different religious beliefs: Protestant, Catholic, and Jewish. The non-WASP whites represent different ethnic groups: Polish, Jewish, and Irish. They are racially mixed: white, black, Latino, and Filipino. According to Jeanine Basinger, *Bataan*'s "mixed" team constitutes an early cinematic symbol of the "American melting pot," which helps to qualify it as "the seminal film of the formation of the [WWII combat] genre."[7]

To repulse the much larger and better-equipped Japanese force, the film's hastily formed patrol must bond into a coherent fighting unit by overcoming the numerous social differences that, outside of wartime circumstances, would likely divide them. The hand-to-hand combat sequence near the film's end stages Roosevelt's plea for Americans to "rally around the standard of their country." As the Japanese creep up to the heroes' encampment, the remaining soldiers—a black, a Jew, and three WASPs—show their team discipline by waiting to fire until they get close enough to see the faces of the enemy. Several shots

Figure 1.1 *Bataan*'s Sergeant Bill Dane (Robert Taylor) addresses his combat team: actors left to right, Lloyd Nolan, Thomas Mitchell, Tom Dugan, Barry Nelson, Kenneth Spencer, Desi Arnaz, Phillip Terry, Alex Havier, and Robert Walker.

depict the men helping each other in battle, cooperation that serves as proof that the men have bonded. Then the volunteers scramble in different directions to meet the enemy on their own. The rest of the sequence features a series of scenes that follow each patrol member on a solo run against the Japanese. Each man displays his courage and fighting skill by single-handedly killing multiple enemy soldiers. After beating the larger Japanese force into retreat, the survivors crawl back to the foxhole to reassemble as a unit.

Bataan reproduced Roosevelt's unity formula so faithfully it prompted Walter White of the National Association for the Advancement of Colored People (NAACP) to comment that the film "shows how superfluous racial…problems are when common danger is faced."[8] Contrary to White, Roosevelt's pleas for domestic unity saw no color distinctions. "In time of crisis when the future is in the balance," he intoned in a February 1942 radio broadcast, "we come to understand, with full recognition and devotion, what this nation is and what we owe to it."[9] By *we*, Roosevelt meant undoubtedly all

Americans, regardless of race. However, many nonwhite citizens at the time—African Americans in particular—had a much different sense about what they owed the United States.

By WWII, most African Americans knew that the nation had never managed to translate what the Republican Party chair called America's "beautiful and worthwhile" ideals into practice for them. Because whites as a group had produced such a paltry fund of social capital with blacks, Roosevelt, as the executive in chief, sometimes incited an angry response from blacks. Published in *The Crisis*, the NAACP's official journal, shortly after white mobs killed twenty-five blacks in a 1943 Detroit race riot, the following poem by Pauli Murray illustrates the bitterness many blacks felt toward white America.

> What'd you get when the police shot you in the back,
> And they chained you to the beds
> While they wiped the blood off?
> What'd you get when you cried out to the Top Man?
> When you called the man next to God, as you thought,
> And you asked him to speak out to save you?
> What'd the Top Man say, black boy?
> Mr. Roosevelt Regrets....[10]

Judging from her poem's tone, if Mr. Roosevelt had posed the questions of "what this nation is, and what we owe to it" directly to Ms. Murray, her answers would probably have disappointed the president. In a federal government poll designed to measure the effect of black anger on the war effort, an interviewer asked Harlem residents the following: Is it "more important right now to beat Germany and Japan or to make democracy work at home[?]" Fifty percent of the Harlem residents agreed; 38 percent prioritized domestic democracy, a reference to the black struggle against white America for civil rights; and 11 percent could not decide. By contrast, another poll that posed the same question to poor whites yielded a 90 percent agreement. Only 5 percent preferred equality at home. Another survey taken shortly after the start of the war reported "formidable evidence" that "racial grievances have kept Negroes from an all-out participation in the war effort."[11]

The long history of white mistreatment of blacks posed a problem for *Bataan*'s mission to tailor Roosevelt's unity plea for two different domestic racial audiences, each of which held a very different evaluation of the promise of the American Creed. On the one hand, the majority of whites still favored formal segregation. Such a stance, however, contradicted the WWII rhetoric of American democracy as the foundational ideology of the nation's foreign policy. On the other hand, black frustration due to white mistreatment had accumulated to the point that some blacks even advocated that African Americans side with the Japanese enemy on the common ground of nonwhite status. The sociologist Horace R. Cayton, for example, reported a sense of ambivalence about his allegiance. "The mighty white man was being humiliated," he writes in his autobiography, "by the little yellow bastards he had nothing but contempt for." "It gave me a sense of satisfaction," he continues, "a feeling that white wasn't always right, not able to enforce its will on everyone who was colored."[12] Writing for the Harlem-based *Amsterdam News*, Roy Wilkins put black and Japanese on the same side of the white and black divide by attributing the lack of military preparedness at Pearl Harbor "to the stupid habit of white people of looking down on all non-white nations."[13]

As a tonic for such ambivalence, the federal government began to enforce systematically the theme of national unity within the film industry in June 1942. Citing "the right of the American people and of all other peoples opposing the Axis aggressors to be truthfully informed about the common war," Roosevelt created the Office of War Information (OWI), charging the agency with "authority over dissemination of all official news and propaganda."[14] As the official intermediary between the federal government and the film industry, the OWI established a Motion Pictures Bureau (MPB) in Hollywood to aid the "industry in its endeavor to inform the American people, via the screen, of the many problems attendant on the war program."[15] Because some Hollywood films had, in the MPB's estimation, "unwittingly hindered the war effort [through] their dialogue and subject matter," the agency requested that studio chiefs "submit screen treatments and finished scenarios of all pictures" to their reviewers prior to production.[16] The MPB wanted to intervene before the studios had spent "too much money," according to OWI director Elmer Davis.[17] The Office of Censorship denied foreign distribution licenses to any script lacking MPB approval, ensuring studio compliance to OWI demands.[18]

To forestall fights over script content, in 1942 the OWI wrote the "Government Information Manual for the Motion Picture Industry" for the studios, addressing "basic information on government aims and policies in the war effort" through a long list of topics ranging from blood donation to economic inflation. The manual functioned to help the studios prepare the citizenry for war. "No amount of legislation," it reads, "will create the kind of unceasing war-mindedness that makes every man, woman, and child govern each act throughout the day with a single question: 'Will this help or hinder the war effort?'" "Words alone are frequently inadequate," the document continues. Only "motion pictures [can] effectively [provide] a graphic demonstration of the what, why, and how." The American public, it predicts, "will take their cue from what they see on the screen."[19]

The manual's emphasis on projecting racial comity supports film historian Thomas Cripps's claim that the word *unity* stood as code for *racial integration* during the WWII era.[20] The document instructs Hollywood to represent the country as "a melting pot, a nation of many races and creeds," whose citizens "have demonstrated that they can live together and progress....Discrimination between peoples because of their race, creed, or color must be abolished." To its readers, all of whom it assumes to be white, the manual said, "In this war for freedom, alien and minority" group members "fight side by side with us....Can we not portray on the screen the fact that under the democratic process the underprivileged have become less underprivileged?"[21] A military spokesman echoes the manual's dictates in a 1942 address to the studio heads. "Only military, mental, and moral unity with our allies will bring victory," he states. "To contribute by any act or word toward the increase of misunderstanding, suspicion, and tension between peoples of different racial or national origin in this country is to help the enemy!"[22]

Despite dictates from Washington, white racism toward blacks persisted into the war years, casting doubt on America's commitment to democratic values. Japanese radio broadcasts used the 1942 Cleo Wright lynching to tell East Indians what to expect if the Allied countries won the war.[23] According to a *New York Times* account, a white Missouri mob "dragged [Wright] through the Negro district," then, in front of a crowd of 300, "set the body afire."[24] Shortly after the Wright lynching, white Mississippi mobs lynched three black men in the space of a week. The widely reported events made the United States appear hypocritical. "In the eye of unfriendly foreigners," a *New York Times* editorial reads, "the State of Mississippi, and with it the United States, must stand condemned as not practicing what our spokesmen preach."[25] That same year, Pearl S. Buck advised that, because Japan uses "that most vulnerable point in our American democracy, our racial prejudice, as her weapon," strategy if not morality dictated that

white America eradicate its racist ways. "Our most numerous allies
in the war against the Axis," Buck reminded a New York audience,
"are in the Far East....Japanese propaganda [repeats] in a thousand
forms [that] the colored peoples" of Asia should possess "no hope of
justice and equality from the white peoples because of their unalter-
able racial prejudice."[26]

Perhaps the persistence of white racism owed something to
Roosevelt's profound ambivalence regarding black civil rights. In
a 1933 radio address, he called lynching "a vile form of collective
murder," yet in 1935, he refused to endorse widely supported federal
legislation to ban it.[27] He felt that he could not take any significant
legislative strides toward black civil rights because he needed votes
from the southern wing of his party for his New Deal projects.[28] "If
I come out for the [Costigan-Wagner] antilynching bill," the president reasoned, the southern Democrats "will block every bill I ask
Congress to pass to keep America from collapsing."[29] Roosevelt sur-
mised, correctly, that the majority of Americans feared the prospect
of black advancement. A 1943 OWI poll, for example, reported that
"whites overwhelmingly endorse segregation," noting a particular
aversion to mixed-race dining: 99 percent of southern whites and
70 percent of northern whites favored Jim Crow for restaurants.[30]
Thus, as the historian Harvard Sitkoff notes, a "liberal interracialism
[that] all too easily accepted the appearance of racial peace for the
reality of racial justice" defeated a more comprehensive agenda for
black equality.[31]

Hollywood picked up the gauntlet that Roosevelt felt he could
not. Prior to WWII, the industry typically represented blackness as a
degraded form of humanity. In a 1943 essay entitled "Is Hollywood
Fair to Negroes?" Langston Hughes writes, "For a generation now, the
Negro has been maligned, caricatured, and led about on the American
screen....To judge from the Hollywood [representation] nobody
would think there was an educated, well-groomed, self-respecting
Negro in America."[32] "The usual Hollywood concept of the Negro
[and] the tolerance of the color line in pictures [constitute] a grave
social abuse," writes Bosley Crowther in 1943. Hollywood shows the
Negro as either "a bowing and scraping menial," the *New York Times*
reviewer continues or a "Sambo designed mainly to tickle the white
folks with his japes."[33] "All we ask," said Lena Horne in 1943, "is that
the Negro be portrayed as a normal person."[34] During the NAACP's
1942 annual conference hosted by Daryl Zanuck and Walter Wanger
on the Twentieth-Century Fox lot, Walter White "urged Hollywood

to have courage enough to shake off its fears and taboos...to depict the Negro [as] an integral part of the life of America."[35] "The program of casting colored persons in more normal roles," Zanuck responded, will "be put into effect at an early date." "We will definitely portray the colored," Jack Warner pledged, "the same as any other human being is portrayed."[36]

Among Hollywood WWII combat films, *Bataan* (along with Archie Mayo's 1943 *Crash Dive*) responded first to the manual's command by including a black character in the American fold. Engineer Corps private Wesley Epps was played by the singer-turned-actor Kenneth Spencer.[37] "Wanting to break the color barrier in American war films," says Dore Schary, then MGM's production chief, "I cast one of the soldiers as a black."[38] "It really was inaccurate," he says, "because there were no combat solders who were black" in 1943.[39] Schary had anticipated criticism, but to his credit, he carried through with his plan. "I said 'to hell with it, we're going to have one Black,'" he reports, "we got a lot of letters from people complaining."[40]

Bataan's representation of Epps avoids the sheer racist caricature of earlier Hollywood films. Rather than a "bowing and scraping menial" or a "Sambo," the film portrays Epps as "an equal soldier in the ranks," according to one review, a smart, skilled soldier who participates in all the strategy discussions. A theology student before the war, Epps is asked by Dane to say a prayer for Captain Lassiter's burial. In a dignified baritone, he evokes a Christian afterlife shared by both white and black. Unlike his white American, Filipino, and Latino peers, Epps never uses a racial epithet to refer to the enemy. Spencer called the role "the most satisfying experience of his career—a Negro playing a grown-up man's part."[41] The shift in representation did not go unnoticed. The NAACP gave the film an award for its progressive portrayal of a black figure.[42] Crowther, the *New York Times* reviewer, described Epps alternately as "a character whose placement in the picture is one of the outstanding merits of it" and "a fine and dignified notation of the share of his race in the war."[43]

The OWI manual tells exactly what constitutes this black "share" to which Crowther refers. "Each word an American utters," the manual implores, "either helps or hurts the war effort." Movies must prompt the citizen to "challenge the cynic[s] [and] poison-peddlers in our midst."[44] In compliance with the manual, one of *Bataan*'s scenes features a disagreement between Epps and the film's only pessimist, Corporal Barney Todd (Lloyd Nolan), which shows how cynicism degrades group morale, making it harder for the soldiers to rely on each other. As a last-ditch effort to save the patrol from the surrounding Japanese, Yankee Salazar (Alex Havier), one of the Filipino soldiers, tries to slip away from the patrol's base to summon bombers from General MacArthur in the south. "The General ain't got any planes," Todd mutters, "and he ain't gonna get any," implying that the rest of the American forces have abandoned them. Epps interjects immediately, "I reckon that the U.S. is sendin' help as best they can, as fast as they can." Todd refuses to relent. "You'd better bury the rest of us face down," he mocks, "so we don't keep lookin' up for the planes that ain't gonna come." As on two other occasions, his sarcasm provokes a fistfight.

The squabble between Epps and Todd constructs a kind of "reversed reality," to use Anne Rice's term, in which a black man with an abiding faith in both God and country challenges a white man with a destructively cynical attitude.[45] Off screen, however, black soldiers serving in a Jim Crow military felt considerable pessimism, while many whites suspected that blacks lacked the requisite loyalty and self-sacrifice to serve. Letters written to the black press by many African Americans in basic training voice anger and frustration over the contradiction between the American theory and practice of democracy. "We are Jim Crowed in everything we do," an African American soldier writes in 1944 to the *Chicago Defender*. "We're here only to be slaves for the white man." Despite "this so called unity and National emergency," a private notes with irony, "the age-old Monster of Prejudice has raised his head high in the Army." "If this is Uncle Sam's Army," writes another soldier in 1942 to the *Baltimore Afro-American*, "then treat us like soldiers not animals or else Uncle Sam might find a new axis to fight." There are "three hundred of us," he adds, "and we all feel the same."[46]

Paradoxically, *Bataan* represents black pessimism through the white figure of Todd. In a sense, Todd is a mirror image of Epps. One seems to have every good trait, the other, every bad one. Todd is selfish, the only soldier shown napping in a hammock. He lays down on the job, literally—a remarkable act, given that the Japanese have already killed several of his mates. His selfishness blocks his ability to feel unity with others. As opposed to Epps or Dane, Todd reveals his unwillingness to sacrifice for the greater cause of democracy when he threatens to desert. Like a good field leader, Dane promises to shoot him if he were to try. "Sacrifice was a big thing in the forties movies," according to the actor Van Johnson. "Those who didn't sacrifice," he continues, "were enthusiastically torn to pieces by those who did."[47]

The "good black and evil white" configuration solves an important dilemma. The film cannot make its only black character the cynic because that would raise questions about the context that feeds such cynicism, namely, segregation. But also the film must give viewers a virtuous black character to show whites that African Americans deserve equal treatment.

Todd seems irredeemable, but the film restores his character in accordance with what Ed Guerrero terms the "white male" buddy formula, a familiar combat film trope wherein two antagonistic white men bond in the face of a common enemy (127). Two other popular WWII Hollywood offerings include the same figure. John Farrow's *Wake Island*, which garnered four 1942 Academy Award nominations, features a rivalry between a Marine commander and the white ethnic chief of the civilian construction company building the island's airfield. In Howard Hawks's *Air Force*, the 1943 drama about a B-17 "Flying Fortress" crew, an aerial gunner feuds with the crew chief. When the gunner hears of the Japanese attack on Pearl Harbor, he forgets his differences with the crew chief and becomes a valuable member of the team.

Like the films above, *Bataan*'s two white male leads meet initially as antagonists. Dane suspects that Todd is not the person he claims to be. Earlier in the war, Dane took custody of a soldier named Danny Burns, a suspect in a murder case. Under Dane's watch, Burns took advantage of some sort of kindness proffered by Dane (the film does not identify what the kindness was) to escape. "I felt kind of sorry for him," Dane explains, "same as I would for any soldier who gets into a jam." Burns "double-crossed me," says Dane. "His getaway cost me my stripes [along with] my chance for officer's school." Dane pledges that if Burns is ever caught, he will "personally see to it that [Burns] stands up on a parade ground scaffold and hangs." Dane suspects, correctly, that Todd is Burns, but despite numerous questions, he cannot prove it.

Dane's reference to hanging reflects the OWI manual's warning against rivalry, which it deems selfish. "We must all hang together," it quotes Ben Franklin, "or most assuredly we shall all hang separately." It further urges, "Past grievances must be forgotten in the urgent necessity to present a solid, militant front against the common enemy." Then, in a reference to the Lincoln versus Douglas debates that featured two men at rhetorical war against each other, the manual states, "The enemy thoroughly understands that a house divided against itself cannot stand."[48] Dane starts his relationship with Todd by vowing to hang the man he knows as Burns. By the end of the film, however, Dane has a change of heart. Todd wins Dane's respect through his performance under enemy fire. Todd proves himself to be a tough fighter, bare-handedly killing several Japanese soldiers in the hand-to-hand combat scene. In another example, Todd and Dane team up for a dangerous mission to blow up an enemy bridge.

However, to conform to the manual, the film must punish Todd for his selfishness. "This great war effort," the manual quotes a Roosevelt radio address, "must not be impeded by those who put their own selfish interests above the interests of the nation."[49] After the hand-to-hand combat scene, Todd checks the bodies of the enemy dead to see if any are playing possum. He spots a cigarette in the pocket of a seemingly dead soldier. While bending over to take the cigarette, the Japanese stabs him in the back with a samurai sword. As Todd lays dying, Dane forgives him. "As far as I'm concerned," says Dane, "your name is Todd," implying that even though he knows Todd's real identity, he would keep his secret if he were to survive. In a final bonding gesture, just before Todd dies, he reaches out to Dane in an embrace that is sufficiently awkward to ward off the specter of homosexuality.[50]

As a necessary condition for bonding, the film creates a qualitative distance between the Japanese and the Allies that trumps any differences that may reside between the diverse combat unit members on the one hand and the two white men on the other. Specifically, the film degrades the Japanese third point of the triangle by representing them as inhuman. The camera shows the face of the enemy close up only twice, which gives the impression of the Japanese as "an impersonal, faceless enemy," according to Basinger (55). With the exception of Epps, whose credibility requires a sense of decency, all the Allied soldiers refer to the Japanese exclusively through epithets that designate the subhuman: "no tail baboons," "yellow-skinned, slanty-eyed devils," "Mr. Monkey," or simply "Japs." As they watch the enemy creep up, just before the film's hand-to-hand combat scene, Dane orders the white and black survivors to hold their fire until the enemy gets close to their foxhole. A smiling Purckett jokes "do Japs have whites in their eyes?" a reference to the 1775 Battle of Bunker Hill. The establishing shot shows Epps crouching next to Purckett in the foxhole, manning a similar machine gun. The "eyes" conversation emphasizes the Japanese as more alien to the Americans than white and black are to one another. In another example, Purckett stays his bayonet during a fight with a Japanese soldier when the enemy raises his hands in surrender. But the surrender turns out to be a ruse when the Japanese takes advantage of his sense of fair play by taking a stab at Purckett. Despite the trick, the young Kansan prevails, strangling the man to death with his bare hands. The scene reinforces the notion of Japanese as dirty fighters, a reference to many accounts of the Japanese in the immediate aftermath of Pearl Harbor.

The film's representation of the Japanese as abject arose from a growing tendency on the part of blacks to openly urge their fellow African Americans to identify with the Asian foe as another non-white race. The Ethiopian Pacific Movement urged black "soldiers and others to resist service in the armed forces of the United States [because] Japan was going to liberate the darker races."[51] The group foresaw "an Africa ruled by 20,000,000 American Negroes under the benevolent protection of a Japan, after the Rising Sun empire had conquered all Asia and overridden the United States."[52] Richard Wright notes "the possibilities of *alliances* between the American Negro and other people possessing a kindred consciousness." He writes, "Looking at the dark faces of the Japanese generals" enabled blacks to "dream of what it would be like to live in a country where they could forget their color [playing] a responsible role in the vital processes of the nation's life."[53]

Predictably, given the wartime atmosphere, whites feared an alliance between black and Japanese. "There is a question whether Negroes have identified themselves with other colored peoples," observes Gunnar Myrdal, "as much as Southern whites have identified American Negroes with Japan."[54] In the successful 1942 congressional bid to put persons of Japanese ancestry—two-thirds of whom were American citizens—into concentration camps, a Mississippi representative accused "Japanese fifth columnists [of] stirring race trouble in this country for a long time." The saboteurs had been "so successful among the Negroes in Harlem," he added, that New York "city authorities [had] entirely lost control." He recited for the record that, if left unchecked, those of Japanese ancestry in America would incite "20,000,000 Negroes [to] rise in revolt and create chaos."[55] A 1943 survey penned by a University of North Carolina sociologist reports the "common rumor" that blacks "sympathize with any colored races and believe that the Nipponese are their kindred."[56]

In the early years of the war, the OWI Bureau of Intelligence conducted surveys to measure African American identification with the Japanese enemy. One Harlem survey showed significant contrast between attitudes toward Japan and those toward Germany. Black interviewers asked Harlemites whether a Nazi victory would improve their lives; 1 percent responded positively, 63 percent negatively. A surprisingly high 22 percent replied that their lives would not change. In another poll taken in 1942, 18 percent replied that the Japanese would treat them better, leading the pollsters to hypothesize that, because "the Japanese are also colored," blacks believe that they "would not discriminate" against them. The poll concluded that many blacks exhibited a "pan-colored feeling," regarding the Japanese as "fellow people of color" and themselves as "brothers of the colored Asiatics who are assailing the white man's civilization."[57]

The OWI manual countered the possibility of an alliance between black and Japanese by painting the latter as antiblack. "The Negroes," it states, "have a real, a legal, and a permanent chance for improvement of their status under democracy [but] no chance at all under a dictatorship."[58] Stuart Heisler's 1944 documentary *The Negro Soldier*, which every American soldier viewed as part of basic training curriculum, translates the manual's warning that blacks would have "no chance at all" under Japanese rule by depicting the death of a black hero at the hands of the Japanese.[59] Heisler's narrator, a black preacher played by the filmmaker Carlton Moss, introduces the threat to American unity. "There are those who will still tell," he announces, "that Japan is the saviour of the colored races." The camera cuts to a dramatization of Dorie Miller's heroic effort at Pearl Harbor.[60] Even though the Navy segregated its forces by relegating most blacks to noncombat duty such as the mess hall, Miller defended his ship, the *West Virginia*, by manning an antiaircraft gun. In real life, he survived the attack to receive a medal for bravery. But in Heisler's version, Japanese bullets kill Miller as he fires at the invading airplanes. The depiction of one of the few black heroes as a victim of the Japanese helps the African American viewer to imagine that "if he loses the war," as the OWI manual reads, "he loses everything."[61]

Bataan's treatment of African American death mirrors that of Heisler's in *The Negro Soldier*. The gruesome decapitation of *Bataan*'s Epps, America's first black figure "to break the color barrier in American war films," exemplifies the filmic effort to integrate blacks into civic consciousness by displacing antiblack racism from whites onto the Japanese. During *Bataan*'s hand-to-hand combat scene, Epps runs from frame right at a Japanese soldier running from frame left. When they engage in the middle, Epps puts the enemy on the ground and bayonets him, exposing his back. Another Japanese soldier rushes at Epps from frame right, swinging a sword. The film cuts to a medium close-up looking up at the black soldier, his face contorted into a grotesque grimace as the sword hits him squarely in the back of the neck. The shot stops just as the blade cuts the flesh. The soundtrack finishes the decapitation with Epps's "marrow-chilling" death scream.[62]

Epps may be the first on-screen African American to integrate the military, but he never had a chance to survive the war. *Bataan* reflects the same ambivalence that stymied Roosevelt's will to push anti-lynching legislation through Congress. The racial politics of the time required a deft hand. Epps's presence mirrors the country's desire to dispel the notion of American hypocrisy about democracy, but his death ensures that the film does not emphasize too strongly black equality with whites. For the sake of the white audience, the film must punish Epps for rising above his station. His decapitation counts as a castration. Traditionally, most understand the head as the seat of the mind. Thus, Epps's death informs the audience about the limits of black social advancement, giving the message that blacks may rise, but not too far. Thus, *Bataan*'s inclusion of the first equal African American character ultimately amounts to tokenism.

At least two important critics characterize *Bataan*'s general treatment of death as especially violent for its period. "Although we do not actually see the head fall, or blood spurt out," Basinger observes, Epps's decapitation "is one of the most graphic and violent killings of the pre-sixties period of film history." Basinger adds, "Involving [the viewer] as it does in the swift action, the effect, even today, is breathtaking" (54). Stephen Prince notes that the film's "grim" depiction of war prompted remarkably heavy censorship for a film outside the crime or horror genres.[63] The sequence in which Japanese airplanes bomb a line of retreating Filipino civilians features several graphic shots. A wounded man, blind and with bloody bandages over his eyes, crawls frantically for cover. When a burning house crushes him, he emits a high-pitched scream. Another shot shows debris raining down from the sky, including a child's hand and a man's leg, the aftermath of a direct hit. Prince identifies the hand-to-hand combat sequence as an "orgy of killing," calling it "one of the most sustained, brutal, and vividly depicted episodes of violence in all of Hollywood film prior to the late 1960s," including horror or gangster movies of the pre-Code era before 1934 (160–1). The sequence features many shots of bayonet stabbing. Dane simultaneously stabs and shoots one Japanese soldier in the stomach. The camera registers the flash of the discharge as well as the recoil of the body. Todd winds the shoulder strap of his rifle around a foe's neck, drags him a few feet, hacks at him with his short sword, then props up his body as a decoy so that the enemy machine gun shoots at the body's head.

Bataan gives the nonwhite Allied deaths much more graphic treatment than the white ones. The most graphic portrayal of a white soldier's death, for example, uses squibs to simulate machine gun bullets striking Feingold in the chest (Prince 160). Basinger notes that "the minority figures of the film [suffer] the most brutish deaths" at the hands of the enemy, which "act as fodder for the film's narrative." But Basinger's otherwise excellent analysis overlooks how the graphic portrayal of nonwhite Allied death serves to cultivate a bond between white and black at the expense of the Japanese. Her reading is not sure whether the Japanese soldier uses a sword or a bayonet to kill Epps (52, 53, 54).[64] Likewise, Prince mistakes the sword for a bayonet (160). Despite the uncertainty, however, we know that it is a sword because of the way the enemy uses it to decapitate Epps. A bayonet, a short-bladed weapon affixed to the end of a rifle, is used for thrusting, not chopping. In the shot, the Japanese soldier holds the weapon like an ax or a baseball bat (two hands close together at the weapon's handle), rather than a lance (two hands farther apart along the shaft), swinging down at Epps's head as if splitting a piece of wood.

The weapon is no ordinary sword. It is a samurai sword. The film introduces the enemy weapon during the scene in which the patrol discovers Private Katigbak (Roque Espiritu), one of the two Filipino soldiers, dead in the jungle. The soundtrack plays a lugubrious tune, a convention borrowed from horror films, marking the gruesome nature of the discovery. The scene's main function, it seems, involves giving the viewers a long look at the samurai sword. Heavy white mist, also taken from the horror genre, blankets the jungle floor. The white mist emphasizes the samurai sword. Visually, it offers a perfect contrasting background for the dark sword. The mist completely obscures Katigbak's body so that the viewers see only the vertical sword, presumably anchored by the body below. A close-up of the sword starts at the handle then tilts down the length of the blade. In contrast to the Allied soldier's unadorned sword, a distinctive black ornamental tassel hangs from the Japanese handle. "I don't know if you know it," Dane says to another soldier, "but that was a samurai sword."

The sword's provenance may seem a trivial point, but the samurai sword plays an important role in the film's strategy to discredit the Japanese as a possible ally to nonwhite Americans, blacks in particular. The samurai sword is distinctively Japanese, an icon of essential national character signifying Japan's archaic military aggression. It sets the Japanese apart from the American and Allied heroes who, by contrast, use only conventional weaponry: guns and bayonets. The Japanese kill differently. The film represents their methods of killing, according to Basinger, as "barbaric" (55). Thus, the film deploys the samurai sword as a type of signature or calling card. It emphatically names the aggression directed against the nonwhite bodies of Epps and Katigbak as an expression of Japanese nature.

Dane's early threat to hang Todd never materializes, but someone does hang before the film ends. The film's yellow peril kills the second Filipino soldier, Yankee Salazar, through one of the more "barbaric methods of killing" in the annals of American history (Basinger 55). The viewer experiences Salazar's death in large part through the youngest soldier, the naïve Kansas boy turned Navy trumpeter, Leonard Purckett (Robert Walker). Purckett's lack of combat experience feeds his insecurity, which he expresses indirectly throughout the film by constantly repeating his desire to "get his first Jap." While on guard duty, he spies what he takes to be an enemy soldier in the clearing in front of his foxhole. "First Jap I've seen," he shouts, "standing right out there in the open!" Eagerly he aims his machine gun at the immobile figure, talking to himself, "OK Mr. Monkey, you're going to get it," but Dane stops him. The four remaining patrol members, all white men, take a closer look. They see that the figure in the killing zone is not an enemy soldier, but one of their own, Salazar, who stole away into the jungle to get help from General MacArthur. The dead Filipino soldier hangs by his neck from a tree, swinging slowly just above the misty jungle floor. Streaks of blood run down the length of the partially naked body, making it glisten in the moonlight.

Understanding the film's portrayal of Salazar's death as it operated in 1943 requires reading it within the context of lynchings in the United States. *Bataan*'s audience in its debut year would have been familiar with the image of a nonwhite man hanging from a tree, his neck snapped so that his head sags at a grotesquely sharp angle. Whites, mostly men, lynched more than 2,500 African Americans, mostly men, between 1880 and 1930.[65] Another study puts the national number at roughly 5,000 between 1882 and 1946. Lynchings occurred on average no less than two to three per week during that time.[66] In 1929, the high rate prompted the NAACP's Walter White to characterize lynching as "an almost integral part of our national folkways."[67]

White mobs staged most of the extralegal killings between Emancipation and WWII in public. Called spectacle lynching, the organizers advertised the protracted killings in newspapers and chartered special trains to swell the white crowd, which included all classes and women and children as well as men. Such lynchings, which Mary Church Terrell in 1904 described as a "wild and diabolical carnival of blood," proceeded according to ritual.[68] First, the mob hunted the unfortunate black person down or removed him or her from jail for identification by the alleged white victim. After bringing in a crowd by public announcement, the lynchers choreographed the killing. It began with a period of mutilation and torture to elicit a confession. The climax involved death by hanging, shooting, stabbing, burning, or some combination of the above. The denouement consisted of "a frenzied souvenir gathering," usually parts of the cadaver or bits of the deceased's clothes, and the display of the body.[69] For those who failed to secure their own bit of flesh or cloth, some photographed the principal mob members posing around the body. After the event, many sold the photographs as postcards.

The racial politics of WWII, however, limited *Bataan*'s options for depicting a lynching. The film could not have shown the lynching of a white soldier. Such an image would have evoked the loss of the Philippines, subordinating white American masculinity to that of the Japanese yet again. Nor could the film have depicted the lynching of a black man. The image of a black man hanging by his neck would have reminded the white audience of its history of sin against blacks. Conveniently, Epps dies heroically before the lynching scene. His presence as a witness to the lynching would have rekindled discomforting visions of whites lynching blacks. Likewise, directors often deployed what Clayton R. Koppes and Gregory D. Black call "writing out," eliminating altogether the potentially controversial character rather than taking the time to retool the script in accordance with the manual's dictates, as the easiest way to deal with black representation in a highly charged environment. For example, a Bureau of Motion Pictures (BMP) reviewer advised MGM to cut the black figures from a 1943 project because the viewer might read them as slaves. "The fact that slavery existed in this country is certainly something which belongs to the past," writes the BMP reviewer, something "which we wish to forget at this time when unity of all races and creeds is all-important." The director of *Action in the North Atlantic* (Lloyd Bacon, 1943) removed black servants from the script to avoid recalling segregation.[70]

These same constraints, however, made Salazar a good candidate for *Bataan*'s lynching victim. As an Asian, he signifies as a nonwhite, enabling the film's visual rhetoric to accuse the Japanese of racism in a plausible manner. As a non-Japanese Asian, his brutal death reminds the viewer of Japanese colonialism in Asia, justified by the Japanese ideology of superiority over other Asians. "The people of Korea and of Manchuria know in their flesh the harsh despotism of Japan," the OWI manual reads.[71] But Salazar's Filipino status requires the film to erase the memory of U.S. colonization of the Philippines, particularly its brutal quelling of the Filipino insurrection (1899–1913), in which a quarter of a million to a million civilians died, according to some accounts.

The film counters American imperialism's black mark by representing Salazar as hyper-American. He is a soldier in the Philippine Scouts, a detachment of the American Army originally raised to help quell the turn-of-the-century insurgency. His very name, "Yankee," is slang for "American." Slang, an insider's language, reinforces his American status. The film connects him to an American cultural icon when he imagines what will happen when MacArthur sends air support. "Planes drop bombs on Japs!" he exclaims, "Bang! Fourth of July!" His first words tell the viewer that he is a boxer, connecting him to the period's most well-known icon of African American heroism, Joe Louis, who in 1938 beat the German champion Max Schmeling in Yankee Stadium.[72] "It seems to me I saw you box somewhere," says Dane when the two meet. On "Thanksgiving" at the "Manila Olympics Club," Salazar affirms, "knocked him out in the fourth."

The depiction of Salazar's death scapegoats the Japanese by transferring the sin of antiblack racism from whites to the foreign enemy. In doing so, however, the film ran the risk of reminding the viewer of the pleasure many whites took in lynching blacks. The theme of white pleasure runs through many literary representations of lynching. Anne Spencer's 1923 poem "White Things," for example, includes a chilling description of sadism.

> They pyred a race of black, black men,
> And burned them to ashes white; then,
> Laughing, a young one claimed a skull,
> For the skull of a black is white, not dull,
> But a glistening and awful thing.[73]

Spencer wrote the poem to protest the 1918 Georgia lynching of Mary Turner, who, according to the *Atlantic Constitution*, had "made unwise remarks" in response to the lynching of her husband, Haynes Turner.[74] "The best show, Mister, I ever did see," boasted one eyewitness to Walter White during his investigation for the NAACP. "You ought to've heard the nigger wench howl."[75] These details highlight the profound change in white public behavior toward blacks after the WWII period.

In 1943, *Bataan*'s audience knew about lynching in large part through the circulation of the many souvenir photographs produced as part of the spectacle. Like the Spencer poem, many of the photographs register pleasure: white people smiling as they pose next to the body. A postcard from the *Without Sanctuary* collection of lynching photography serves as a good example. In 1916, a Texas mob lynched the "mentally retarded" Jesse Washington in a public square before a crowd of 15,000 whites. The mob beat the seventeen year old with shovels and bricks, cut off his ears, fingers, and sexual organs, then burned him alive. Several of them used a chain suspended over a tree limb to lift him up and down by his neck as the crowd roared in response to each dip into the fire.[76]

In her 2004 analysis of the Washington postcard's "morning after" photograph, Shawn Michelle Smith notes the smiles of the white men and boys who gather around the charred body, rigid and brittle, hanging by the neck from a wooden post. "This is the Barbecue we had last night," a young man writes on the back of the postcard. "Your sone [sic] Joe." "Where are the stunned and sickened faces of shock?" Smith asks. "Why are the children not confused and overwhelmed?"[77] "For people to smile," said one visitor to a 2000 lynching photography exhibit in Manhattan, "to be actually jostling to be in the picture, that's more stunning than anything else.[78] The sight of all the white people, maskless, milling about, looking straight at the camera as if they had nothing to be ashamed of, often smiling," writes a *New York Times* reporter, "takes the breath away."[79]

WWII changed the meaning of racism, especially white racism toward black people. For the first time in history, treating nonwhites, especially blacks, as fellow human beings became an unofficial prerequisite for being American. The national rhetoric of democracy made it impossible for white Americans to act in an overtly antiblack fashion. Spectacle lynching stopped, for example, with the advent of WWII.[80] Acts of antiblack racism by whites served as counterevidence for America's claims as the most democratic nation on earth, an ideological mantra repeated endlessly to reinforce American resolve to win the war against the Axis. In 1943, the wartime project of representing the nation as unified could scarcely abide the traces of white racism against black people that a lynching depiction would revivify. The Pennsylvania state censor, for instance, eliminated all views of Salazar's hanging body (Prince 162).

After the start of WWII, the change in racial politics turned the white smiles in the lynching photographs into a liability, evoking stunned disbelief. Post-WWII, the white smiles, which signify a lack of remorse, stand as an indictment of the white viewer, a reminder of "white culpability," in the words of historian Amy Louise Wood.[81] This admission, in turn, initiates the desire to make amends for the sin of lynching. A *New York Times* article describes the reaction to the NAACP's 1935 Manhattan lynching photography exhibit. "The large crowd," the reporter writes, behaved as "one going to some sacred shrine, to some high and holy place of atonement [rather] than to just 'another' exhibit."[82]

Bataan did not so much atone for white misbehavior as disavow it by producing its own version of the souvenir lynching photograph, one that conditioned the white viewer to respond differently to lynching in particular and racism in general. "That's no Jap," Dane informs Purckett after he misidentifies the body hanging by the neck from a tree, "that's Salazar." Or "what's left of him," Feingold adds, implying a protracted period of torture. Then the "sickened faces of shock" that Smith finds missing from the Washington photograph surface on the movie screen through a series of reaction shots. The four white men look up at the slowly swinging body with horror. Their faces all register shock and disgust. The director emphasizes young Purckett's reaction by placing him at the center of the frame. His mouth agape in disbelief, the viewer sees a series of emotions run across his face: disbelief, anger, and then horror. "Japs probably got him last night," says Todd, "worked him a long time before they finally strangled him." Todd's dialogue suggests the same drawn-out sadism reminiscent of the American lynching ritual. The camera pushes in to a medium shot of Purckett. Transfixed, he whispers through gritted teeth his own description of what he sees. "Dirty, dirty, dirty, dirty," he repeats obsessively. The horror arrests his ability to process psychologically the event. The film makes a good choice in Purckett as the figure to convey the shock of the lynching. The youngest of the group, he is less likely to have seen anything so horrible. His naïveté, which is also read as a product of the Midwesterner's "natural" moral cleanliness, underscores the disgusting nature of lynching.

Bataan's "dirty, dirty" scene recuperates whites as a nonracist people and thus rewrites the narrative of racial oppression in the United States as conveyed by artifacts such as the many surviving lynching photographs of the pre-WWII era. By simultaneously depicting the lynch mob as Japanese rather than as Euro-American and displaying the white soldiers' horrified faces fixed on the nonwhite hanging body, the film helps to erase the memory of white America's lynching of blacks. Thus, *Bataan* stands as prime example of how the white and black binary that dominates American racial discourse positions the Asian to play not only the foreigner but the scapegoat as well.

White and Black to the Brink: *China Gate* (1957), *Pork Chop Hill* (1959), *All the Young Men* (1960)

The worse things get, the better they are.

—Winston Churchill on Mutually Assured Destruction (MAD)

The previous chapter argued that Tay Garnett's 1943 WWII combat movie *Bataan* is a precursor to the Orientalist buddy film in that it represents race in a triangulated fashion, pitting white and black against a yellow enemy in the form of Japanese forces that have invaded the Philippines. Chapter 1 shows that the era's emphasis on national racial unity prompted the film to include, for the first time in Hollywood history, a sympathetic black American figure, Private Wesley Epps, as part of its combat unit, even though the nation's military did not abolish segregation until well after the war. The present chapter has two parts. The first establishes a historical pattern for the Orientalist buddy film by identifying three early examples of the type. Continuing the previous chapter's focus on the war film genre, it shows how three period combat movies, Samuel Fuller's *China Gate* (1957), Lewis Milestone's *Pork Chop Hill* (1959), and Hall Bartlett's *All the Young Men* (1960), try to build, at least cinematically, racial unity between white and black by repeating *Bataan's* triangulation of race. Like *Bataan*, these three films feature a mostly white combat team, integrated with one or two black figures, battling an Asian threat. Unlike the WWII era *Bataan*, however, each of these Cold War era films elevates a black figure to play one side of the "white male" buddy duo, to use Ed Guerrero's term again, found in *Bataan*, thereby putting tension between white and black, and eventually the transcendence of that tension, at the center of the plot. Reflecting the American military's desegregation of the late 1940s, this promotion of the black soldier from bit player to main character establishes for the first time the Orientalist buddy film formula: two Americans, one white and the other black, bonding through the vehicle of a common Asian enemy.

The second part of this chapter sets these early Orientalist buddy films in the historical and geopolitical context of the Cold War to show that their narration of white and black on the brink of disaster—what I call the discourse of mutually assured racial destruction—produces an important political advantage for white Americans. This mode of narrating race relations tells the viewer, both white and black, that conflict between the races must stop immediately or else both groups will perish. Such an urgent emphasis on the cessation of conflict between white and black counters the early activism of the nascent civil rights movement, thereby giving the advantage to the racial top dog, in this case, white America.

As a group, the combat films of the 1950s have received less critical attention than those of the WWII era. The category's inauspicious status is due, in part, to the fact that Hollywood did not produce very many. The decade's major military conflict, the Korean War, "never became a popular subject for filmmakers," according to the war film historian Lawrence Suid, "most likely because of the nature of the conflict." It was one "shaded in gray instead of painted in the easily defined black and white of World War II." The relative few that Hollywood did make were largely derivative of their WWII predecessors. "The American experience in World War II," Suid continues, "remained the model on which most directors, producers, and screenwriters based their military portrayals during the 1950s."[1]

The three Cold War combat films at the center of this chapter mirror the WWII era *Bataan* in a variety of ways. Predictably, the yellow peril enemy in Fuller's *China Gate* is Asian communism. Set in 1954 Vietnam, the movie follows a French Foreign Legion combat squad on a mission to destroy a Viet Minh munitions depot located somewhere along the mountain range from which the movie takes its name. Ho Chi Minh's army has "stocked in secret tunnels" a cache of bombs that, according to the anonymous narrator in the main title sequence, "was winning the war for the communists." The sequence characterizes the legion as "the barrier between communism and the rape of Asia," a reference to the Cold War era concept proposing that if the free world allowed one country fall, then all the other nations in the region would fall as well. The French squad leader suggests that the domino theory applies beyond the region. If Asia falls to communism, the West will likely follow. "This time the foreign legion mercenary is not fighting for money or the French government alone," the commander states. "This time they're fighting for the whole western world against a common enemy."

Like *China Gate*, *Pork Chop Hill* and *All the Young Men* unfold against an Asian backdrop. Both movies are set during the Korean War. *Pork Chop Hill* follows an American Marine unit's fight to liberate a hill that neither the Americans nor the North Koreans deem strategically important, given that peace negotiations have commenced at Panmunjom. When a soldier questions the wisdom of sending Americans during the last stage of the war to die for "a stinking little garbage heap [with] no military value," his commander, Lieutenant Joe Clemons (Gregory Peck), likens the negotiations to a poker game. "Pork Chop is just a chip in the big game," he surmises, "every time the Reds win a chip here, they raise the ante there. I guess we've got to convince them we're not about to give up any more chips." *All the Young Men*, which is set early in the war during the winter of 1950, focuses on a Marine team moving in advance of a battalion on return from a strike in North Korean enemy territory. The scouting unit must commandeer a remote farmhouse that overlooks a strategic mountain valley, a snowy choke point through which the battalion's one thousand men must pass on their way back to home base. "If you don't [take] that farmhouse," the squad leader stresses to his men, the Communists will use it to "cut the battalion in half." After securing the farmhouse, the unit, without a working radio or an adequate supply of food and ammunition, must hold it against a much larger enemy force until the main body arrives.

Like *Bataan*, these Cold War films dehumanize the Asian foe, which by contrast defines the shared ground on which white and black will eventually bond. Like *China Gate*, *Pork Chop Hill* and *All the Young Men* portray the enemy as a yellow peril that, if left unchecked, would engulf the free world. Both films end with a last-stand battle in which an overwhelming number of enemy soldiers, Chinese and North Korean, surround an American combat unit (Basinger 27). During *Pork Chop*'s final encounter, one American screams, "They're behind us everywhere, a million of them." "Sounds like all of China's coming," yells another. After the Americans take the hill, the final scene's voice-over tells the viewer, "Millions live in freedom today because of what they did." Just before *All the Young Men*'s climactic battle, a Marine (played by the comedian Mort Sahl) surveys the North Korean territory. Implying that the sheer size of the Asian force alone constitutes a menace to Western civilization, he jokes nervously that there are "about six hundred and fifty million" Chinese, all of whom are "draft age." *All the Young Men* highlights how essentially foreign the Americans find Korean culture. One exchange emphasizes how poorly the Koreans mimic an American staple. "Korean coffee," one soldier jokes as he hands a cup to another, "it'll crack your tongue." Excusing his men's aggressive behavior toward a Korean farmhouse owner, a Marine explains, "We have had to bury our friends, in places we can't even pronounce." Visually, the film evokes a sense of dehumanized inscrutability through several close-ups of the Asian Communists. The identical goggles, scarves, and winter hoods that completely mask their faces make them into the same "impersonal, faceless enemy" that Jeanine Basinger identifies in *Bataan* (55).

Pork Chop Hill represents its Asian Communists as callous enemies who fail to respect human lives, even those of their own soldiers. During the negotiations at Panmunjom, the American negotiators signal that they want peace to spare their own men at Pork Chop. "This insignificant little hill is of no importance to you and no importance to us," pleads one, "how can it be worth any man's life?" Cementing the message that the Asian foe lacks the emotions of normal human beings, the North Korean negotiator abruptly cuts off his counterpart in mid-question, removing the translation feed from his ear, looking straight up at the ceiling in an ostentatious refusal to listen. "They're willing to spend lives for nothing," the American says. "They want to know," he continues, if we are "as willing to do that as they are." The film answers its own question when American reinforcements appear on the hill, risking their lives to rescue their fellow soldiers. *China Gate*'s North Vietnamese major who directs the bomb depot, Cham (Lee Van Cleef), echoes the North Korean negotiator's inhumanity. In contrast to the French, whose civilized values dictate that they "don't bomb villages or temples," the Viet Minh "bomb everything." Cham boasts, "That's why we'll win all of Asia." "I don't know how you can talk so indifferently about killing women and children," one Westerner responds, incredulously. "How can you sleep nights?"

The rest of Major Cham's profile constitutes an early version of the model minority Asian. He is one-dimensional, obsessed with his career and future success. Trying to win back a former mistress, he brags, soon "I'll be in line to direct the Viet Minh politburo." "Imagine me," he continues, "a general stationed in Moscow." In a bid to win her hand in marriage, he takes her on a tour of the bomb depot. "If all this fails to convince you that you'd be marrying the winner," Cham presses her, "I can only catalogue you as a fool." In contrast, she reacts with abhorrence, calling the bomb warehouse "a butcher shop before the slaughter." When she reminds him that he used to oppose the Viet Minh, he reveals a moral relativism born of his desire to climb to the top of the Communist administrative hierarchy. "It's all according to your point of view. You get caught in a political upheaval, you're hanged as a traitor. If you lead a successful revolt, future generations will worship you as the father of your country."

Like *Bataan*, these Cold War era films showcase an Allied combat team whose members hail from diverse social backgrounds. In *China Gate*, the members of the legion's detachment come from several different Western nations: France, Germany, Greece, Hungary, and the United States. *Pork Chop Hill*'s combat unit incorporates Lieutenant Tsugi Ohashi (George Shibata), a Japanese American figure who calls attention to his non-European ancestry by noting that his "ancestors were pretty good at" fighting, what he terms "this banzai business."[2] In *All the Young Men*, the Marines come from a variety of regions (urban and rural, Deep South, Southwest, and Midwest), religions (Protestant and Jewish), and even nations. To reflect the United Nations' involvement in the conflict, the director recruited the boxer Ingemar Johansson to play a Marine recently emigrated from Sweden.[3]

The social diversity in each of the Cold War combat films includes a descendent of Private Wesley Epps, *Bataan*'s WWII era African American figure who integrates a mostly white American combat team fighting a yellow peril. *China Gate* has Goldie (Nat "King" Cole), an ultrapatriotic American who fought in both WWII and the Korean War. Unlike Goldie, though, *Pork Chop Hill*'s Private Franklin (Woody Strode) is a soldier whose cynicism toward his own country makes him fake an injury to avoid fighting in the key battle. Finally, *All the Young Men*'s Sergeant Eddie Towler (Sidney Poitier) is a self-described urban dweller, born and raised "right in the middle of a million people," a reference to the black ghetto.

In 1943, critics hailed *Bataan* as politically progressive for its sympathetic portrayal of Epps. Compared in retrospect to these three African American figures, however, Epps seems like a token. Whereas Epps appears in only a few scenes, the last of which depicts his beheading at the hands of the Japanese, the black characters in these Cold War combat films not only survive the entire movie, each has an initial conflict with one of the white soldiers on the team. This transformation of *Bataan*'s triangular formation from two white men to a white man and a black man bonding in the face of a mutual Asian threat creates the first set in a series of Orientalist buddy films that will appear up to the end of the century and beyond.

As in *Bataan*, *All the Young Men*'s Asian enemy kills the American team leader early in the movie, establishing the buddy duo. Gravely wounded, the unit's only officer orders the only black soldier, Sergeant Towler, to take the command. "I'm turning these men over to you," he gasps, reiterating the mission: "Get that farmhouse!" Towler's promotion to the top position sets him against the squad's longest-serving member, Private Kincaid (Alan Ladd), who, according to one of the soldiers, "know[s] more about getting us out of here than all the rest of us put together." As a recent transfer on his first mission with the team, Towler hesitates. "I can't take over this outfit, sir," he balks, "Kincaid's the one," deferring to the de facto leader, who is white. But the dying lieutenant quickly settles the issue by insisting on Towler, the Marine whose rank puts him next in the line of succession. "You're not wearing those stripes on your sleeve for nothing," he tells Towler. In a diplomatic gesture, Towler acknowledges Kincaid's informal authority. "You ought to be calling the shots," says Towler to Kincaid, "they know it and so do I....I need your help."

Emulating *Bataan*, the film's two protagonists do not get along, initially. Instead of assistance, Kincaid promises Towler only an adversarial surveillance. "When you start cracking up" under the stress of command, Kincaid warns Towler, "I'll be right on top of you." Kincaid's baiting culminates in a fistfight with Towler. "[I'm] sick of you right down to my guts," Towler exclaims before he attacks the white man. "Every time I turn around you're watching me, waiting for me to make a mistake." Likewise, when *Pork Chop Hill*'s Franklin feigns an injury during the major assault, Clemons recognizes the ruse immediately, promising to prosecute him for desertion. Concerned that Franklin might shoot him from behind rather than spend "ten years in Leavenworth," Clemons orders him to the front of the charge. The tension between white and black comes to a head when Clemons stumbles onto Franklin's hiding place just before the last battle with the Communists. "Don't you move," Franklin threatens to kill Clemons, "I'm aiming straight at your belly."

Including the black man as half of the buddy pair allows the films to put racism at the center of the conflict between the two soldiers. In *China Gate*, the dispute between Goldie and the white Sergeant Johnny Brock (Gene Barry), the squad's explosives expert, stems from the latter's racism toward his own son, a product of his marriage to a "half-caste," Asian and white, bar owner named Leah (Angie Dickinson), nicknamed "Lucky Legs." Before the birth, he believed that the child would look white due to the mother's Caucasian appearance. "You don't look like a thirty-buck Chinese bride," he insists. But, to the father's dismay, the son looked "Chinese all the way down the line." "I saw his eyes," he tells Leah, "I got sick inside, so ugly." Disgusted, Brock abandoned both of them. The mission to destroy the bomb depot reunites husband and wife when the legion recruits Leah to act as the team's guide. On learning of the estrangement, Goldie takes Leah's side, refusing to sit near Brock on the trail, which leads to a shoving match between the two men. "What's eating you, Goldie," Brock yells, "you've been snapping at me every chance you get." "The only other American on this patrol," he tells Brock, "and it had to be a weasel like you." *Pork Chop Hill*'s black soldier declares himself to be a victim of white America. Franklin explains to Clemons that, for a black man, racial injustice at home renders sacrifice for the United States a ridiculous proposition. "You think I'm stupid," he yells. "What do I care about this stinking hill?...You ought to see where I live back home," he says, linking racism to poverty. "I ain't gonna die for Korea," he promises, "or serve ten years for it, neither."

In *All the Young Men*, Kincaid's resentment toward Towler's promotion includes racism as well as professional envy. Kincaid exposes his prejudice during an argument with Towler. The team secures the farmhouse according to plan. But when the reinforcements fail to reach them on schedule, the two men discover that they have contradictory agendas. In the close quarters of the farmhouse's courtyard, the men huddle around Towler as he diagrams the defense of their position against the much larger and better-equipped enemy force. Kincaid reminds Towler that the Communists will likely slaughter the company's handful of surviving soldiers if they remain. "If we don't pull out now," he says, "you can cross off ten men." In spite of Kincaid's appraisal, Towler holds the soldiers to their original orders. "We're sitting on" the pass, he says, "right where we're supposed to

Figure 2.1   Goldie (Nat "King" Cole) and Sergeant Brock (Gene Barry) in *China Gate*.

be." Appealing to the soldiers' sense of duty, Towler tells them that they must stay to "prove" that "there are ten marines" on the mission. In response, Kincaid suggests that Towler's talk of honor hides an ulterior motive that would make the unit's whites bear the cost of black progress. Kincaid returns Towler's correction. Rather than ten soldiers, suggests the white warrior, they have "nine marines and one black man with an ax to grind." If they pull out, Kincaid says sarcastically to the black man, "you'll be a hero....When all your people hear what you've done, they'll build a statue for you in the cotton fields."

All the Young Men disfigures the white buddy with a racist remark only to transfer the stigma of American racism from white to yellow by repeating a crucial feature of *Bataan*'s racial narrative: a lynching. The scene stages the execution of the team's Native American tracker, Chief (Leonard Mountain Chief), the movie's analog to *Bataan*'s Yankee Salazar, the Filipino soldier whose attempt to contact General MacArthur for reinforcements ends in disaster. Like Salazar, Chief is neither white nor black. Just as Salazar claims a special relationship to the wilderness that serves as the stage for the team's entrapment, the

Bataan jungle, Chief maintains that the rugged mountain geography is, in a sense, home territory for him. "This is Indian country," he tells Towler, who wants to accompany the tracker on a mission to reconnoiter thickly wooded area around the farmhouse's perimeter. "They'll never know I'm around.... You're a city boy," he continues, "you'll just get in the way."

Chief's death at the hands of the Asian Communists duplicates a key detail of Yankee Salazar's murder in *Bataan*. After capturing him, the Asian Communists force Chief to act as a human shield, making him walk in front of their column as they advance toward the farmhouse for their next attack. As the enemy soldiers drive him forward with savage blows from the butts of their rifles, they choke him with a rope around his neck. Like a dog on a leash, they yank him upright whenever he stumbles in the heavy snow or advances too far ahead of the column. The iconic detail of a rope around a nonwhite man's neck qualifies Chief's death as a lynching. Recalling the history of racist brutality against black Americans, the scene serves as a bonding moment for white and black, as a white Marine and Towler watch the yellow enemy drive their friend to his death.

All the Young Men's lynching scene qualifies the movie as a precursor to many 1980s and 1990s white and black buddy films or what Robyn Wiegman calls "interracial male bonding narratives" (117). Rather than through a lynching, however, many of them transfer the stigma of racism from the white buddy to a common enemy through a scene in which the villain calls the black buddy a "nigger" in a fit of anger. *In the Heat of the Night* (Norman Jewison, 1967, Rod Steiger and Sidney Poitier), *Silver Streak* (Arthur Hiller, 1976, Gene Wilder and Richard Pryor), *Trading Places* (John Landis, 1983, Dan Ackroyd and Eddie Murphy), and *White Nights* (Taylor Hackford, 1985, Mikhail Baryshnikov and Gregory Hines) fit this profile. The Confederate general (Kenneth Branagh) in *Wild Wild West* (Barry Sonnenfeld, 1999, Kevin Kline and Will Smith) shows his disdain for the black buddy through various equivalents such as "coon." Other white and black buddy films mark their villains as antiblack racists by tying them to one or another icon of white America's long history of the mistreatment of black people. In *Beverly Hills Cop* (Martin Brest, 1984, John Ashton, Judge Reinhold, and Eddie Murphy), when the black detective tries to follow the elitist art dealer villain into one of his all-white haunts, a posh 90210 restaurant, the maitre d' will not let him pass. The African American man links the villain to Jim Crow segregation by exclaiming, "no niggers allowed in there," after which the villain's goons throw him out through a plate-glass window. In *Enemy Mine* (Wolfgang Petersen, 1985, Dennis Quaid and Louis Gossett, Jr.), the alien race that threatens both of the protagonists trades in slaves. In *Rocky IV* (Sylvester Stallone, 1985, Stallone and Carl Weathers), a Communist official lauds his government's policy of breeding fighters with superior "genetics," a reference to the long-discredited practice of American eugenics of the early 1900s. Likewise, in *Philadelphia* (Jonathan Demme, 1993, Tom Hanks and Denzel Washington), cross-examination reveals the oppressors as not only intolerant of gays but of African Americans as well, while the white buddy's mother (Joanne Woodward) hails her gay son as a kind of latter-day Rosa Parks. "Fight for your rights," she says. "I didn't raise my kids to sit in the back of the bus."

Like *Philadelphia*, *All the Young Men*'s discord between white and black reflects the struggle for civil rights, including the bid to desegregate the American military in the late 1940s. Shortly after WWII, white American leaders reanimated Henry Luce's prewar ideology of American Exceptionalism to authorize Cold War foreign policy to win hearts and minds around the globe, especially the nonaligned Third World. But yet again, the horribly fraught domestic issue of relations between whites and blacks posed a political bind for U.S. leaders. What Gunnar Myrdal characterized in 1944 as America's "Negro Problem," the glaring contradiction between the country's democratic ideals and its long history of black mistreatment, threatened to destroy the crusading spirit of U.S. foreign policy for the entire Cold War era. By the time the Soviet Union launched Sputnik in 1957, the situation facing whites had not changed since the WWII period. On the one hand, various national figures continued Luce's idea from the early 1940s, which advocated the global spread of U.S. influence, authorized by American Exceptionalism. On the other, the rest of the world heard media reports about the ongoing struggle for black civil rights, for example, the 1954 *Brown v. Board of Education* decision and the Montgomery bus boycott of 1955.

In the late fifties, white America faced the same dilemma that Roosevelt encountered over antilynching legislation as recounted in the previous chapter on the WWII era. The first horn involved ameliorating the Negro Problem. This option, however, required whites to cede institutional power to blacks, historically an unpopular move in the United States. When Truman called for federal legislation to ban Jim Crow, lynching, and poll taxes, one Virginia senator characterized his presidency as a "dictatorship," likening the sitting commander-in-chief to "Hitler and Stalin."[4] A Mississippi member of the House warned, "We're not going to stand idly by and watch the South mongrelized."[5] Only a few weeks before his order to desegregate the military, the entire Mississippi delegation of twenty-two and half of the twenty-six Alabama delegates walked out of the Philadelphia national convention in protest of the party's plank on civil rights. A *New York Times* article called the walk-out a "spectacular gesture, [the] political equivalent in the modern Democratic party of the shots that fell upon Fort Sumter."[6] "All of a sudden," noted another newspaper, black rights had "split a great national party."[7] Most of the southern Democrats formed their own ticket based on a states' rights plank, naming themselves Dixiecrats, with South Carolina Governor Strom Thurmond as their candidate. Although Truman went on to win a second term, Thurmond continued his virulent anti–civil rights stance well into the 1950s. As a Democratic senator in 1957, he set a record for holding the floor, over twenty-four hours, in an attempt to block a civil rights bill.[8]

The second horn of the dilemma involved leaving the racial status quo intact. But this avenue entailed terrible public relations beatings from rival nations on the world stage, especially the Communist ones. Like the WWII era, various presidents throughout the Cold War period addressed this point of vulnerability and the need to remedy it. "Our civil rights record has been an issue in world politics," a 1950s presidential commission appointed by Harry Truman notes. "Those with competing philosophies…have tried to prove ours an empty fraud and our nation a consistent oppressor of underprivileged people." It continues, "This may seem ludicrous to Americans, [but] the final triumph of the democratic ideal is not so inevitable that we can ignore what the world thinks of our record."[9] Truman himself came to his own conclusion: "The top dog in a world which is half colored ought to clean his own house."[10] In 1957, the Arkansas governor's mobilization of the National Guard to block school desegregation in Little Rock prompted Truman's successor to warn the American public, "We face grave situations abroad because of the hatred that Communism bears toward a system of government based on human rights," Dwight Eisenhower intoned on national television. "It would be difficult to exaggerate the harm that is being done to [our] prestige and influence….Our enemies are gloating over this incident," he continued, "using it everywhere to misrepresent our whole nation."[11] Such presidential examples illustrate the "top dog" leadership's elevated anxiety over incidents publicizing the Negro Problem. When facing China and the Soviet Union in the struggle for world supremacy, the nation's democratic identity could not afford what Eisenhower deemed a gross misrepresentation.

To win equality, early civil rights leaders exploited the dilemma posed by the Negro Problem. For example, A. Philip Randolph, president of the Brotherhood of Sleeping Car Porters, used the glaring contradiction between the democratic discourse and the long history of American white supremacy as leverage to obtain political concessions. In 1941, Randolph threatened to organize a massive march on the Capitol to protest a lack of legal protection. In response, in June of that year, the federal government took an early legislative step against racial discrimination in the workplace by opening defense industry jobs to black people through Executive Order 8802, the Fair Employment Act. Franklin Roosevelt's administration had no choice but to accede. Randolph's plan to mount a "black invasion of lily-white Washington restaurants and hotels" would have underscored the Jim Crow practices of the nation's capital, greatly damaging the United States' position of ideological superiority over its WWII rivals. One historian called Randolph's gamesmanship "one of the most brilliant power plays ever executed by a Negro leader."[12]

Randolph's success in manipulating the contradiction for the cause of black civil rights extended to the postwar era. In March 1948, Truman's White House hosted a number of black leaders, Randolph among them, to discuss black compliance with the draft in a segregated military. As he had with Roosevelt, Randolph pointed out the gap between American theory and practice regarding the treatment of African Americans. According to the *New York Times*, Randolph said to Truman, "In my recent travels around the country I found Negroes not wanting to shoulder a gun to fight for democracy abroad unless they get democracy at home."[13] Later that month, Randolph told the Senate Armed Services Committee, "I personally pledge myself to openly counsel, aid, and abet youth, both white and Negro, to quarantine any Jim Crow conscription system." Randolph sounded the same refrain in a letter to Truman in June 1948. He warned the president, "Negro youth will have no alternative but to resist a law, the inevitable consequence of which would be to expose them to un-American brutality so familiar during the war."[14] Soon after, Randolph created the League for Non-violent Civil Disobedience Against Military Segregation to push Truman to desegregate the military through executive order. In July of that year, Truman issued Executive Order 9981, which promised "equality of treatment and opportunity for all persons in the armed services without regard to race, color, religion, or national origin."[15]

Of course, actual discord between white America and its black counterpart did not abate with the 1948 desegregation of the armed forces. On the screen, though, these three Orientalist buddy films resolve such tension by representing the warring parties at the brink of mutual destruction. Friction establishes the buddy relationship, but white and black soon learn that the yellow threat will kill them both if they do not transcend their racial differences. Immediately after the spat between Brock and Goldie, *China Gate*'s Communists ambush the patrol, forcing the feuding soldiers to cooperate. When a sniper pins down Goldie, Brock rushes to his aid, yelling to the rest of the team, "They got him zeroed-in." After the pair dispatches the sniper, Goldie, in turn, covers Brock. "Keep them off me while I grenade them," he tells Goldie as he attacks the enemy patrol. The only two to survive the mission, the black American embraces the white one, softly caressing his head. At the end of the film, Brock overcomes his anti-Asian sentiment enough to take his mixed race son home with him to the United States.

In *Pork Chop Hill*, the white soldier makes the black one realize that they belong to the same nation after all. In response to Franklin's threat to shoot him, Clemons reminds the black man of the likelihood that both will die in the next skirmish. "At least we've got a chance to [die]...in pretty good company," says Clemons. "A lot of men came up" the hill, he reminds Franklin, the majority of whom made the ultimate sacrifice for American freedom. He continues by observing that the remaining twenty-five "don't care any more about Korea than you do." He reminds Franklin of the black soldiers who served and, in many cases, died for their country. They were fellow citizens who "had it just as rough at home as [he] did." Domestic racism does not entitle him to excuse himself from the fight for America's freedom, the white man implies. Clemons offers redemption: "You can still join up if you want to." Franklin does. During the battle, he helps Clemons by carrying the wounded and fortifying the command post with heavy timbers. "Welcome to the club," Clemons smiles, just before their reinforcements arrive.

All the Young Men literalizes *Pork Chop Hill*'s notion that white and black belong to the same club. The rumble of a Communist tank compels Kincaid and Towler to end their fistfight. "We've got to stop that tank before it gets to the house," Towler tells Kincaid, "or we've had it." If the two do not put aside their differences, the enemy will destroy the combat team and then the thousand-man battalion. Working as a team, the two disable the tank, but not before the tank crushes Kincaid's leg, nearly killing him. To save Kincaid, Towler volunteers to give him his blood, which is the only match on the team. A close-up within the makeshift operating theater focuses on the black man's blood flowing through a transparent tube into Kincaid's arm. When help finally arrives, Towler registers his relief by invoking an important icon that both men share as Americans. "Merry Christmas," Towler says, with a smile. "Same to you, Sergeant," Kincaid replies, acknowledging Towler's superior rank as a sign of respect. The soundtrack for the final scene plays a brassy rendition of "When the Saints Go Marching In" while Towler sprays the enemy with his machine gun.

By projecting a fantasy of harmony between white and black, of course, these buddy films are meant to alleviate the eruption of public discord between the two races sparked by the long-standing racial inequities in American democracy.[16] Robyn Wiegman observes that such felicitous endings constitute a form of tokenism. Even though they may at first seem progressive for their deliberate and often ostentatious acknowledgment of blackness as integral to U.S. identity, in the long run they constrain black demand for equality. The 1980s, she states, produced a transformation of the decade's "visual terrain *toward* more clearly inclusive representational images [without reshaping] in politically progressive ways the status of [actual black] bodies in the economic and social spheres." Such "integrationist aesthetics," she writes, "emerged as the strategic and contradictory means for reframing and securing the continuity for white racial supremacy [by replacing] the question of political power [with] a vapid fetishization of" the black image (116; emphasis in the original).

My supplement to Wiegman's analysis shows exactly how the Orientalist buddy film's narration of white and black at the brink of mutual destruction elides what she calls "the question of political power." Well before the Cold War era, prominent critics of American culture narrated race relations as a discourse of disaster, emphasizing with remarkable consistency the seemingly intractable differences between white and black in ways that foreground the possibility of devastation for both races. In the early 1800s, Thomas Jefferson spoke of an ominous dilemma. "We have the wolf by the ears," he said of the black slave. "We can neither hold him, nor safely let him go." The author of the Constitution observed, "Justice is in one scale, and self-preservation in the other." Emancipation, he feared, would "divide us," producing "convulsions" that would "probably never end but in the extermination of one or the other race."[17] In 1862, Abraham Lincoln invited a group of African Americans to the White House to discuss shipping blacks "back" to Africa. "We have between us a broader difference than exists between any other two races," said the Great Emancipator. "This physical difference is a great disadvantage to us both," he told his guests. "Your race suffer very greatly, many of them by living among us, while ours suffer from your presence."[18] Touring the United States in the late 1830s, France's Alexis de Tocqueville read the possible emancipation of southern blacks in terms of a terrible dilemma. Whites must keep blacks in the total submission of slavery or enter into a race war. "Any intermediate measures," warns Tocqueville, "seem to me likely to terminate, and that shortly, in the most horrible of civil wars, and perhaps the extermination of one or the other of the two races."[19] Bill Clinton's 1997 inaugural speech illustrates that this dominant theme of American racial discourse persisted at least until the end of the millennium. Echoing Jefferson, Lincoln, and Tocqueville, he foregrounds the potential for fatal fragmentation. "The divide of race has been America's constant curse," Clinton warns, "the challenge of our past remains the challenge of our future." "Will we be one nation," he asks, "one people, with one common destiny—or not?" If whites and blacks do not submerge their differences—the union, the nation, the citizens—will suffer, once again, the horrible consequences of white and black at odds. With rhetoric reminiscent of Rodney King's 1991 plea to the nation, the self-proclaimed "healer of the breach" asks, "will we all come together, or come apart?"[20]

Not only does the discourse of mutual destruction provide white America with an image of how to defeat the long-standing dilemma posed by the nation's Negro Problem, it offers a remedy that counters the kind of civil rights activism typified by Randolph's career. *All the Young Men* in particular encapsulates the narrative of mutual destruction in a single scene. When Kincaid and Towler arrive at an impasse about whether or not to abandon the farmhouse and therefore the mission, the black buddy wins his way by manipulating the risk of shared obliteration posed by the Asian enemy. Rather than accede to Towler's plan, Kincaid openly defies his authority by initiating a retreat. "Saddle up, boys," he orders the men, "we're moving out." When the men start to decamp, Towler yells as he brings

Kincaid close, "stay where you are," shoving a grenade into the white soldier's face. If you move, he threatens Kincaid, "I'll pull this pin and push it down your throat." With his suicidal gesture, Towler signals that he would rather run the risk of destroying everyone, including himself, to get his way. Without a doubt, the grenade would kill most of the men crowded in the cramped space; the fast-approaching Asian Communists would surely kill whomever the grenade did not.

Setting this Hollywood scene of white and black at the brink of mutual destruction within the context of the Cold War illustrates the advantage that such a discourse produces for white America. Scholars of the period commonly represented geopolitical conflict, namely, the nuclear stalemate between the United States and the Communist world, in terms of brinkmanship, a trope that bears a striking resemblance to *All the Young Men*'s depiction of the black buddy's threat to blow up both himself and his rival. Brinkmanship "means *manipulating the shared risk of war*," Thomas Schelling, a leading Cold War nuclear strategist, writes in the 1966 *Arms and Influence*. "It means exploiting the danger that someone may inadvertently go over the brink...dragging the other with him." He likens brinkmanship to the familiar game of "chicken," in which two adversaries speed directly toward each other in their cars.[21] The one who loses his nerve first, the one who swerves away from the head-on crash, loses face and is labeled the "chicken." The one who does not lose his or her nerve in the face of impending doom wins the day.

All the Young Men is a relatively recent movie, but brinkmanship is an old idea. Schelling traces the concept back to the ancient period. As one of the earliest instances of it in Western literature, he cites a showdown between two horse-drawn chariots in Homer's *Iliad*.

> The road here led through a gully, and in one part the winter flood had broken down part of the road and made a hollow. Menelaos was driving in the middle of the road, hoping that no one would try to pass too close to his wheel, but Antilochos turned his horses out of the track and followed him a little to one side. This frightened Menelaos, and he shouted at him: "What reckless driving Antilochos! Hold in your horses. This place is too narrow, soon you will have more room to pass. You will foul my car and destroy us both!" But Antilochos only plied the whip and drove faster than ever, as if he did not hear...[Menelaos] fell behind: he let the horses go slow himself, for he was afraid that they might all collide in that narrow space and overturn the cars and fall in a struggling heap. (Schelling 117)

Brinkmanship, then, requires a number of conditions. There must be two antagonistic parties who face the possibility of mutual disaster. That is, the parties must be tied together in some way such that whatever affects the one will affect the other equally, as in mutually assured destruction, a head-on collision, or a race down a narrow gully road. Finally, the essence of brinkmanship entails one of the parties manipulating the other into doing his or her bidding by using the shared risk of disaster as leverage.

I stress the Orientalist buddy film's narration of white and black locked in a relationship of mutual destruction because such a discourse binds the nation together in terms that privilege whites. The nagging contradiction between democratic theory and America's practice of it opened a window of opportunity for black civil rights activists, like Randolph, during both the WWII and the Cold War eras. Hollywood took seriously Truman's warning that America's "top dog" in a nation "that is half-colored" could no longer ignore how the rest of the world read America's record on civil rights, especially the Communist world. The characterization of white and black in a conflict that could destroy them both worked to close that window. By frightening viewers in much the same way that Antilochos frightened Menelaos, the films renarrated the relationship between white and black in terms of a disaster that was close at hand.

The figure of white and black fighting against the backdrop of mutual destruction narrates the conflict as if white and black shared equal standing on the register of social and political privilege. But Hollywood's characterization throughout the late 1950s and the early 1960s did not match actual American conditions. Jim Crow and extralegal racism put blacks underneath whites in no uncertain terms. Given the power differential, any outcome that perpetuates the status quo benefits the group that enjoys structural dominance. By narrating white and black conflict in terms of brinkmanship, "both sides are under similar pressure to settle the game" as it stands, according to Schelling (102). Thus, to convince the viewer that disaster looms imminently gives the political advantage to whites. In other words, representing the relationship between the white and the black worlds in catastrophic terms amounts to a "win" for the "top dog," to use Truman's words. Such a narration freezes the political play between white and black in a manner that allows whites, as a group, to preserve their edge.

Brinkmanship was a topical figure during the 1950s, surfacing in popular media around the middle of the decade. In reports on the containment of Asian communism, a 1956 *Life* magazine article, for example, describes how Secretary of State John Foster Dulles "brought [the] U.S. back from the brink" of war on three separate occasions: Korea in 1953, Vietnam in 1954, and Formosa (now Taiwan) in 1954.[22] The concept of brinkmanship held an especially high currency for scholars of strategic interactions between the United States and the USSR during the heyday of nuclear stalemate. In 1964, roughly two years after the Cuban Missile Crisis, U.S. leadership abandoned its hopes of fighting and surviving a limited nuclear war with the Soviet Union. Instead, the United States opted for a strategy of "mutually assured destruction" or "MAD," defined by Secretary of Defense Robert McNamara as "the capability to destroy the aggressor as a viable society, even after a well-planned and executed surprise attack on our forces."[23] McNamara predicated his peacekeeping logic on the likelihood of mutual ruin. Neither the United States nor the USSR would dare start a nuclear war because of the high risk of an unbearable outcome—total destruction for both sides—regardless of which country struck first.

All the Young Men was not the period's only movie to use the trope of mutually assured destruction in its portrayal of relations between white and black. Robert Wise, a winner of four Academy Awards, directed *Odds Against Tomorrow* in 1959. Nominated for Best Film Promoting International Understanding at the 1960 Golden Globe Awards, its plot revolves around two desperate men brought together to rob a bank. The white half of the dyad (Robert Ryan) is an unemployed ex-convict; the black, a lounge singer (Harry Belafonte). The white man's numerous expressions of racial hatred ("pickaninny," "nigger," "monkey") bring the two men to the threshold of several fistfights.

Whereas the white-black duos in the three Orientalist buddy films avoid annihilation by eventually recognizing their essential similarity, the two men in *Odds Against Tomorrow* fail on this score, enacting Thomas Jefferson's worst fear about America's racial fate, the mutual extermination of white and black. When the white man's hatred of black people causes the robbery to go awry, the two men turn on each other. Engaged in a gunfight, the robbers chase each other atop a series of multistory gasoline tanks until an errant bullet sparks a huge conflagration. Amidst the smoking ruins, a policeman, unable to tell the two charred bodies apart, asks his partner, "Which is which?" The other cop responds, "Take your pick."

Consideration of a film that received a great deal of attention in 1958, the year of its debut, serves as further evidence that the concept of mutually assured racial destruction enjoyed a fairly widespread currency in Hollywood. Stanley Kramer's allegory of white and black relations, *The Defiant Ones*, in which Poitier also stars, enjoyed critical success as one of the first Hollywood films to tackle explicitly the issue of race relations after the Hollywood blacklist era.[24] *The New Republic*'s film reviewer described it as "easily one of the best American pictures of the decade."[25] It won two Academy Awards (for best original screenplay and best black and white cinematography) and nine nominations (including best picture, best director, and best actor). The film has proven to be highly influential in the sense that it has served as a model for a welter of subsequent white and black buddy movies in the latter part of the twentieth century.[26] *The Defiant One*'s plot of two escaped convicts, one white and one black, chained together at the wrists resurfaces in movies such as *48 Hours* (Walter Hill, 1982, Nick Nolte and Eddie Murphy), *Fled* (Kevin Hooks, 1996, Stephen Baldwin and Laurence Fishburne), and *I-Spy* (Betty Thomas, 2002, Owen Wilson and Eddie Murphy).

The Defiant Ones may have served as the template for *All the Young Men*'s brinkmanship scene in which a black character played by Poitier breaks a stalemate by leveraging the risk of mutual destruction. Just after having made their escape through the woods, the two prisoners stop to try to break the heavy iron chain that binds them together. When this fails, a disagreement erupts about which direction to flee. Each has a plan. Noah Cullen (Poitier) wants to go north to try to hitch a ride on a train bound for Ohio. John "Joker" Jackson (Tony Curtis), the white convict, wants to go south, to an old girlfriend who lives in a nearby town.[27] "I don't go South," proclaims Cullen. "I'm a strange colored man in a white south town. How long you think before they pick me up?" Momentarily forgetting his fetters, Jackson asserts his right to act independently. "Get off my back," screams the white man, "I ain't married to you!" Cullen, holding up the chain, quickly reminds Jackson of their situation of forced dependence on one another, "You're married to me all right Joker, and here's the ring." "But I ain't going south on no honeymoon now," Cullen continues, "we going north." In response, Joker tries again to yank Cullen southward by the chain. But when the black man refuses to budge, Jackson starts a fistfight.

Like Poitier's Towler in *All the Young Men*, his Cullen in *The Defiant Ones* wins his way by manipulating the looming common threat. As he holds Jackson's fist closely between the two of them, Cullen responds by delivering an ultimatum: "Either we go north together or together we gonna go them ten miles right back on to Dead Street." "Dead Street" refers to the possibility of facing a brutal white Southern posse whose members do not acknowledge "the difference between hunting men and rabbits." For better or for worse, the iron chain ensures that whatever happens to the black man will also visit the white one. Thus, Cullen wins his way by running the risk of going back to meet the posse, an act that may ultimately kill them both.

The Defiant Ones narrates the movement from hatred to tolerance in accordance with the same formula employed by the three Orientalist buddy films examined in this chapter. A common threat forces the two men to cooperate. One scene, for example, begins with the escaped convicts jumping into a deep clay pit to avoid capture. A heavy rain has filled the bottom of the pit thigh-deep in water. The scene's staging suggests that if the convicts cannot get out of the pit, they'll drown. Initially, the two convicts try several times to climb out on their own. But the rain makes the walls loose and slick. Because they are chained together, when one of them slips and falls, he takes the other down with him. Eventually, the pair decides to cooperate rather than act independently. The white convict tells the black one that he will stand on his shoulders, using the stable foothold to get a good grip of the tree roots jutting out of the crumbling earthen wall. Through great effort and patience, they climb out of danger, together.

The sense of solidarity between the two men reaches its zenith near the film's end. Eventually, the convicts manage to break the thick metal chain, freeing them to go their separate ways. Despite their history of discord, they discover that they cannot break the psychic bonds of mutual obligation that result from their shared experience. When the pair reaches their vehicle to freedom, a freight train headed north to Ohio, Cullen runs and jumps on the train. The white man Jackson, hobbled by a gunshot wound, cannot make the leap. The black man finds that he cannot leave the other to perish, even if it means foregoing his final chance at freedom. Instead of staying on the train, Cullen jumps off so that his white partner would not have to face the bloodthirsty posse alone. In the final scene, the two former enemies wait calmly for the militia while the black man cradles the injured white man, soothing him with a softly vocalized Negro spiritual.

Many reviews at the time of its debut praised *The Defiant Ones'* ending as producing racial progress rather than racial subordination. "It is a measure of the film's excellence," writes *The Catholic World*, "that the fade-out, in which the two men await capture by the sheriff's posse because one would not leave his injured companion, seems like a happy ending."[28] "Brotherly love," *The New Republic* states, "makes the triumph." The review continues, "At the end they lie together panting. The white man says that their attempt didn't come to much, and the Negro replies, with a little smile: 'We doin' all right.' And we understand the victory."[29] A *New York Times* review has a similar reading:

> These two men, who think they are so profoundly different, are in basic respects the same. Each is the victim of cruel oppressions, each has his hopes and dreams, and each, as a consequence of frustrations, has committed crime...after perilous fording of streams...or hair-breadth escape from a mob, [the director Kramer] has them slash at each other with bitter accusations that reveal...their complete commonality. In the end, it is clear that they are brothers, stripped of all vulgar bigotry.[30]

Disaster chases both men in the form of a redneck sheriff's posse. The series of shared hardships that constitute their flight act as a solvent that strips away racial prejudice to reveal "their complete commonality." Just beneath the surface of skin tone, we find that white and black "are in basic respects the same."

At least one review differed from the main, anticipating Wiegman's critique of 1980s buddy films. *The Nation*'s review suggested that if *The Defiant Ones'* allegory had been true to life, the film would have let the two convicts beat each other to death. "The whites and blacks of the South have been chained together for a good many years," the reviewer wrote, "and they have not grown notably sweet toward each other because of the confinement." The review continues,

> It is easy to commend Mr. Kramer for the skill with which he uses popular melodrama to elucidate a social problem, but his oversimplification may give people the notion that prejudice is just a big, unhappy misunderstanding and that it can be solved by a little effort at a common goal. Prejudice is a tougher root than that, and sentimentality is a poor weapon in a good cause.[31]

As the review so nicely points out, characterizing racial problems in the United States circa 1958 as a spat between two brothers promotes little more than individual introspection. Sentimentality, searching our hearts and souls, is not a modality that brings institutional change.

One African American intellectual put an even finer point on his critique of *The Defiant Ones*' (and by extension the Orientalist buddy film's) self-serving sentimentality, interpreting the ending as a symptom of the white "American failure to face reality." "I saw that movie twice," writes James Baldwin. "I saw it downtown with all my liberal friends, who were delighted when Sidney jumped off the train." Then "I saw it uptown with my less liberal friends," he continues, "who were furious." In terms of Manhattan geography, Baldwin uses "downtown" and "liberal" as code words for *white*, "uptown" and "less liberal" as code for *Harlem* and *black*, respectively. To Baldwin, an ending in which the black man sacrifices his chance for freedom because the white man cannot keep up seems ludicrous. "Why is it necessary at this late date," Baldwin asks the white reader, "to prove that the Negro doesn't really hate you"?[32] Recalling what was for Baldwin a contemporary event helps to explain his sarcastic tone. Only three years earlier, the national and world press gave extensive coverage to the sort of "reality" that so many whites failed to "face," when two white Mississippi men lynched and disfigured fourteen-year-old Emmett Till for allegedly whistling at a white woman. Baldwin answers his own question. "Liberals are so delighted by the movie" because it assuages their guilt regarding white mistreatment of blacks.

3

The Blaxploitation Buddy Film

The villains in the 1974 Blaxploitation film *Three the Hard Way* (Gordon Parks, Jr.) are members of a latter-day Nazi group who plan to poison the nation's water supply with a chemical lethal to blacks but harmless to whites. "Just like sickle cell anemia," the toxin's creator boasts, "this little mixture of mine is as lethal as cyanide, [but] will not affect the people of the Caucasian race." "It took God seven days to create the world," another member exalts, "we can cleanse it in just three." Evoking memories of WWII Jewish genocide, the paramilitary group kidnaps African Americans to use as guinea pigs for the chemical's development process. One of the film's three black heroes, a Vietnam veteran and martial arts expert named Mister Keyes (Jim Kelly, the international karate champion of the 1970s) recruits a friend and fellow black belt, an Asian American man called Link (David Chow), to help him save African America. Unarmed and vastly outnumbered, the interracial pair intercepts the villains at a Detroit water treatment plant. On defeating the white supremacists, black and yellow reaffirm their bond with a Black Power handshake.

The previous chapter analyzes three Cold War era Hollywood combat films that are early examples of the Orientalist buddy film's triangular representation of race: white and black bonding in the face of a mutual Asian threat. This chapter demonstrates the flexibility of the racial triangle as I describe it by analyzing one of the Orientalist buddy film's cognates, another type of interracial buddy movie that surfaced as a result of America's changing racial politics in the 1960s and 1970s. In particular, this chapter sharpens my profile of the Orientalist buddy film by showing how black demand for social change at home and an unpopular war in Southeast Asia generated moments of political and cultural solidarity between African

Americans and Asian Americans. This sense of unity forged between black and yellow by the common enemy of white supremacy did not dispel Hollywood's Orientalist buddy film. *Black Mama, White Mama* (Eddie Romero, 1973), for example, has a white and black buddy duo (Margaret Markov and Pam Grier) fighting a Filipino drug dealer who refers to Grier's character as "that black bitch." Rather, the shifting political landscape, in tandem with Hollywood's 1969–1971 financial crisis, forced a crucial reconfiguration of the racial triangle as it appeared during the 1950s, producing yet another type of interracial buddy movie: what I call the Blaxploitation buddy film. An offshoot of the larger Blaxploitation genre of the 1970s, it features black and yellow joining forces to defeat a racist white villain.

The Blaxploitation buddy film echoes the Orientalist buddy film in several respects. Both have a tripartite racial content of white, black, and Asian. Both follow the same general formula. Two buddies, each of a different race, join forces to defeat a villain who signals racist belief through an epithet or an association with slavery or both. The Blaxploitation buddy film and the Orientalist buddy film, however, differ in crucial ways. The former has a black and yellow buddy dyad, a black hero and an Asian sidekick, rather than a white and black pairing. In *Way of the Black Dragon* (Chih Chen, 1978), for example, the African American Interpol agent Billy Eaton (Ron Van Clief) teams up with the working-class Chan (Carter Wong) to break apart a drug ring.[1] *The Dynamite Brothers* (Al Adamson, 1974) couples Stud Brown (Timothy Brown), an African American who wants to rid his Watts neighborhood of heroin, with Larry Chin (Allan Tang), a Hong Kong native who has traveled to Los Angeles in search of his brother. A derivative of Stanley Kramer's *The Defiant Ones* (1958), one of *Dynamite*'s scenes has the two men escape from police custody, running through woods while handcuffed together at the wrists. Two of this chapter's Blaxploitation buddy films put a black woman in the leading role, a reflection of the increased visibility in African American political and cultural movements of women such as Angela Davis and Cecily Tyson.[2] A sequel to Jack Starrett's popular *Cleopatra Jones* (1973), Chuck Bail's *Cleopatra Jones and the Casino of Gold* (1975) has a dyad consisting of the movie's namesake (Tamara Dobson), a U.S. government agent who travels to Asia "to bust a drug ring that makes over 100 million dollars a year," and an Asian female police officer, Mi Ling Fong (Ni Tien). Anticipating popular interracial buddy films of the 1980s and 1990s such as *Lethal Weapon* (Richard Donner, 1987), Jones resists the initial order to collaborate with the new colleague, explaining that she would rather work "alone than with some partner who's going to screw up and get me knocked off." Jones, however, changes her mind when Fong saves her from a fatal stabbing. In *TNT Jackson* (Cirio Santiago, 1975), the movie's namesake, Diana "TNT" Jackson (Playboy Playmate Jeannie Bell), searches for her brother who, unknown to her, has been killed by a heroin syndicate. During her search, she befriends a Chinese night-club owner, Joe (Chiquito), who assists her.

A change forced by the civil rights movement, the Blaxploitation buddy film has a white racist villain rather than the Orientalist buddy film's Asian one. The white nemesis in *Dynamite Brothers* is a crooked narcotics detective, Lieutenant Burke (Aldo Ray), supported by bribes from heroin dealers. He establishes himself as racist by repeatedly calling blacks and Asians "niggers" and "chinks," respectively. In addition to calling an African American underling (Stan Shaw) a "dirty black bastard," the white chief of *TNT Jackson*'s drug syndicate, Sid (Ken Metcalfe), expresses his hatred of blacks by telling the heroine that he doesn't want her color to "rub off" on him. Led by a white boss (Robert Blackwood), *Way of the Black Dragon*'s heroin

Figure 3.1 Tamara Dobson in *Cleopatra Jones and the Casino of Gold*.

syndicate kidnaps unsuspecting women to use as mules to smuggle drugs. Once the dealer receives his contraband, he sells the women as sex slaves. Likewise, *Casino of Gold*'s white villain (Stella Stevens), a lesbian who deals drugs in her posh Macau casino, trades in flesh. Calling herself the "Dragon Lady," she "adopts," to use her word, young orphan Chinese girls to sell as slaves.

The blonde-haired Dragon Lady mistreats African Americans as well as Asians, making the white American an enemy to both groups. In one scene, she greets two of Jones's fellow government agents (Caro Kenyatta and Albert Popwell), a pair of black American brothers, as they enter her establishment. "Welcome to my casino, boys," she says, underscoring the fact of her ownership. Surprised to see black people in Hong Kong, her Caucasian casino guests react dramatically to the brothers. One woman chokes on her drink. Others point and gawk. "Oh my God!" a woman says to her husband, "they've got spades here [in Asia] too." Invoking what one film critic calls "the potent racial fear of the over-endowed negro," still another white visitor asks in a salacious tone, "Do you think it's true what they say [about black men]?"[3] The Dragon Lady reacts to these comments with a silent smile that signals tacit consent. Even though the remarks do not come directly from the villain, the white gamblers' talk reinforces by extension the drug dealer's standing as a racist: her casino, her patrons, her racism. In a different scene, the villain addresses the black men as "boys" again, to which one of them quips, "Did she say Roy?" The remark refers to the fact that "boy," a common epithet for an African American man, rhymes with the proper name "Roy." The play on words aims at the viewers who have seen the first *Cleopatra Jones* film. In it, the same brothers use the same rhyme to playfully draw attention to the fact that some whites use "boy" to assert a supposed superiority over a black man.

The villain in the Blaxploitation buddy film exists so that the hero may punish him or her for being racist, a function that derives from its parent genre. With "liberal doses of gratuitous sex and drugs," as Ed Guerrero glosses it, the standard Blaxploitation film's definitive theme centers on a "bad nigger," a black hero "who challenges the oppressive white system" through violence "and wins." Three early movies that establish Blaxploitation—*Sweet Sweetback's Baad Asssss Song* (Melvin Van Peebles, 1971), *Shaft* (Gordon Parks, 1971), and *Super Fly* (Gordon Parks, Jr., 1972)—illustrate the genre's hallmark, what Guerrero calls "black victory over white evil" (86, 104). In *Shaft*, a Harlem crime boss hires the black private detective of the film's title to rescue his daughter, kidnapped by the Italian Mafia. After killing the mobsters and recovering the girl, the black hero ends the film with a loud and gloating laugh. *Super Fly*'s Youngblood Priest (Ron O'Neal), a Harlem cocaine dealer, wants to leave New York's largest drug syndicate. But the white man who secretly runs it, the city's deputy police commissioner, will not let him quit. Priest frames his desire for a new life in terms of slavery. "I want to be free," he declares to the commissioner, "you don't own me, pig." Before escaping, Priest pummels the boss and his two henchmen, throwing one headfirst into a garbage can. In *Sweet*, the young black man of the title (the film's director, Melvin Van Peebles), escapes from Los Angeles into Mexico after killing two white LA cops.

The Blaxploitation hero or "bad nigger" stands in stark contrast to the type of roles played by Sidney Poitier, Hollywood's first black leading man. A Hollywood dominated by whites celebrated Poitier. One of the most successful stars of 1967, irrespective of race, for his work in *Guess Who's Coming to Dinner* (Stanley Kramer), *In the Heat of the Night* (Norman Jewison), and *To Sir with Love* (James Clavell), he contended for the 1959 Best Actor Academy Award for *The Defiant Ones* (Stanley Kramer, 1958) and won it in 1964 for *Lilies of the Field* (Ralph Nelson, 1963). But as black protest movements grew during the 1960s and the 1970s, so did criticism of Poitier from some in the black artistic community. The two most scathing reviews of his career are playwright Clifford Mason's 1967 "Why Does White America Love Sidney Poitier So?" and theater scholar Larry Neal's 1969 "Beware of the Tar Baby," both in the *New York Times*. Calling him "a showcase nigger" and "a million-dollar shoe shine boy," respectively, Mason and Neal argue that Poitier's career in an industry run by "gutless white liberals" represents that of an emasculated racial token. Viewed as obstacles to black advancement, his fame and success obscured "what black people must understand," Neal writes. "We are ruled by Beasts," referring to whites, "whose final perceptions and attitudes are antihuman," he continues. "It will take more than a public relations struggle or a Black studies program to change them." Instead, "for nearly two decades," Mason remarks, the black community has had "the same old Sidney Poitier syndrome: a good guy in a totally white world, with no wife, no sweetheart, no woman to love or kiss, helping the white man solve the white man's problem," "good nigger that he is."[4]

African America's growing political consciousness during the 1960s and 1970s created a taste and a market for a new kind of black male lead, "a viable black-power sex figure," as Donald Bogle puts it.[5] In Isaac Julien's 2002 documentary about the genre, *Baad Asssss Cinema*, Fred Williamson, a former professional football player and star of *Hammer* (Bruce D. Clark, 1972), *Black Caesar* (Larry Cohen, 1973), and *That Man Bolt* (Henry Levin, 1973), describes the "three rules" that constitute Blaxploitation's antidote to Poitier: "you can't kill me, I win all my fights, I get the girl at the end of the movie if I want her."[6] Another former football pro, Jim Brown, made a career out of playing the *bad nigger* in a number of Blaxploitation movies: *Slaughter* (Jack Starrett, 1972), *Black Gunn* (Robert Hartford-Davis, 1972), *Slaughter's Big Rip-Off* (Gordon Douglas, 1973), and *Three the Hard Way*. "A crystallization of physical potency," writes his biographer, "young black children in the ghetto liked" Brown "because he was a black man who could shove back to whitey the violence whitey had originally dealt out."[7] The civil rights and the black power movements gave Brown what Hollywood denied to Poitier, Guerrero asserts: the freedom "to act in a violent assertive manner and express his sexuality openly and beyond dominant cinema's sexual taboos" (79).

To function as a foil to the bad nigger, Blaxploitation depicts whites as villains who express an extreme hatred of black people. Film scholar Daniel J. Leab describes the genre's white characters as "moral lepers," who represent "the oppressive white system" and whose "rhetoric of bigotry" and "psychotically antiblack" behavior signify the long history of injustice borne by black America.[8] *Sweet* vilifies its white characters even more relentlessly than *Shaft* and *Super Fly*. Aside from voicing countless racial epithets, the film's collective villain, the entire LA police force, menaces or murders all of the black people who help Sweet during his escape. In separate scenes, white police torture a black man by discharging a gun next to his ears, which deafens him, and beat another black man with the butt of a gun for sleeping with a white woman.

The movie's caricature of white racism intensifies the act of vengeance that comes inevitably by the end of the movie. *Sweet*, the founding movie of the genre, makes its desire for black retaliation against white America explicit (Guerrero 86).[9] Just before the credits roll, a title card celebrates the fact that the black protagonist "gets away with it"—that is, the killing of several white cops—while simultaneously warning white viewers of more black revenge to come. "Watch out," another title card reads, "a baad asssss nigger is coming back to collect some dues." In a 1971 *Life* magazine interview, the director Melvin Van Peebles explains his film's angry mood, describing it as "not what the man wants to hear." *Sweet* "shows a *nigger* that busts a White man's head *and gets away with it*!" White viewers may not enjoy it, he continues, "but Black folks do....They scream and cry and laugh and yell at the brother on the screen. For the Black man, Sweetback is a new kind of hero. For the White man, my picture is a new kind of foreign film."[10] Even though produced independently of the major studios, *Sweet*'s box office success enabled it to set the tone of Blaxploitation's racial politics.

Sweet's message reflects the feelings of many black Americans at the time. Remembering the prominence of the civil rights and the black power movements in their heyday contextualizes Van Peebles's anger. Rather than rehash this familiar history, it suffices to say that black demands for social change created a rising political consciousness among an African American population losing patience with white intransigence toward meaningful policy changes. Fred Williamson hints at the frustration fueling the revenge fantasy's appeal for African American audiences in the 1970s. "If there were more than five blacks on the corner they considered it a riot," he recounts, "so they'd bring out the dogs and they'd turn the water hoses on....All of this stuff was still happening in the 70s," he continues. "If you fought back you went straight to jail....The only way we could get away with it was on the screen."[11] Williamson's "dogs" and "hoses," of course, refer to the violence dispensed by angry white mobs on black Americans during 1960s civil rights protests such as the southern Freedom Rides and "Bloody Sunday" in Selma, Alabama.

It seems unlikely that a Hollywood run by whites would offer revenge fantasies like *Sweet*, *Shaft*, and *Super Fly*, movies in which a black protagonist causes so many whites so much pain. On the business side, one development in particular primed the pump for Hollywood's production of the roughly sixty films marketed primarily to a young black male urban audience during the period (Guerrero 69). Economic factors both inside and outside Hollywood created the industry's financial crisis of 1969–1971, to use film scholar David A. Cook's definition of the emergency. In 1965, Fox made *The Sound of Music* (Robert Wise) for $10 million, an expensive figure at the time, but it unexpectedly drew $135 million in revenue in the two years after its debut. Hoping to replicate its box office success, the major studios adopted a big-budget philosophy, which produced a glut of expensive films leveraged by money borrowed at high interest rates. With the advent of a national recession in

1969, the industry's markets shrank precipitously and "Hollywood nearly collapsed," as cinema scholar David J. Londoner puts it.[12]

Cook and Londoner may explain why white Hollywood turned to black American audiences for relief during an economic crisis, but they fail to mention a third racial element that prevents some Blaxploitation films from fitting neatly into the dominant white and black binary of American racial discourse. Often, Blaxploitation films establish their bad niggers, to use Guerrero's term again, as fierce fighters through brief scenes that show them practicing martial arts (Japanese karate or Chinese kung fu), marking their mode of violence as Asian. A scene in *Super Fly* shows the Harlem drug dealer Priest, clad in a white karate uniform, flipping his sparring partner onto the mat several times in a row. Several subsequent Blaxploitation movies follow *Super Fly*'s example. The protagonist (Paul Winfield) of *Gordon's War* (Ossie Davis, 1973), a Vietnam veteran who vows to rid Harlem of drugs, drops into a martial arts fighting crouch, hands forward and palms open, just before he pummels the neighborhood dope dealer. A James Bond imitation, the title's namesake (Fred Williamson) in *That Man Bolt* (Henry Levin, 1973) practices a lengthy karate routine in the opening scene. Similarly, *Foxy Brown*'s main title sequence (Jack Hill, 1974) features its heroine (Pam Grier) in silhouette, rehearsing karate forms.

The Asian martial arts theme plays a central role in the Blaxploitation buddy film. Numerous fight scenes portray one or both of the buddies as martial artists who decimate unbelievable numbers of enemy thugs in equally unbelievable ways. One can trace this martial arts motif to what film scholar David Desser calls the 1970s "kung fu craze," which refers to the popularity, especially with urban black American audiences, of Hong Kong-produced action movies that feature martial arts fighting. As evidence of the trend, Desser cites *Variety*'s May 16, 1973, weekly ticket sales tally, which lists three kung fu movies at the top—*Fists of Fury* (Wei Lo, 1971), *Deep Thrust: The Hand of Death* (Feng Huang, 1972), and *Five Fingers of Death* (Chang-hwa Jeong, 1972)—"perhaps for the first and only time in history of the American cinema." Desser then explains the "connection between kung fu films and black audiences." Spotlighting an "underdog of color, [a] lone, often unarmed combatant" who defeats an enemy who represents an oppressive status quo, be they "colonialist enemies, white culture, or the Japanese," he writes, such films "offered the only nonwhite heroes" available to black viewers "alienated by mainstream film and often by mainstream culture."[13] "These films focus," cultural studies scholar Amy Ongiri notes, "on either the triumph of the little guy...or the nobility of the struggle to recognize human-ity and virtue in all people....This familiar formula," she continues, helps to explain "African American interest in martial arts culture" during the 1970s.[14]

The link between African America and the kung fu film produced in Hong Kong gave rise to two variations of the Blaxploitation buddy film that drop the Asian buddy yet retain the black and yellow dyad. The first variation unites black and yellow in the form of a single black hero who is a martial arts expert. In the first *Cleopatra Jones* film (Jack Starrett, 1973), Tamara Dobson works alone. She conquers a villain named Mommy, yet another white American lesbian drug trafficker (Shelley Winters), who calls her a "trouble-making coon" and a "goddamn black bitch." In *Black Belt Jones* (Robert Clouse, 1974) and *Black Samurai* (Al Adamson, 1977), Jim Kelly deploys his karate prowess to vanquish, respectively, white mobsters who refer to blacks as "ape[s]" and a white witch doctor (Bill Roy) who sells young women as sex slaves. The other variation features one or more black Vietnam veterans who, on their return to the United States, defeat white American racists by using the combat training learned in Southeast Asia: *Slaughter* (Jack Starrett, 1972), *Gordon's War* (Ossie Davis, 1973), *The Black Six* (Matt Cimber, 1974), and *Brotherhood of Death* (Bill Berry, 1976). This version reflects African American disaffection with the Vietnam War. In a 1967 speech, for example, Martin Luther King, Jr. noted the irony experienced by blacks when forced to a faraway fight for rights that their own country denied to them at home, a repetition of WWI and WWII. "We were tak-ing the black young men," he said, "crippled by [white] society and sending them eight thousand miles away to guarantee liberties in Southeast Asia which they had not found in Southwest Georgia and East Harlem."[15]

These Blaxploitation buddy films that tie together black and yel-low either as a buddy dyad or as a black hero who does martial arts or applies combat skills learned in Vietnam echo the views of some prom-inent social justice advocates of the period who urged an alignment of black and yellow to fight a United States run by racist whites. In a 1963 Detroit speech, for example, Malcolm X urged black Americans and Asian Americans to bond in the face of domestic racism. "The white man," he told the crowd, represents "an enemy to all [nonwhites], be you black, brown, red or yellow, a so-called Negro....We have a com-mon oppressor, a common exploiter, and a common discriminator."

He said, "Once we all realize that we have a common enemy, then we unite."[16] At the 1969 Vietnam War moratorium demonstration in Washington, DC, Black Panther Connie Matthews instructed African Americans to look to the East for a role model for defying oppression. "The Vietnamese are a good example of the people being victorious," she said, "with all of America's technology and her greatness she has been unable to defeat the Vietnamese. Every man, woman, and child has resisted." Echoing Indonesian President Sukarno's speech at the 1955 Bandung Conference in which he reminded Africa and Asia of their "common detestation of racialism" and "colonialism," in the early 1960s Marxist sociologist Immanuel Wallerstein suggested that, under the banner of anticolonialism, China and the African continent unite against the white "Western world."[17]

In the late 1960s and early 1970s, news of Vietnam War atrocities strengthened Malcolm X's claim that blacks and Asians occupied the same position relative to the "white man" by providing the American public with an actual white villain whose racism toward Asians constituted his infamy. The 1971 court-martial of Lieutenant William "Rusty" Calley for his part in the 1968 My Lai massacre serves as a prime example of how the period's racial politics created a cultural context that made it not just feasible but also profitable for Hollywood to screen black and yellow joining forces against a white menace. In March 1968, an Army company of roughly 115 soldiers attacked a small village in South Vietnam thought to be sympathetic to the Viet Cong. Despite meeting no resistance at My Lai, the company proceeded to kill hundreds of villagers. All of them, according to a 1969 *Time* magazine article, "were either elderly men, women or children."[18] An Army report states that the American soldiers committed "individual and group acts of murder, rape, sodomy, maiming, assault on noncombatants, and the mistreatment and killing of detainees."[19] Estimates of the body count vary. The Army's initial March 1969 press release mischaracterizes the massacre as a "running battle," which resulted in 128 enemy dead. The 1969 *Time* article states a range of 109 to 567. One scholarly history of the event estimates between 400 and 500, another, "well over 300."[20] The memorial at the site of the massacre lists 504 names.[21]

According to one historian, news of the "the massacre dominated public discourse within the United States"[22] from fall 1969, when the Army charged Calley, the ranking officer at the site of the massacre, with the premeditated murder of 109 South Vietnamese civilians (the official charge reads "Oriental human beings") at My Lai, to spring 1971, when it sentenced him to life in prison at hard labor.[23] Seymour Hersh, the reporter who would many years later in 2004 break the Abu Ghraib torture story in *The New Yorker*, broke the My Lai story in the Chicago *Sun-Times* and the St. Louis *Post-Dispatch* in November 1969.[24] An April 1971 *Time* article claimed that "the Calley affair" had produced a "crisis of confidence" more grave than "the horror following the assassination of President Kennedy."[25]

The most graphic record of the massacre appeared in a December 1969 issue of *Life* magazine as a series of pictures taken by Ron Haeberle, a military photographer traveling with the company.[26] One photograph shows a group of Vietnamese women and children cowering with fright.[27] Eyewitness testimony, which revealed that Haeberle took the photograph an instant before their murder, makes it particularly haunting. The witness, a soldier in the company, described at least three other soldiers cornering a group of women and infants, which included a "girl [of] about 13...wearing black pajamas." Intending to rape her, "a G.I. grabbed the girl and with the help of others started stripping her." During the commotion, her mother tried to intervene, "scratching and clawing at the soldiers.... Another Vietnamese woman," the witness continued,

> tried to stop the woman from objecting. One soldier kicked the mother and another slapped her up a bit. Haeberle jumped in to take a picture of the group of women. The picture shows the 13-year-old girl, hiding behind her mother, trying to button the top of her pajamas. When they noticed Ron, they left off and turned away as if everything was normal. Then a soldier asked, "Well, what'll we do with 'em?" "Kill 'em," another answered.[28]

Illustrative of both the brutality enacted by the American soldiers and the terror experienced by the Vietnamese civilians, this and the rest of Haeberle's photographs caused a worldwide uproar.

The only person convicted of murder at My Lai, Calley stood at the center of the controversy. A White House poll measuring the public's awareness of his verdict registered 96 percent, "the highest we've gotten on any subject in any of our polls," according to Chief of Staff Bob Haldeman.[29] Many Americans supported Calley. The White House received more than 5,000 telegrams, which favored clemency by a ratio of 100 to 1. After three days in jail, President Richard Nixon transferred him to house arrest, prompting "a spontaneous round of applause on the floor" of the House of Representatives.[30] Supporters even produced a song, "The Battle Hymn of Lieutenant Calley," which broke the Billboard chart's top 40.[31] Even though he received the maximum sentence, such support ensured that Calley would not spend much time behind bars. Within half a year, in August 1971, the Army reduced his life sentence to twenty years; in April 1974, to ten years. Roughly three years after the verdict, in November 1974, Secretary of the Army Howard Calloway pardoned Calley.

Identified as "an all-American boy" and "an average American boy"[32] by the American press, Calley "came to embody" the issue of anti-Asian sentiment on the part of U.S. troops in Vietnam.[33] A 1971 *Time* article quotes from the court's psychiatric report that Calley "did not feel as if he were killing humans, but rather that they were animals with whom one could not speak or reason." "The tension of being feared and hated in a remote, racially different Asian country has pushed many Americans toward a tribalistic logic," the article continues, "all 'gooks' are enemies and therefore killable."[34] Many mainstream news sources characterized Calley's attitude as typical and American mistreatment of the Vietnamese as widespread. In "Why Civilians Are War Victims in Vietnam," a 1969 article in *U.S. News and World Report*, the Yale psychiatrist Robert Jay Lifton noted that the American soldiers at My Lai referred to the Vietnamese as "gooks" and "dinks," terms that signify subhuman status.[35] A 1969 *Newsweek* article noted that "many U.S. fighting men" harbored such "antipathy," calling it the "dink syndrome." "It's much easier to kill a 'dink' than it is to shoot a 'Vietnamese,'" it observed.[36] A 1971 *Time* article called the same phenomenon the "'mere gook' rule."[37] A 1969 *Nation* editorial claimed that U.S. soldiers exhibited "the most horrifying opinions of the Asians among whom they were serving."[38]

Because it incorporates elements of the interracial buddy films that I discuss above, Bruce Lee's star vehicle, *Enter the Dragon* (Robert Clouse, 1973), the most popular of the "kung fu craze" films for American audiences of all races, seems a fitting movie to end this chapter on the Orientalist buddy film's Blaxploitation cognate. In this joint production from Warner Bros. and Raymond Chow's Golden Harvest film company based in Hong Kong, the British Hong Kong government recruits a kung fu expert to infiltrate a major opium ring under the pretext of a martial arts tournament held on the drug pusher's island fortress.

Echoing both the kung fu film and the standard Blaxploitation film, *Enter the Dragon* employs the revenge motif so attractive to 1970s black audiences. The hero, Lee, named after the film's leading man, is Chinese and a disciple of the Shaolin Temple, the martial arts monastery made famous in the United States by the ABC television show starring David Carradine, *Kung Fu* (1972–1975). In *Enter the Dragon*, Lee bests a fighter named Parsons (Peter Archer), a white New Zealander who menaces a group of Hong Kong servants. When the bully tries to bait Lee into a fight, the Shaolin priest outwits Parsons, then humiliates him in plain view of the servants who enjoy a vicarious revenge. The film stages yet another confrontation between Lee and a white bully, a karate champion named Oharra (Bob Wall). Lee wants to avenge his sister, Su Lin (Angela Mao), whom Oharra had killed years before. When he and Oharra meet in a tournament fight, Lee wins the bout in a spectacular fashion. At one point he kicks Oharra in the jaw while doing a full body flip. The fight ends when Lee kills him. With a catlike leap and growl, one of his signature kung fu moves, Lee lands on a prone Oharra, crushing his neck.

Lee is the film's protagonist. But he splits the fight scenes with two other heroic martial arts fighters, one white and the other black, in supporting roles. Roper (John Saxon), a white American deeply indebted to the Mafia, enters the tournament for the prize money. Williams (Jim Kelly), an African American, operates a South Central LA karate school. Revenue concerns motivated the decision to write Roper and Williams into the script. According to film scholar Gina Marchetti, the movie's producers employed heroic characters of three different racial types "to draw in as much of the international action audience as possible from Hong Kong to black America."[39] By covering the racial spectrum from white to black to Asian, *Enter the Dragon*'s three-way split enables the film to combine thematic elements of not only the standard Blaxploitation film and the kung fu movie, but of all the interracial buddy film variations that I examine in this chapter: the white and black buddy film, the Orientalist buddy film, and the Blaxploitation buddy film.

The black character, Williams, is the key that enables the film to incorporate elements from a variety of film types. Like so many Blaxploitation movies, the film salts its sets with numerous icons that connect him to the black protest movements of the 1960s and 1970s. A shot of Williams's quarters on the island shows a wall poster with a line drawing of the Black Power salute, a raised fist, made famous by the 1968 Summer Olympics medalists John Carlos and Tommie Smith. One scene follows Williams into his LA karate school where he greets another black man with a Black Power handshake. The camera pans the interior, showing a large logo painted on the *dojo* wall. It is the crest of the Black Karate Federation (BKF), an organization started in the 1960s to teach karate to the poor black youth of the South Central Los Angeles. The crest has a coiled cobra against a red, black, and green background. The colors refer to the flag designed by Marcus Garvey in 1914 for the Universal Negro Improvement Association (UNIA), which many Black Power organizations adopted in the 1960s and 1970s as a symbol of liberation and pan-African unity.[40]

The movie exhibits definitive elements of the interracial buddy film in its various iterations. Roper and Williams, friends since their military service in the Vietnam War, constitute the white and black dyad of the standard interracial buddy film and of the Orientalist buddy film. As in *The Defiant Ones* (Stanley Kramer, 1958), which follows a relationship between a white man and a black man from initial animosity to a loving friendship, theirs is an unlikely bond. Race aside, Roper and Williams are complete opposites, which leads the viewer to presume that they did not begin as friends, but instead forged a friendship in the crucible of a war against a common Asian enemy. The film signals this opposition through the ridiculous amount of luggage that Roper brings to the tournament: more than fourteen suitcases. Roper requires five rickshaws to travel the streets of Hong Kong: one for himself and four for his baggage. Props that make several appearances, his luggage signifies hedonism. "A man's strength can be measured by his appetites," he says, justifying his inability to control his desire for what he calls "first class" living (golf, gambling, and fancy clothes). "Indeed, a man's strength flows from his appetites." By contrast, Lee and Williams suffice with modest loads that befit the modest lifestyles of a temple monk and of a community role model who wants to uplift South Central's black youth through the discipline of karate.

Williams's presence allows the martial arts film to mirror yet another type of interracial buddy film. Through him, the film exhibits the Blaxploitation buddy film's theme of solidarity between black and yellow on the basis of shared social oppression. While sightseeing in Hong Kong, Williams identifies one of its poor neighborhoods as analogous to his own in Los Angeles. "Ghettoes are the same everywhere," he remarks, "they stink." All three kung fu heroes take the same tour, but Williams is the only figure to make a personal connection with the ghetto denizens. To their delight, he waves at a group of Chinese children peering at him from their hovel. A subplot joins Williams and Lee together as a black and yellow buddy dyad, completing the movie's likeness to the Blaxploitation buddy film. In defiance of the head of the drug ring, Han (Shih Kien), Lee steals away from the palace at night to reconnoiter. By coincidence, Williams observes Lee's night maneuvers. In a show of solidarity with the Asian fighter, however, the black man refuses to name Lee when questioned by Han. For his recalcitrance, Han savagely kills Williams.

What Han does with Williams's body marks him as the racist Asian villain of the Orientalist buddy film. To intimidate Roper, Han hangs the black man's body. The manner in which he does so makes it resemble a lynching, a display similar to the scene in *Bataan* (Tay Garnett, 1943) in which the Japanese hang a Filipino soldier by the neck from a jungle tree, as I discuss in an earlier chapter. Wrapped in chains and ropes and suspended from a lifting hook joined to an industrial hoist, Williams's half-naked body glistens with fresh blood. While the soundtrack plays a horror movie refrain, a close-up of his upper torso reveals his battered head hanging forward at a grotesque angle as if hanging by the neck. The film completes its portrait of Han as a racist by depicting him as a slave trader. "He selects attractive girls and methodically builds their dependence on" opium, explains the British agent (Geoffrey Weeks) who briefs Lee, "then sells them to an elite clientele around the world." Lee discovers two such women on Han's island, both white and blonde. One begs him to free her from her jail cell, informing him that she comes from California and is only seventeen. The other one acts like a zombie, her unblinking eyes staring into the distance.

Williams's death allows the film to transform into still another type of interracial buddy film: what we might call the kung fu buddy film, which features a yellow and white buddy dyad. In this sense, *Enter the Dragon* stands as a precursor of *Shanghai Noon* (Tom Dey, 2000) and its sequel, *Shanghai Knights* (David Dobkin, 2003), both starring Jackie Chan and Owen Wilson. *Enter the Dragon*'s Roper and Lee follow the classic buddy dyad trajectory as rivals who form a friendship in the face of a common enemy. A quick scene that involves an insect fight, a common form of gambling in China, establishes the two as rivals. The fighting insects serve as proxies for Roper and Lee. While bettors try to predict which bug will win, two praying mantises fight in a small bamboo box that serves as a ring. Roper challenges Lee to a bet, "I'll lay you fifty bucks on the big" mantis, which is also a style of kung fu. Roper loses the bet, prompting him to warn Lee,

"I plan to win [the money] back." Williams's death, however, makes room for the two kung fu fighters to transcend their rivalry. When, near the film's end, Han commands his army of kung fu guards to kill Lee and Roper, the two former rivals seal their bond, fighting side by side against the mutual enemy.

4

The Orientalist Buddy Film in the 1980s and 1990s: *Flash Gordon* (1980), *Lethal Weapon* (1987–1998), *Rising Sun* (1993)

America is one coherent society, with bonds that are stronger than its internal dif-ferences. We understood this instinctively during World War II, but not enough since then.

—James Fallows, More Like Us: Making America Great Again[1]

Chapter 2 shows how three Cold War era combat films—*China Gate* (1957), *Pork Chop Hill* (1959), and *All the Young Men* (1960)—established the Orientalist buddy film blueprint by elevating a black character to occupy one of the two buddy slots of the standard "white male" buddy dyad (Guerrero, 127). Chapter 3 shows how Hollywood transformed the triangular representation of race into a black and yellow dyad buddy pair with a white figure that functions as the racist villain. This chapter considers several movies of the last twenty years of the millennium—*Flash Gordon* (Mike Hodges, 1980), the *Lethal Weapon* series (Richard Donner, 1987–1998), and *Rising Sun* (Philip Kaufman, 1993, based on the 1992 Michael Crichton novel of the same name)—that illustrate the triangulated figure's reversion back to the Cold War configuration of the Orientalist buddy film: white and black buddies who bond through a common Asian enemy.

The Orientalist buddy film template structures the campy science fiction film *Flash Gordon*. From his remote planet of Mongo, Emperor Ming the Merciless (Max von Sydow) seeks to destroy humanity by setting the moon on a crash course with the earth. Von Sydow's yellowface portrayal of the extraterrestrial villain instantly strikes the viewer as a generalized Asian threat. Heavy black mascara makes the Swedish actor's eyes appear angular and narrow. An Asian actress plays Ming's daughter, Princess Aura (Ornella Muti). Her body, a biological marker of the Asian, underscores the father as yellow. The Emperor Ming's title and name sound Chinese. The round portals of his ornate palace mimic the style of traditional Chinese architecture; his native planet is a contraction of "Mongol." If Ming's name and planetary address have Chinese referents, the identical robots that comprise his vast army signify as Japanese, futuristic samurai armored in shiny gold metal. The film's heavy reliance on the two most common metonyms for the Asian—Japanese and Chinese—without acknowledging any difference between the subgroups conforms to the old Hollywood pattern of treating "Asian" as a catchall term. Thus, it reinforces the familiar stereotype that all Asians are essentially the same despite different body types and national origins.[2]

Flash Gordon vilifies Ming by depicting him as an amalgam of two common stereotypes of the Asian: the yellow peril and the model minority, its fraternal twin. Numerous details establish the emperor as a yellow peril, an Asian with ambitions to rule humanity. Ming's makeup, his talonlike fingernails, and wispy black mustache

Figure 4.1   Emperor Ming the Merciless (Max von Sydow) in *Flash Gordon*.

and beard link him to Hollywood adaptations of pulp novelist Sax Rohmer's Chinese arch villain, Fu Manchu.[3] The model minority stereotype associates Asians with wealth, ruling class status, and control of cutting-edge science and technology. The sumptuous interior sets of the ruler's palace signal a sultan's life of luxury. Robots and other forms of advanced technology that perform a myriad of fantastic functions fill the emperor's world. Some machines float in defiance of gravity. Others reprogram the minds of his enemies or enable him to communicate telepathically. Still others allow Ming to create natural disasters on earth.

Ming's dual-sided profile fits those drawn by several important works in Asian American Studies. Gary Okihiro observes that the yellow peril and the model minority represent two halves of an interlocking pair of stereotypes, forming "a circular relationship." "The model minority," he explains, "if taken too far, can become the yellow peril."[4] Other scholars note that the combination of profiles generates animus toward Asian Americans. "The 'model minority,'" Nazil Kibria writes, "becomes the 'yellow peril' as the connotation of Asian achievement becomes cause for resentment and so takes on an inhuman, even species-different character....Hostilities towards Asians often focus on their [so-called] inhuman, robot-like and one-dimensional qualities, thus underscoring their essential distance from what is 'normal.' "[5]

Ming stands in stark contrast to a variety of sympathetic characters played mostly by Caucasian actors. The hero, Flash (Sam Jones), and his girlfriend, Dale Arden (Melody Anderson), rocket to Mongo to thwart Ming's plan. Once there, they discover that, unlike earth's single moon, Mongo has many in its orbit. "Every moon of Mongo," explains Princess Aura, "is a kingdom." The film codes this social difference as racial in that the natives of each moon share a distinct body type that sets them apart from the other kingdoms' inhabitants. The Hawkmen, for example, are Nordic-looking warriors, space Vikings with enormous wings sprouting from their backs. In addition to the wings, the men wear identical costumes, establishing the idea that a shared biological profile translates into a shared cultural profile. Members of another Caucasian race, the Arborians, wear green uniforms and hail from a moon populated by giant trees.

Apart from its depiction of the Asian, the film incorporates the more customary alter ego to American whiteness by incorporating a few token black actors into its nearly all-white cast. Barefoot and naked from the waist up, the inhabitants of the moon called Ardentia wear stereotypical "African" costumes (headdresses and skirts made of strips of shimmering gold metal), making them look like a cross between sub-Saharan tribesmen and ancient Egyptian priests. Even though the black Ardentians appear in just one scene, they fulfill the crucial function of conveying the master trope of U.S. racial discourse: conflict between white and black. As the representatives from each moon gather in Ming's palace to present their annual tributes to the emperor, a fight nearly erupts between the Nordic-like Hawkmen and their black counterparts. On seeing one another, the white and black Mongo citizens express their mutual animosity by grabbing their swords and growling. The scene reinforces the sense of a chronic state of war between the tribes by staging a sword fight between the two princes of the hawk and the tree tribes.

The palace scene begins with discord between what the film represents as races, but it concludes by transferring the scene's depiction of racial animus between the white and black characters onto a third figure who is neither white nor black. Princess Aura explains to Flash that Ming is the ultimate cause of the planet's pervasive strife, engendering division among Mongo's various breeds to maintain his rule over them. "My father keeps them fighting each other constantly," she says. "It's a really brilliant strategy." To counter the display of mutual hatred between white and black, the film poses the autocratic Asiatic ruler as an even more menacing threat to the ersatz Africans than any of the white tribes. When the emperor asks for his tribute from the black Mongos, their prince (George Harris) pleads with outstretched arms, "I can offer you nothing this year except my loyalty." Ming responds to the offer with a diabolical punishment, commanding the black man to prove that loyalty by taking his own life. "Fall on your sword," he orders. Initially, the prince pretends to comply with the suicide command, but instead of turning the sword on himself he lunges at Ming with the cry, "Death to Ming!" Anticipating the thrust, Ming freezes the black man with one of his machines and then sadistically kills him.

Ming's inhuman cruelty toward the film's only black figure with a speaking part begets unity between the feuding Mongo tribes. Before Ming's entrance, the Hawkmen and the Arborians regard each other as fundamentally different. But Ming's sadism bonds the two white princes by making them loathe the emperor, which transforms them into similar beings, into Ming-haters. Just after Ming plunges the sword into the black man's chest, a series of close-ups of the principal white characters' faces visually bonds them in sympathy for the black victim while simultaneously revealing their revulsion for Ming. Inserts of the two white princes show shock and disbelief. Incredulous, Flash whispers, "This Ming is a psycho," emphasizing his outsider status. Inspired by the black man's courageous revolt, Flash urges the divided Mongo tribes to bury their acrimony to "team up and overthrow" Ming. At first the two Caucasian clans refuse, but eventually they realize that they must emphasize their common interests rather than their differences to defeat the emperor. United, Flash and the erstwhile enemies lead their forces to victory against the Asian threat. The film ends when one of the white princes ascends to the throne with a pronouncement of racial comity. "From this day on," the new ruler declares, "let every breed of Mongo live together in peace."

Like *Flash Gordon*, *Lethal Weapon* (1987), the first film in Richard Donner's extremely popular series, highlights conflict between white and black. Initially, LA homicide detectives Martin Riggs (Mel Gibson) and Roger Murtaugh (Danny Glover) hate one another. Forced to ride together as partners, the two have contradictory agendas. Distraught over the recent death of his wife, the white cop Riggs has what Murtaugh calls a "death wish," which translates into a chronic willingness to put both himself and his partner into potentially fatal situations. Close to retirement, the black cop Murtaugh does not want to take any unnecessary risks. The tension between the two detectives comes to a head when Murtaugh pushes his enormous six-shooter into Riggs's mouth, daring him to fulfill his suicidal desire so that he can reach his retirement intact.

Despite the dramatic confrontation, the two principals eventually forget their seemingly insurmountable differences when threatened by the movie's villain, a heroin dealer called Mr. Joshua (Gary Busey), whose monstrous behavior delineates the ground on which the two detectives will eventually bond. The management of his drug business requires Mr. Joshua to commit a variety of heinous crimes. He lures pretty young women into the pornography industry, kills several innocent people, tortures the white detective, and kidnaps the black one's entire nuclear family. His lurid ransom note, which includes a snapshot of Murtaugh's teenager, reads, "YOUR DAUGHTER LOOKS REALLY PRETTY NAKED." The degenerate's blind loyalty to his drug ring boss makes him appear robotic, lacking a will of his own. Mr. Joshua's traits—sadism, homicidal mania, sexual perversion, and a complete lack of normal human emotion—render Mr. Joshua into a foil. "The only way to make a good guy really good," the film's producer Joel Silver remarks, "is to make a bad guy really bad."[6] With simultaneous draws of their guns, Riggs and Murtaugh kill Mr. Joshua at the film's climax. By way of a denouement, the former enemies cement their newly forged brotherhood by sharing Christmas dinner, an icon of American familial bonding. "After all we've been through," the black man says to the white one, "if you think I'm eating the world's worst Christmas turkey by myself," a reference to his wife's bad cooking, "you're crazy."

Donner's next two movies in the series, *Lethal Weapon 2* (1989) and *Lethal Weapon* 3 (1992), repeat the formula of the first—a salt-and-pepper duo pitted against a common foe—but with one important difference. Racism, particularly racism against black people, establishes the bad guy as "really bad." The second film, which debuted five years prior to South Africa's first multiracial elections, features Afrikaner villains, diplomats stationed in the United States who use their official status to smuggle drugs into Los Angeles. Linking the case to American history, the black cop compares the apartheid officials' scam of "drugs to dollars to Krugerrands" to the eighteenth century "triangle trade" of "molasses to rum to slaves." The drug peddlers call Murtaugh a "*kaffir*," the Afrikans' equivalent of "nigger," and Riggs a "kaffir lover." The third movie's white villain is an arms dealer who sells guns to young black gang members in South Central Los Angeles, who in turn use them to kill each other. The black detective claims that the relay constitutes genocide for the next generation of African Americans, a reference not only to the black experience, but also to Native American and Jewish victimization by racist whites.[7]

Like the second and third movies, the last of the series, *Lethal Weapon 4* (Donner, 1998), makes its villains into racists by linking them to an icon of white domination over black people. *Lethal Weapon 4* depicts its villains as modern-day slave traders who smuggle impoverished refugees into the country. Unlike the villains of the two previous movies, however, the villains in the fourth film are Asian rather than white, members of a Hong Kong gang called the Chinese Triad, headed by a deadly martial arts expert (Jet Li). After the pair discovers the mob's operation, an immigration agent explains that the thugs transport their human cargo by sea, "like slaves... [to] sell them as cheap labor" in the United States. The film emphasizes the link to white America's history of racism when the black detective gives asylum to one of the Chinese families. Murtaugh justifies his illegal action to Riggs by appealing to the African American experience. "Those are slave ships," he exclaims. "I'm freeing slaves like no one did for my ancestors."

One scene in particular rehearses common visual tropes associated with black slave narratives, particularly the Middle Passage. After Riggs single-handedly kills the entire Chinese freighter crew, the white protagonist opens one of the ship's holds. A medium shot reveals a small area under the decks packed tightly with illegal Asians of all ages and both sexes. A medium close-up shows numerous dirty faces looking up at Riggs through the square frame of the hatch. As in popular American narratives of slavery, Murtaugh's comments emphasize the masters' inhuman cruelty, remarking that the boat people "sure look raggedy." "Six weeks locked in a hold with one toilet," the INS agent explains, with only "rice and a little fish to eat." As a policy, the mob executes one immigrant in every boatload, the agent continues, to show "the rest what'll happen if they run off."

Despite a sentimental scene between Murtaugh and the patriarch of the Chinese immigrants that bonds black and yellow through an appeal to shared histories and aspirations, *Lethal Weapon 4*'s final sequence includes none of the smuggled Asians. After the two policemen team up to kill the martial arts expert in hand-to-hand combat, the LA detectives rush to the baby ward. Both Riggs's wife and Murtaugh's daughter deliver babies at the same time in the same hospital. In celebration, the two families, one white and the other black, gather in the hospital corridor for a group photograph. "Are you all friends?" a passerby asks. "No," they all shout back in unison, "we're family," an exclamation of their devotion to one another. After the camera in the diegesis flashes, a medium shot freezes the group as an image of the nation: two families merged into one big and happy family. By excluding the sympathetic Asian characters, the finale constructs an exclusively white and black portrait of the larger American nation.

The white and black "family" photograph carries the appearance of racial harmony into the credits. As the credits roll, the camera moves slowly over the pages of what, in the DVD commentary, the director calls a "family photo album" of the film's cast and crew, an artifact that includes a small photograph of every individual in the production. The album shows that the people who made the film do not only create representations of racial harmony, they also practice it in real life. As images of smiling industry personnel working together run across the screen, the soundtrack plays a song whose lyrics make an explicit appeal for racial unity, "Why Can't We Be Friends," by War, the 1970s rhythm and blues band. The chorus reinforces the film's message of a racially integrated nation by echoing Rodney King's 1991 plea seven years earlier in Los Angeles.

The Orientalist buddy film replicates itself yet again with the 1993 blockbuster *Rising Sun*. The film resurrects *Bataan*'s WWII enemy by depicting the mutual threat to white and black Americans as yet another invading samurai force. But rather than a military peril of sword-wielding soldiers, the film registers the historical particularities of its time by representing its Japanese as an economic threat. Reflecting the widespread paranoia in the United States during the 1980s and 1990s of a Nipponese industrial conquest, the movie's villain is an army of model minority businessmen who work for a wealthy Japanese multinational corporation.

Like *Bataan*, *Rising Sun* frames its Japanese enemy in terms of the yellow peril stereotype: "the belief that the West will be overpowered and enveloped by the irresistible, dark, occult forces of the East."[8] The main title sequence begins with two successive images: the first, large red Japanese *kanji* (two characters that mean "rising sun," which taken together signify "Japan"), which then transform into the English version of the main title. Simultaneous to the twin titles, the soundtrack booms with traditional taiko drumming, the beat that feudal Japanese armies used to bolster their troops during battle. The track punctuates the motif of Japanese aggression with a male voice issuing a loud warlike cry (what the DVD format's subtitles call "Japanese man yelling") and the bang of a gong.

The rest of the title sequence emphasizes the sense of an Asian invasion of the west coast by placing Japanese actors in a Western movie set, an iconic tableau in which the viewer expects to find whites but not Asians. After the gong, the camera cuts to an establishing shot of a boiling sun, a visual reference to Japan's national flag (a bright red circle on a stark white background) and moniker ("the land of the rising sun"). With details such as cowboys on horses, mission-style ruins, cacti, and sagebrush, the setting is a stock high-desert scene of the American West. The soundtrack reinforces the geography's emblematic identity with a Cole Porter song. "Give me land, lots of land under starry skies above," a voice sings, "don't fence me in.... Let me ride through the wide open country that I love," it continues, "don't fence me in." An American viewer may associate the lyrics and the landscape with a John Ford western, but instead of John Wayne, the cowboy hero is Asian, a yellow "Marlboro Man." Thus, instead of signifying the national myths of western America's humble cowboy origins and rugged individualism, the director's choice to repopulate such a nostalgic American scenario with a Japanese man suggests an Asian occupation. The sequence repeats the theme of a yellow invasion by revealing the Asian cowboy as a figure on a television screen in a LA karaoke bar; a jump cut shows that the voice delivering the "give me land, lots of land" lyrics with a heavy "Oriental" accent belongs to a Japanese man, with four of his countrymen singing behind him.

Fed by memories of WWII, widespread paranoia of Japan as an economic threat to U.S. sovereignty during the 1980s and 1990s established the context for *Rising Sun*'s vilification of Asians. Beginning roughly in the mid-1970s, a considerable number of Americans worried that the Japanese were poised to dominate certain key commercial sectors, especially automobile manufacture, home electronics, and the burgeoning computer industry. By the late 1980s and early 1990s, cries of another Pearl Harbor had reached a crescendo. One prominent 1992 poll, just a year before *Rising Sun*'s debut, reported that "Americans rank the Japanese economic threat higher than the Russian military threat," even though Japan ranked third behind England and Holland in foreign investment in the United States. At the time of the poll, the U.S. economy had been in a recession for eighteen months.[9] Three years prior to the poll, Japanese corporations had bought several high-profile American businesses and real estate concerns. Matsushita, Sony, and Mitsubishi acquired MCA, Columbia Pictures, and Rockefeller Center, respectively. Prompted by a $41 billion trade deficit with Japan, Democratic Congressman Dick Gephardt introduced a 1991 trade bill that sought to bar the importation of Japanese cars.[10] The United States "is running a $20 billion trade surplus with Europe," noted a *New York Times* editorial in response. "Does Mr. Gephardt believe Europe should retaliate?"[11] During the same period, another *New York Times* article quoted a television ad run by a New York area Pontiac dealership. The ad typified how many Americans at the time knit together the twin fears of an economic and cultural takeover of the nation. "Imagine a few years from now," the announcer grimly intones. "It's December, and the whole family's going to see the big Christmas tree at Hirohito Center....Go on," the announcer goads, "keep buying Japanese cars."[12]

Rising Sun's convoluted plot revolves around a Japanese corporation's bid to buy a leading-edge American computer company, Microcon (a play on Microsoft), which develops vital technology for the U.S. military. The Nakamoto Group's proposed takeover falters, however, when it creates a hotly contested national debate. Many Americans, including some powerful people in the Capitol, believe

that Japanese corporations are buying too many strategically important domestic companies. The film uses a fictional U.S. senator from
California, John Morton (Ray Wise), as a mouthpiece for this concern.
Morton believes that the computer firm's research should not fall into
the hands of a foreign government, especially the Japanese. "Look
what happened to our TV industry," says Morton. "If the Microcon
sale is approved then they will control the market and use the research
and technology to compete against our own companies." As a member of "the Senate finance committee which sets all Japanese import
regulations," Morton announces that he will "vote against the sale of
Microcon" to the Nakamoto Group, effectively killing the Japanese
corporation's gambit to acquire the American computer firm.

Morton's is not the only killing in the movie. Kaufman's film completes its triangulated representation of race by pitting its Japanese
corporate raiders against a white and black buddy duo. The plot
pairs two homicide detectives, Captain John Connor (Sean Connery)
and Lieutenant "Spider" Web Smith (Wesley Snipes), to investigate
a murder committed during a lavish party celebrating the opening
of the Nakamoto Group's LA headquarters. The victim is a pretty
Kentucky blonde named Cheryl Lynn Austin, a mistress to one of
the Japanese businessmen with an interest in acquiring Microcon.
Connor surmises that he "probably offered her to the senator as a
form of hospitality." To blackmail him into changing his vote, one
of the Nakamoto employees murders her, then tricks Morton into
believing that he accidentally strangled Austin during an episode of
rough sex on the Nakamoto boardroom table.

Like every other interracial buddy film, *Rising Sun* portrays the relationship between the buddies as one marked by conflict and, eventually, the threat of physical violence. Initially, the two detectives do not
get along. Each believes that the other cop is "on the take," as Smith
puts it. Connor knows that Smith has a history of taking bribes from
drug dealers. Before meeting Connor, Smith's precinct colleagues had
warned him "that [Connor] couldn't be trusted" because of his long-
time residency in Japan. Another detective on the case, Smith's former
partner, Tom Graham (Harvey Keitel), is Connor's most vocal critic.
"The department put him on leave because he's too good a friend of
Japan," reports Graham. "He's not a team player....Stay on your toes"
he cautions Smith, "the guy's trouble." The mutual distrust between the
two culminates when the black detective challenges the white one to a
fistfight. "I'm tired of your shit," he shouts when Connor confronts him
about the drug bribery. "I'll pimp slap you up and down this street!"

Initially, *Rising Sun* frames the tension between white and black in terms of white American racism toward black people, specifically, the stock binary of twentieth century civil rights narratives: the white southern master and the black southern slave. When Connor, the older white detective, gives the younger black one an order, Smith registers his dismay by hailing his white partner as the stereotypical master of the Old South. "Massa," Smith wryly comments, "wants me to get the car." The binary resurfaces when the elder Connor addresses Smith as the *kohai* or the junior man. "Every aspect of your appearance and behavior will reflect on you, on the department," explains Connor, "and on me as your *sempai*, [the] senior man who guides the junior man." Annoyed by Conner's lectures about how to behave like a Japanese, Smith correlates the sempai and kohai binary with that of the white master and black slave. "My sempai," the black man responds, "that wouldn't happen to be anything like 'massa,' now would it?"

Rising Sun recalls the storied master and slave binary only to transfer the "massa" title from Caucasian to Asian, thereby making the Japanese into scapegoats. One scene, for example, initiates this transfer through a cognate of "nigger," branding the Japanese and anyone affiliated with them as racist against black people. In a conversation with the African American Smith, Connor's girlfriend, Jingo Asakuma (Tia Carrere), tells her story of growing up in Japan as half African American and half Japanese. She explains that, because of her black blood, the Japanese shunned her as a member of the society's lowest class, an "untouchable." Do "you know that word *niguro*?" Asakuma asks Smith. "Oh yes," he nods in sad recognition, "I know that word." Regarding "niguro," the 1993 Hollywood blockbuster took its direction from Michael Crichton's controversial 1992 detective novel of the same name. In the novel, when Smith asks Connor why he left Japan after so many years of living there, the white detective responds, "I got tired of being a nigger." Connor describes the Japanese as "the most racist people on earth" (370–1).

One of the Nakamoto Group's white American employees, Bob Richmond (Kevin Anderson), a former U.S. State Department negotiator who opportunistically switched to the Japanese side, performs the sort of racism recounted by Asakuma. As Smith waits for Connor outside the Nakamoto building after the extravagant party, Richmond, attending to Senator Morton, mistakes the black detective for a parking lot attendant. "Hey you," Richmond shouts to Smith, "quit loafing!...Get the senator's car!" Aside from revealing that Richmond equates black bodies with servitude, the command exposes Richmond's belief that black people are lazy. "Wrong guy," Smith shouts back angrily, "wrong fucking century," identifying the Nakamoto employee as an anachronism that properly belongs to a distant era.

The film links the Japanese businessmen to the culture of slavery by portraying them as top dogs in an undemocratic caste system. Ugly Japanese elitism materializes as soon as the detectives arrive at the crime scene. When Ishihara (Stan Egi), a Nakamoto minion, tries to shield the corporation's opening reception from the detectives' potentially embarrassing murder investigation, he expresses grave concern "about the attempt to link this girl's death to our reception downstairs." When Smith suggests that she was in the building to attend the party, Ishihara callously dismisses the woman's death. "This is a very important evening for the Nakamoto Corporation," he insists in heavily accented English. "We don't want it marred by unfounded allegations concerning the death of a woman of no importance," assuming that the detective takes the victim's low social position for granted.

The film reinforces its transfer of "massa," or the sign of the master, from white to yellow through its representation of late twentieth century U.S. class relations. Specifically, the film characterizes the Japanese as a model minority: a profile that stereotypes Asians and Asian Americans as an emerging but corrupt ruling class, as un-American. Every detail of the Nakamoto skyscraper headquarters, for example, conveys a sense of Japanese wealth and corporate power. In polite Japanese, a soft female voice in the elevators tells riders when they arrive at their floor. The interior sets signal opulence, featuring gleaming metal, dark hardwood, and immaculately polished glass and mirrors. A fancy circular stairway leads up to an expansive boardroom (where Austin meets her demise), which itself hides a luxury bedroom suite, a trysting place for company men and their clients. All the younger Japanese characters wear expensive clothes and drive luxury automobiles.

The model minority stereotype first surfaced in the mainstream media in 1966 with the publication in *U.S. News and World Report* and the *New York Times Magazine* of two articles. The pieces praise Chinese Americans and Japanese Americans, respectively, for their successful assimilation into American society through hard work, independence from government aid, transcendence of past racism from whites without political protest, and their so-called Confucian values.[13] The *U.S. News* piece praises Asian Americans to discipline 1960s African Americans by making an explicit comparison between yellow and black. "At a time when it is being proposed that hundreds of billions be spent on uplifting Negroes and other minorities," the article exclaims, "the nation's 300,000 Chinese Americans are moving ahead on their own with no help from anyone else."[14]

In short, the model minority version of yellow America seeks to prove that mainstream or white American society is not fundamentally racist, thereby setting Asian America against African America, two racial groups aligned as victims of white supremacy prior to the 1960s advent of the model minority stereotype. "The 'model minority,'" Nazil Kibria writes, "becomes the 'yellow peril' as the connotation of Asian achievement becomes cause for resentment."[15] Claire Jean Kim's 2000 *Bitter Fruit: The Politics of Black-Korean Conflict in New York City*, for example, gives an account of how the model minority stereotype exacerbated conflict between yellow and black in Brooklyn, resulting in the 1990 African American boycott of local Korean grocery stores. "Ideologically, the model minority becomes a scapegoat," notes Viet Thanh Nguyen, "drawing the ire of other minorities for the systemic inequities that they experience."[16]

The position of the model minority Asian or Asian American relative to the white and black binary of American racial discourse fits the profile of what René Girard terms the "marginal insider."[17] Girard argues that every society eventually reaches a crisis as a result of competition between its members (in this case white Americans and black Americans), a dynamic that he calls mimetic rivalry. When society reaches this critical point, its members develop a desire to scapegoat one or a few of the community, believing that "they can be purged of their various ills and primarily of their internal violence through the immolation of a victim."[18] In spite of running counter to intuition, the perception of wealth and privilege can transform a group into a scapegoat. "No doubt," Girard writes, "some people will be shocked to find the rich and powerful listed among the victims of collective persecution under the same title as the poor and weak." "The rich and powerful," he continues, "exert an influence over society which justifies the acts of violence to which they are subjected in times of crisis." "Extreme characteristics," he explains, "ultimately attract collective destruction at some time or other." "The further one is from normal social status of whatever kind," he continues, "the greater the risk of persecution."[19] Echoing stereotypes of Jewish people, *Rising Sun*'s model minority Asian connotes a money-grubbing nascent ruling class. "In today's America," Slavoj Zizek observes in 1990, "a role resembling that of the Jew is being played more and more by the *Japanese*."[20]

Rising Sun exploits the animosity between black and yellow created by the model minority stereotype by representing blacks as economic slaves who languish under the new yellow masters. One scene has Smith driving through nighttime Los Angeles during a heavy rain. One of the shots shows a group of homeless people on the sidewalk, three black men (one shirtless) living among trash and cardboard boxes, exposed to the elements. Phillips, the blue-collar security guard that works for Nakamoto's surveillance team, represents black America's dread of falling into the underclass. His Japanese employers dominate him to the point that he behaves like a cowering slave. Wracked by the anxiety of dismissal, the poor man cannot help but stutter and sweat when the detectives interrogate him about Austin's murder. "Come on, brother," he pleads with Smith to stop the questioning. "These people have been good to me....Don't fuck with these guys," he whispers to the policemen while motioning up toward one of the corporation's ubiquitous surveillance cameras. "They're too good."

The backdrop for the film's car chase sequence reinforces the association between black people and poverty. With *yakuza* (Japanese mobsters, hired by Nakamoto) chasing them, the buddy duo drive into Smith's childhood neighborhood, South Central Los Angeles. The black district made infamous by the 1992 Rodney King riots is a very different America from the clean, shiny, and high-tech corporate world inhabited by the Japanese. Markers of poverty abound in the low-tech world of postindustrial rust and decay: high chain-link fences topped with barbed wire, mismatched corrugated metal walls, old broken-down cars, a defunct water tank. Racial (but not Asian) markers saturate the scene. Multicolored graffiti, a form of cultural production associated with young, urban blacks and Latinos, covers the walls of the nearby buildings.[21] A low-rider car passes through the frame, a stereotypical signature of young West Coast Latinos. The soundtrack sounds a blast of hip-hop music. Simultaneously with the music, the viewer sees a group of young black men and Latinos peering into the detectives' passing car from the stoop of a house. Their costumes and props reflect their poverty: sweatpants, hooded sweatshirts, and shirts with cutoff sleeves. Some drink from bottles wrapped in brown paper bags.

The film's correlation of black America and poverty reflects another shift in the discourse of race that occurred about the same time as the model minority stereotype. James Morone's *Democratic Wish: Popular Participation and the Limits of American Government*, for example, argues that the widespread demand for black entitlement, starting with the WWII era and continuing through the 1960s, not only presented black Americans with a window of opportunity for social advancement, but also initiated a semiotic shift in racial discourse. The very "meaning of the word race was reconstructed" during the civil rights era. Specifically, by the early 1970s, "black" came to signify "poverty." Prior to the 1970s, in the wake of Michael Harrington's popular *The Other America: Poverty in the United States*, published in 1962, "poor" signified white West Virginians, Pennsylvanians, and Appalachians. At that point in history, the "stereotypical juvenile delinquent," Morone asserts, "was a member of a white youth gang."[22]

But soon thereafter the civil rights movement gave poverty a darker cast while simultaneously giving race a new economic dimension. "While we see the poverty problem today as almost coal black," Adam Yarmolinsky wrote in the 1969 anthology *On Fighting Poverty*, "it was [earlier] at most light gray."[23] "For the next decade," Morone argues, "*poverty* became an ironic political euphemism for *black*." In public documents and political rhetoric, "*poor* meant *black*, regardless of income" (219; emphasis in the original). In 1969, the journal *Public Administration Review* published S. M. Miller and Martin Rein's "Participation, Poverty and Administration," which characterized "the term 'poor' [as] misleading," because those to whom it referred "were of the poverty neighborhood, but not necessarily poor." The authors conclude that, in both official policy documents and public discourse about the issue, "'poor' meant black."[24] Published in the same journal in 1972, John Strange's "Citizen Participation in Community Action and Model Cities Programs," an essay termed by Morone as "an exhaustive review of the literature," makes a point similar to that of Miller and Rein. "Though the official documents referred to 'poor,'" they write, "'poor' was often interpreted to mean 'black' or 'Puerto Rican' or 'Indian' without regard to income."[25]

Morone's account of the shift in racial discourse rests on a familiar telling of the civil rights movement. In 1954, the *Brown v. Board of Education* case created high expectations for black progress. But the phrase "with all deliberate speed" allowed the South to stall and block implementation of the decision. White intransigence regarding black civil rights created a kind of political dilemma that has haunted every presidential administration since the WWII era. The potential for damaging the democratic image of the United States pushed the federal government to intervene in the South, not only through the mobilization of troops, but also through legislation. But if the White House pushed too hard in favor of black civil rights, the president ran the risk of alienating southerners. This was especially true for Democrats, whose efficacy as a party depended on a fragile coalition between North and South (186–252).

The Johnson administration solved the problem by "transform[ing] racial politics into class politics," thus redressing a racial demand with an economic solution, the so-called War on Poverty launched in 1964 (195). "The Kennedy and Johnson administrations negotiated the black threat to New Deal politics," according to Morone, "in a remarkable fashion," converting "the racial crisis into a class issue.... Complaints about racial oppression were answered with programs designed to ameliorate poverty" (219). As policy makers, they applied a familiar 1930s "New Deal" style, class-based framework of reading to the unfamiliar problem of the civil rights movement.

Not only was this old framework familiar to the policy makers, but also "the redefinition of the racial problem was politically useful" (219–20). According to Morone, this solution worked nicely in the sense that it translated a race problem into terms that offended no one. "Class politics was far less trouble," writes Morone, "poverty programs skirted the American racial cleavage" because they "could be passed without marches or filibusters" (220). Poverty legislation "did not mobilize Southerners protecting segregation, urban elites defending their own power relations, or militant black leaders demanding 'the abstraction of integration.'" In other words, poverty programs could be passed without losing votes in Congress and in the electorate at large. This shift from one discursive register to another, Morone argues, protected the democratic image of the United States by responding to the black demand for entitlement while at the same time avoiding the alienation of the southern democrats and tearing asunder the fragile New Deal coalition within the Democratic Party (219).

Rising Sun reproduces the civil rights discourse that equates poverty with black Americans. At the same time, it revises the discourse by casting some of its white figures as economic slaves, providing a common ground on which white and black may bond. The film uses the murder victim, Cheryl Lynn Austin (Tatjana Patitz), to suture the Japanese to the story of American slavery. Eddie Sakamura (Cary-Hiroyuki Tagawa), the playboy son of "a big industrialist" Japanese automaker, recruited his twenty-three-year old mistress to Los Angeles from Kentucky where she worked on an automobile assembly line. Cheryl "was working in that Toyota plant back there in Kentucky," explains her roommate Julia (Alexandra Powers), a southern blue-eyed blonde like Austin, "then one day who should show up in that small little town but Eddie." In the victim's bedroom, the detectives find a photograph of Austin's rural Kentucky homestead that establishes a profile of economic and social vulnerability. In the photograph, Sakamura, Austin, and her mother pose in front of an old car covered with dust from an unpaved road, marking her humble economic status. Her rural status adds to the photograph's intimation of an innocent upbringing. With an American Gothic look of chagrin on her face, the white-haired mother looks like a figure in a Norman Rockwell print, wearing a modest apron and prairie dress.

The photograph describes a scenario that held a widespread currency at the time of the film's debut, one in which a predatory Japanese automobile industry drives American firms out of the market and replaces American factories with their own. *Rising Sun* amends this narrative by suggesting that such market behaviour creates a large pool of vulnerable white American women for its wealthy businessmen to exploit. While searching through the victim's purse, Lieutenant Graham finds a "nice tight roll of hundred dollar bills... Japanese credit cards... and Japanese cigarettes," suggesting to the detective that she was "well taken care of" by Sakamura. "These little guys eat shit all day long in Tokyo, crammed into subways, working in big companies," Graham sums it up, "suddenly they're rich and free" when "they come over here," and "they all want to fuck a Rose Bowl queen."

Even though the film does not specify whether or not they won the right to appear in a Rose Bowl parade, both Julia and Cheryl are pretty enough to be mistaken for beauty queens. Julia's biography of Cheryl continues by describing a sordid dimension of Nakamoto's business practice that amounts to white slavery. Austin was part of a prostitution ring, an operation run by the Japanese to provide sexual entertainment for its businessmen. Connor instructs Smith that the corporate men living in Los Angeles have their own parallel existence. "This isn't America," Connor says to his partner, "this is their shadow world.... They have clubs, bars, [and] *bettaku* [or] love residence[s] where mistresses are kept." Austin's love residence looks like a college dormitory in which all of the residents are Caucasian women that the Japanese have transformed into lingerie-clad geishas. It's a sort of prison, with a hidden entrance guarded by a menacing *yakuza* dressed in black. As the B-52's "Love Shack" plays in the background, the camera shows the mistresses in various acts of servitude to Japanese men, sitting on their laps while flirting and genuflecting while serving tea. Japanese patriarchy's objectification of white American womanhood reaches its nadir in the film's only sex scene, which shows Eddie Sakamura using a naked blonde mistress as a sushi platter.

Fittingly, the rich Japanese receive their comeuppance for the crime of modern-day slavery from a group of poor black American men, reinforcing the divide between black and yellow created by the model minority stereotype. During the car chase through South Central Los Angeles, Smith pulls up to a group of young black men and Latinos, old neighborhood friends, with a plea for assistance.

> I got a serious situation here. I'm trying to escort this old geezer [Connor] back to the loony farm, stole some sushi from some Japanese cats. Now they chasin' us. So I need you guys to get behind us. Think you can help us out?

"We got your back," they respond. As agents of the white and black buddy duo, the South Centralites ambush the *yakuza*'s car. Trapped by several vehicles, the mobsters cower inside their Cadillac while black and brown men abuse their car, throwing mud on the wind-shield and pulling off the wipers. Before long, the mobsters, dressed in expensive suits, hair slicked back into trendy ponytails, forget about Connor and Smith and flee the scene.

The film's marriage of two stereotypes, one that correlates black with poverty and one that equates yellow with wealth, transforms black and poor neighborhoods like South Central into the ultimate American bulwark against the new Japanese peril. As the police pair drives into Smith's old neighbourhood during the chase, Connor, the only white person around, expresses concern about his safety. The black detective reassures his partner, "we're safe around here," boasting that "rough neighborhoods may be America's last advantage" against the Japanese. Of course, the post–civil-rights viewer understands that "rough neigh-borhood" means black ghetto. The movie's racial discourse that desig-nates who is rich and who is poor makes black ghetto culture, a subset of mainstream American culture, inscrutable to the Japanese. Thus, even though the Japanese exhibit an uncanny ability to penetrate the rest of America, they cannot penetrate the nation's "rough neighborhoods."

An exchange between the *yakuza* and one of South Central's denizens proves Smith's claim about the Japanese inability to read African American culture. Just before the Asian mobsters flee the scene, an interior shot of the *yakuza*'s convertible shows a black man cutting through the fabric top with a knife. As the black man peers through the tear in the Cadillac's roof, he asks one of the Japanese about the car's ownership papers, "Where is the pink slip?" "I was led to believe that this car would be for sale," the black man pauses, "soon," intimating that the *yakuza*'s demise is imminent. The mobster does not know the meaning of "pink slip," responding in heavily accented English, "Why pink srip?" His complete failure to understand the slang signifies him as an outsider bewildered by black American culture.

Of course, the Asian man's inability to distinguish between the spoken *l* and *r* ("srip" as opposed to "slip"), a common mistake made by native speakers of Asian languages, marks him as a foreigner. In this sense, he is typical of the film's other Asian characters, of which there are many. Given the storyline of a Japanese firm vying to buy an American one, the large number of foreign Asians that inhabit the film's diegesis should not surprise the viewer. The film's paucity of Japanese American or Asian American figures, though, is curious. Only two of the movie's Asian characters speak English without an accent, marking them as American. Amy Hill plays a medical examiner who has a short conversation with Connor. Patricia Ayume Thomson makes a very brief appearance as a "Connie Chung" character whom the credits identify as "Female Accident Reporter."[26] Both are very small parts. Both actresses are mixed-race, part white and part Asian. One would expect to find more Asian American figures on the screen given that the film is set in Los Angeles, perhaps the U.S. city with the highest population of Asian Americans. Even Connor's girlfriend, the computer expert Jingo Asakuma, the only figure explicitly marked as both Asian and American, speaks English with a heavy Japanese accent. Like most of the films in this study, *Rising Sun* has so few Asian American characters because one of the grounds upon which the white and black buddies bond is the shared status as Americans.

In the main, the Orientalist buddy film must represent the Asian as non-American. But the fact that the film has two female figures who are both Asian and American and no male ones, not even bit parts, suggests that the film makes an even finer distinction that runs along gender lines. Patriarchy dictates that the two buddies who stand in for the nation are male. Since the two detectives bond not only as

Americans but also as men, the common enemy to white and black Americans must be not only an Asian foreigner (nonwhite, nonblack, and non-American), that foe must also be male. That men measure their value by comparing themselves to other men is a commonplace. "Ideologies of manhood," according to critic David Leverenz, "have functioned primarily in relation to the gaze of male peers and male authority."[27] On a more prosaic note: "Women have, in men's minds, such a low place on the social ladder of this country that it's useless to define yourself in terms of a woman," the movie director and playwright David Mamet states. "What men need is men's approval."[28]

Rising Sun's pattern that includes a few Asian American female characters but excludes male ones entirely is typical of popular film and television of the 1980s and 1990s. For example, Mick Jackson's *Volcano* (1997), starring Tommy Lee Jones and Anne Heche has the Korean American Jacqueline Kim playing a scientist. Yet like, *Rising Sun*, despite the fact that it is set in 1990s Los Angeles, it has no male Asian American characters. Brian Helgeland's *Payback* (1999) has Lucy Liu playing a dominatrix as well as several Asian male actors playing Chinatown hoods. Liu speaks English without an accent, the men with garish "Oriental" ones. Elsewhere, on television, Liu plays Ling, a "dragon-lady" lawyer, on Fox's *Ally McBeal* (1997–2002). As a principal character, Ling appears in every episode. Now and again, though, a male Asian character surfaces to play a bit role. For example, in one episode Billy, Ally's former boyfriend, is diagnosed with a brain tumor. An Asian American actor (Clyde Kusatsu) plays his doctor. But the doctor cannot communicate with Billy because of his "bad Engrish."

Other 1990s U.S. television shows reveal female figures that are both Asian and American. Ming-na Wen plays an overly ambitious model minority medical resident in NBC's *ER* (1994–2009). Wen also played Trudy Sloane, the wife of the title character's best friend in *The Single Guy* (NBC, 1995–1997). Margaret Cho played the protagonist, Margaret Kim, in the short-lived *All-American Girl* (ABC, 1994–1995). Finally, Heather Tom played a stint as Ross' interloper girlfriend, Julie, in *Friends* (NBC, 1994–2004). All of these female Asian characters speak perfect American English, marking them as native speakers and thus as American. Except for Cho, all of these actresses played leading roles as Asian Americans in *Joy Luck Club* (Wayne Wang, 1993).

By contrast, Hollywood from its beginnings to the 1980s and 1990s offers only Asian males whose broken or accented English signifies foreign origin: Jerry Lewis in *The Geisha Boy* (Frank Tashlin, 1958), Mickey Rooney in *Breakfast at Tiffany's* (Blake Edwards, 1961), the evil Fu Manchu, the benign Charlie Chan, and Bruce Lee's martial arts fighters as well as all of his subsequent clones. In terms of newer films, Keye Luke plays an elderly Chinese herbalist who speaks only fortune cookie English in Woody Allen's *Alice*, set in New York city (1990). The only Asian figure in Clint Eastwood's *Absolute Power* (1997) waits tables with a thick foreign tongue. Chow Yun Fat and Jackie Chan play the male lead in two 1990s movies, but these roles have them speak with a heavy accent: *The Replacement Killers* (Antoine Fuqua, 1998) and *Rush Hour* (Brett Ratner, 1998). Perhaps the most durable Asian man in U.S. film history is a king (what could be less American than a king?), played by the Russian-born Yul Brynner, in Walter Lang's *The King and I* (1956).[29]

Television has a few exceptions, but they prove the rule. Sulu (George Takei) of the original *Star Trek* (NBC, 1973–1975) and the San Franciscan Ensign Harry Kim (Garrett Wang) of *Star Trek: Voyager* (UPN, 1995–2001) speak without an accent. But within these shows' diegetic world of intergalactic exploration, the category of nation is supposed to have been transcended in favor of the category of earthling. Robert Ito plays the L.A. County Medical Examiner's assistant, Sam Fujiyama, in *Quincy, M.E.* (NBC, 1976–1983) but the series' setting demands at least one Asian American role to make it realistic. There are also *Kung Fu* (ABC, 1972–1975) and its sequel, *Kung Fu: The Legend Continues* (Warner Bros. Television, 1993–1997) in which David Carradine plays Kwai Chang Caine, the half Asian, half Caucasian Shaolin monk-turned-drifter-of-the-old-west. Caine speaks in the slow and soft cadence of Confucian aphorisms. His half Chinese son in the sequel speaks like an American. But then, the figure's blonde hair and blue eyes code him as European, not Asian. A few other Hollywood films and television programs have Asian American male characters, but each is feminized from the point of view of mainstream masculinity. In one episode, *ER*'s Yosh (Gedde Watanabe) is revealed to be gay. In *The Thomas Crown Affair* (John McTiernan, 1999), the lone Asian American male figure speaks American English, but is the houseboy (James Saito).

In addition to the Asian American male, *Rising Sun* must elide two other figures of the actual Los Angeles landscape in order to bond white and black through an Asian scapegoat. One is a specter from WWII. Both the director and the novelist frame their characterization of the Japanese in terms of war. In interviews, Michael Crichton reports that he wrote his 1992 novel "to make America wake up"[30] to the fact that "the Japanese have invented a new kind of trade—adversarial trade, trade like war, trade intended to wipe out the competition."[31] Kaufman, the director, echoes Crichton's fear, insisting that Americans maintain "vigilance" with respect to the Japanese. "We have to take responsibility for what happens to our businesses," he warns, "and what happens to our country."[32]

The film's plot relies on the figure of WWII. When an African American journalist accuses Senator Morton of "bashing" Japan, a thinly veiled accusation of racism, during an appearance on a television news show, Morton neatly deflects the charge by couching his position in the language of the national interest. He explains that his vote against the Japanese bid to buy the American computer firm stems from a noble concern for national security and the welfare of the American military men and women who enforce that security, not racism against the Japanese. The Senator argues that the Nakamoto Corporation's acquisition of Microcon could potentially cripple national security by "put[ting] vital elements of our advanced military weaponry entirely under control of the Japanese." Evoking Pearl Harbor, Morton implies that the Japanese would betray the United States in a future war, despite its status as an ally. "During the [1990–1991] Gulf War," he explains, "the Japanese suggested that they would deny us that weaponry."

The Japanese confirm the senator's fear by transforming Los Angeles into a kind of war zone. As the detectives drive through a night rain, Connor explains to Smith that the Nakamoto Corporation is part of a *keiretsu*, "a united front of hundreds of powerful companies all acting in partnership to win" economic hegemony. "There's a *keiretsu* war going on," Connor tells Smith. That is, the Nakamoto Group has a competitor, another *keiretsu* that wants to purchase Microcon. Reminiscent of Carl von Clausewitz's famous dictum, Connor implies that the Japanese show the same ruthlessness in business as they did in war. Connor asks, "You ever hear 'business is war' or 'all's fair in love and war'?" "Where," Smith asks, "does that leave us?" "We're in the war zone," Connor replies.

If "we're in the war zone," as Connor claims, then who is the "we" in *Rising Sun*? "We" are white and black Americans in the direct sense that the conversation occurs between Connor and Smith, which buttresses the notion that the nation is white and black exclusively. But "we" signifies not only a white and black nation. It means white and black non-elites caught in the crossfire between two wealthy Japanese corporations at war. Neither Connor nor Smith is an elite. Connor hails from Scotland originally. But when his partner Smith assumes that he came to the LA police force from the elite Scotland Yard, Connor immediately corrects him, "Scotland Backyard," suggesting working-class origins. To underscore the point, the film has Conner living in a remarkably modest apartment above a fishmonger in LA's Japan-town. Smith, the black detective, grew up in the predominantly black and infamously poverty-stricken South Central neighborhood. After the conversation about the *keiretsu* war, the film cuts immediately to a shot of barbed-wire fences, seen through the rain-streaked car window, then to a shot of homeless people aimlessly shuffling around the streets near their makeshift tents. The soundtrack repeats the heavy, labored breathing of the murdered woman's strangulation, what the shooting script calls the " 'gasping' motif," which establishes both the unfortunate Kentucky woman found dead on the Nakamoto boardroom table and the homeless (white and black) as victims of strangulation by the Japanese.[33]

Of course, the last time any Asian or Asian American had any part in transforming Los Angeles into a war zone was during WWII. In the hysteria that followed Pearl Harbor, many feared betrayal on the part of Japanese and Japanese Americans living on the West Coast. "We are at war," declared Lieutenant General John L. DeWitt, the chief of the Western Defense Command. "We have to watch" the Japanese.[34] "This area—eight [western] states—has been designated as a theater of operations," he stated. DeWitt's rationale for internment rested on an idea of racial essence that made no distinction between Japanese and Japanese Americans. "The Japanese race is an enemy race," he explained in a 1942 report to the Secretary of War. "While many second and third generation Japanese born on United States soil, possessed of United States citizenship, have become 'Americanized,' the racial strains are undiluted" (391). A *Los Angeles Times* editorial reflected DeWitt's view: "A viper is nonetheless a viper wherever the egg is hatched" (388).

Roughly sixty years later, *Rising Sun* repeats indirectly WWII era essentialism by displaying an abundance of Japanese characters and a dearth of Japanese American ones, which suggests that all persons of Japanese ancestry on American soil are not American. But because the movie uses the same canard, *Rising Sun*, as an Orientalist buddy film, cannot mention the WWII internment of persons of Japanese ancestry.[35] Any direct reference to the camps would remind the viewer of the history of white American racism towards non-whites, which in turn would destroy its story of white and black as common victims of Japanese treachery.

Rising Sun's last ghost is a black man. This chapter argues that *Rising Sun*, like most of the films in this book, scapegoats the Asian because of historical tension between white and black Americans. In a *New York Times* interview, the director acknowledges the important role that this tension plays in the narration. In Crichton's 1992 novel, Smith is a white man named Peter Smith. Kaufman reveals the reason for changing the race of the *kohai*, the Smith character played in the movie by Wesley Snipes, from white to black. "The movie version of the junior detective was written for a black," the director Kaufman notes, "to heighten the tension between the two characters."[36] (The race change accounts for the name change; "'Spider' Web" is much hipper than "Peter.") The "tension" to which the director refers is racial. The change turns a buddy detective novel into a white and black buddy film.

Kaufman's reference to heightening the "tension between" the white Connor and the black Smith probably refers to the 1991 Rodney King beating and its aftermath, given that *Rising Sun* debuted only two years after the 1992 South Central riots. Many of the film's elements provide an opportunity to mention the beating, yet it does not. The two principal characters work for the LA police department. Nearly all of the film's action occurs within the city of Los Angeles; South Central plays an important role as a backdrop for the bonding of white and black.

It seems unlikely that the director would have forgotten about the beating and subsequent acquittals, which sparked six days of high drama in South Central Los Angeles and was aired by television programs across the globe. By the second day of the riots, thirty-eight people had died, four more than the 1965 Watts riot body count, and more than 4,000 had been arrested. The first president Bush deployed nearly 5,000 troops to the area. The conflagration sparked violence in several other major cities: Atlanta, Miami, San Francisco, and Seattle.

Given its production history and setting, the film must acknowledge the King beating, but it must do so only obliquely. The film must scrupulously avoid any direct references to King, for any explicit mention of him would have evoked the long-standing domestic racial tension between white and black, reminding the viewer that, historically, whites constitute a much older and more durable enemy to black America than any Japanese businessman. The film's only reference to the King beating occurs as Smith and Graham prepare to arrest Eddie Sakamura as a suspect in the murder case. To Smith's surprise, Graham hands him a bulletproof vest. Eddie is a playboy, not a gun-wielding thug. The vest prompts Smith to gain assurance from Graham that the arrest of Sakamura, a nonwhite male, will not result in a police beating. "I thought no violence," Smith responds as he takes the vest. "The guy's a murderer," Graham replies, "LAPD takes no chances." "Yeah," the black detective says, "but we do take prisoners, right?" Smith has his doubts about Graham's professionalism, as the white cop had threatened Sakamura earlier in the film: "I'm going to love breaking your arms."

Since the King beating makes the issue of police racism so fraught, the allusion to police brutality requires another scapegoat apart from the Japanese businessmen. The film must distance its heroic cops, especially the white Connor, from the antiblack violence of the actual LAPD. It does so through Lieutenant Graham, the film's only character that exhibits obviously racist behavior toward the Japanese. Throughout the film, Graham issues a nearly constant stream of epithets such as "Jap" and "Nip." Graham is the bad or racist cop onto whom the film transfers the stigma of the King beating. He absolves Connor, enabling the buddy duo to represent mainstream America's fantasy of racial harmony.

5

The Orientalist Buddy Film and the "New Niggers": *Blade Runner* (1982, 1992, and 2007)

Look at my face,—look at my hands,—look at my body…why am I not a man, as much as anybody?

—*George Harris*, Uncle Tom's Cabin: Or, Life Among the Lowly[1]

I want more life, fucker.

—*Roy Batty*, Blade Runner

In Sir Ridley Scott's immensely popular science fiction film *Blade Runner* (1982; rereleased in 1992 as *The Director's Cut* and in 2007 as *The Final Cut*), Los Angeles in the year 2019 is an Asian city that has gone to hell. The opening aerial shot tracks across a dark industrial wasteland, punctuated by large smokestacks that shoot roiling bursts of orange flame high into the air. A giant Times Square-like video screen fills the side of one skyscraper. The screen runs a Coca-Cola advertisement on a loop, featuring a close-up of the powder-white face of a Japanese geisha popping a little red pill. A loud and menacing *kabuki* soundtrack accentuates the image. Hot neon business signs written in a jumble of kanji (Japanese characters based on Chinese ideograms) and *kana* (Japanese syllabary) are everywhere. Asian people crowd the sidewalks. Most are dressed in stereotypical rice-picker straw hats and black pajama suits, caught by the camera in the midst of running errands. Some run small street stands, selling things like noodles.

In the street, they ride their bicycles in droves, just as in Beijing. The rain-drenched postapocalyptic scene conveys "the feeling that everything is contaminated and everyone will soon die from radiation poisoning," as Danny Peary writes in a 1982 review. "Has WWIII occurred?" he wonders. "Judging by all the Orientals in the streets, could China have defeated America?"[2] The "Oriental" dystopia probably made sense to the viewer in 1982, the film's debut year, as well as in 1992, the year of the highly successful theatrical release of the director's cut version. In fact, many critics read the characterization of the city as a reflection of the period's economic history: the increasing globalization of the national economy with respect to the Pacific Rim, especially Los Angeles, and the widespread "yellow peril" fear of a Japanese corporate invasion.

The few whites, including the retired cop Rick Deckard (Harrison Ford), one of the two heroes, seen in this emphatically Asian Los Angeles are clearly the minority. Not only do Asians vastly outnumber whites, but the city also appears to have been evacuated of black people. "There aren't any in the picture, even in the crowd scenes," another reviewer observes.[3] Taking the same inventory, Kaja Silverman in her essay on the film, "Back to the Future," concurs that *Blade Runner* "contains no black characters."[4] The film's lack of blackness departs from the standard racial representation of an American city, which is based on a white and black binary. At least since the 1968 Civil Rights Kerner Commission report, to pick just one example, *inner city* and *ghetto* have often served as metaphors for the tension between a white majority and a black minority. One would expect to see at least a few black people on the screen, especially since the British Film Institute volume on the film describes the city as "an extended inner-city ghetto environment."[5] It is a curious omission, given the actual black presence in Los Angeles and given the long history of writing about such a presence in U.S. cities. In *Blade Runner's* Los Angeles, however, the racial composition of a white minority and Asian majority replaces that of a white majority and a black minority. Are we to believe that by 2019, all the black people of Los Angeles have left, en masse, for a better life elsewhere in the galaxy? The film never explains. And neither do the critics.[6]

But even though the film contains no black bodies, *Blade Runner* absolutely depends on the category of blackness and its role in the history of American slavery and civil rights. By the year 2019, life on earth has deteriorated dramatically, and most of those with mobility have emigrated to a better life on the off-world colonies of outer space. Industry has begun to manufacture "replicants," robots that are "virtually identical" to humans, as "slave labor" in the "hazardous exploration and colonization" of the new frontier. To ensure human hegemony, replicants are forbidden to return to Earth, "under penalty of death." Special policemen called "blade runners" enforce the law by detecting and killing fugitive slaves. Those fugitive replicants who have made it back to Earth talk of eluding slave catchers by running "north" to freedom. The idiom of the film thus reprises the well-known tradition of African American history and slave narratives.

The film's only direct reference to the existence of black people, earthly or otherwise, was cut from the original 1982 version in its transformation to the 1992 director's cut incarnation. The reference comes by way of the original's noir style voice-over, when the film introduces Deckard's former police boss, Captain Bryant (M. Emmet Walsh). Over whiskey poured from what looks like a Jack Daniel's bottle, Bryant says to the retired blade runner, "I've got four skinjobs walking the streets." Deckard's voice-over comments, " 'Skinjobs'—that's what Bryant called replicants. In history books, he's the kind of cop who used to call black men 'niggers.' " This exchange establishes Bryant and Deckard as stock figures of twentieth century civil rights narratives: the Southern redneck cop and the cynical but nonracist white one. Thus, by 1992, the film has excised all its direct references to black people despite its reliance on traditional African American themes.

This chapter seeks to analyze the curious formula that elides black people yet exaggerates the presence of Asian ones. Critics of the film tend to ignore the transposition of racial terms—from white and black to white and yellow—in one of two ways. Some focus on the film's representation of the Asian as a reflection of the period's economic history, without explaining the lack of blackness.[7] Other critics read the film in terms of a white and black binary structure, while downplaying or ignoring the obviously racist representation of the Asian.[8] Both types of reading strategies are binary, focusing on only two races. Yet it is clear that *Blade Runner* relies on at least three racial categories to construct its narrative. Therefore, any attempt to understand the film's politics must attend to the interplay among all three elements of this racial triangle. Specifically, the film reinscribes white supremacy by displacing the historical tension between white and black onto another type of racial body, namely, the figure of the Asian.

Even as *Blade Runner* presents twenty-first century Los Angeles as a place without African Americans, the city of the film is the site of a new slave system. Humans manufacture replicants to serve as slave labor for the project on which the survival of humanity depends: the colonization of the new frontier of outer space. "Let's go to the colonies!" shouts a recorded message from one of the omnipresent neon blimps that float over the dark streets, "the chance to begin again in a golden land of opportunity and adventure." Certain tasks associated with the vast emigration project require that replicants be virtually identical to humans. (Or at least white humans. There are no nonwhite replicants.) For example, Captain Bryant describes the blonde-haired and blue-eyed Pris (Daryl Hannah), one of the female fugitives, as "a basic pleasure model"—a euphemism for sex slave—"a standard item for military clubs in the outer colonies." The need for android slave labor that passes as human gives rise to the film's central question: what constitutes the difference between what is human and what is not?

The film's answer is the ability to feel emotion. Replicants "were designed to copy humans beings in every way, except their emotions," explains Bryant. Ironically, the robot makers did their job of copying nature too well. "Designers reckoned that after a few years, [replicants would] develop their own emotional responses," such as hate, love, fear, anger, envy, thereby bridging the ontological gap between human and not human. Yet the dividing line between human and replicant must be firmly fixed to justify the twenty-first century slave economy. If replicants become too much like humans, then humans would have no moral justification to enslave them. Thus, the corporation must find a way to block the possibility of any replicant becoming indistinguishable from human. The corporation solves the problem by allowing replicants only a four-year life span. The fail-safe device of "accelerated decrepitude" ensures that, even if replicants were to develop their own emotions, they would not live long enough to pose a threat to the master/slave political economy.

The film's central figure is Rick Deckard, a retired blade runner charged with the mission to kill a group of four Nexus 6 replicants. They are the most technologically advanced, and therefore the most emotionally gifted, generation of slaves. The rebel band has staged a "bloody mutiny" and returned to Earth in the hope of finding a way to lengthen their life span. At first, Deckard is unwilling to comply with the mission. "You're gonna spot them [and then] air'em out," orders Bryant. Deckard balks. Then, in the clipped syntax of noir masculinity, Bryant threatens him, "You're not cop, you're little people," implying that he would use his position as a policeman to force Deckard to comply. Deckard has "no choice" but to accept the assignment.

The scene is important because it makes conceptual room for Deckard's movement from accepting to rejecting the conventional hierarchy of human and replicant. Initially, Deckard sees the replicant as essentially different from his own human kind. For example, he remarks at the beginning of the film that "replicants are like any other machine," displaying his assumption that the replicant slave is a mere thing. When Deckard discovers that the corporation that manufactures the replicants has fooled a female replicant, Rachael (Sean Young), into thinking that she is human, he immediately characterizes her as nonhuman. "How can it not know what it is?" he asks Dr. Tyrell (Joe Turkel), the genius inventor of replicant technology. In a scene from the shooting script that was cut from the final print, Deckard admits to Holden (Morgan Paull), a fellow blade runner, that his sexual liaison with Rachael has intensified his misgivings about his job as replicant killer. "So what?" Holden responds "You fucked a washing machine."[9]

Even without this scene, the film dissolves the opposition between human and replicant almost as fast as it sets it up. When Deckard first meets Rachael, she already intuits that she may be a replicant. Immediately, she challenges Deckard's conviction about the difference between humans and replicants by asking, "Have you ever retired a human by mistake?" The question emphasizes the fact that the naked eye alone cannot distinguish between the two, forcing him to think of humans and replicants in terms of similarity rather than difference. The rest of the film shows replicants having feelings that are just as strong and complex as those of the "real" human figures in the movie, as well as the "real" humans that make up the audience. For example, when Deckard tells Rachael how Tyrell has fooled her into thinking that she is human by implanting someone else's memories into her brain, the camera holds a tight focus on her face, following the slow descent of a tear down her cheek. Deckard begins to sympathize with her plight, so much so that his initial callow treatment of her quickly transforms into love, proving his heterosexual status.

Roy Batty (Rutger Hauer), the leader of the rebel band of slaves, is the other significant vehicle through which the film displays replicant emotion. His sense of irony, for example, marks him as human. Despite living under an overarching power structure that defines him as a nonperson, he still manages to be playful. "Gosh, you really got some nice toys here," the normally formal Roy reacts with campy emphasis on his first visit to the apartment of Sebastian (William Sanderson), the genetic designer who makes animated robots as a hobby. Later, he jokes with Sebastian in an Orientalized accent, "we're so happy that you've found us" while making a comic face with buck teeth and oversized plastic eyes.[10] Roy chokes up with tears of sadness when he recounts Deckard's assassination of fellow replicants Zhora (Joanna Cassidy) and Leon (Brion James). When Deckard kills Pris, Roy's replicant love interest, Roy observes an impromptu funeral by ritualistically painting his face "like a commanche [sic] warrior" with her blood, expressing his sorrow with a long and plaintive howl in the night (Fancher 115). All of these scenes create a sense of complex emotional and intellectual response to the world, in a word, Roy's individual personality.

There is a long tradition of defining human status by the sorts of emotions one has as opposed to the specific body type one possesses. *Blade Runner*'s project of defining humanity through the capacity to feel parallels another literary tradition: the sentimental depiction of blackness within the context of American slavery. The film's use of emotion to create sympathy for the victim parallels Harriet Beecher Stowe's *Uncle Tom's Cabin*, the 1852 antislavery novel whose original subtitle tells us that it is a story about a "man that was a thing."[11] One of the book's central messages is the humanity of blackness. Black slaves are human beings, and as humans, they should not be slaves. Like *Blade Runner, Uncle Tom's Cabin*'s evidence for the claim that slaves are human is emotion. By showing the feelings of slaves, Stowe forges an identification between her white readers and the black slave characters in her novel. She establishes black humanity by convincing whites that black people experience the same joys and pains as they do.

One of the primary examples of suffering humanity is, of course, Uncle Tom. Early in the novel, Tom is sold to the cruel slave trader, Mr. Haley. The scene in which Tom says what he knows to be his final goodbye to his wife and children illustrates Stowe's mode of operation.

> [Tom] leaned over the back of the chair, and covered his face with his large hands. Sobs, heavy, hoarse, and loud, shook the chair, and great tears fell through his fingers on the floor: just such tears, sir, as you dropped into the coffin where lay your first-born son; such tears

woman, as you shed when you heard the cries of your dying babe. For, sir, he was a man,—and you are but another man. And, woman, though dressed in silk and jewels, you are but a woman, and, in life's great straits and mighty griefs, ye feel but one sorrow! (45)

Part of the sentimental technique is to make the reader feel what the victim in the diegesis feels, producing tears in readers themselves. After the description of Tom weeping, the narrator abruptly switches the address. When Stowe's narrator says "sir" and "woman," she hails the white readers of the novel. The switch from omniscient narrative to direct address exhorts white readers to recognize that the black characters that she describes are essentially like them. Both white readers and black characters share a common struggle against "life's great straits" and as a result, both "feel but one sorrow," which in turn proves their common humanity.

Even more than Rachael, Roy convinces both Deckard and the viewer that the replicants do in fact fit the profile of humanity; he proves his humanity by demonstrating that he is physically, intellectually, and even morally superior to everyone else in the film, humans as well as slaves. Because replicants were meant to perform the physical labor for the "hazardous exploration and colonization" of the new frontier, they were created to be "superior in strength and agility, and at least equal in intelligence, to the genetic engineers who created them." Roy literalizes the corporation's motto "more human than human," the promise that replicants will not only pass as human but be better at being human than humans themselves are. "You're so perfect," Sebastian tells Roy. Roy is the smartest, strongest, and most handsome man in the film, thereby giving the lie to the notion of replicant inferiority. He demonstrates his physical superiority by being impervious to subzero temperatures, punching holes through walls, breaking bones, dodging laser bullets, jumping from one high rooftop to another, and catching and lifting up grown men with one hand. Through his skill at chess, Roy cleverly secures a meeting with Dr. Tyrell. Roy exhibits a peerless sense of high culture, being the only character who recites poetry. Just before he kills Chew (James Hong), the elderly Chinese eye-maker who works for the Tyrell Corporation, Roy makes a dramatic entrance by reciting a version of William Blake's epic poem *America: A Prophecy*.[12] Despite the fact that Deckard has killed all of his replicant kin, Roy chooses to save Deckard's life rather than kill him at the climax of the film. According to Scott, if "the roles are reversed," Deckard would be "delighted to blow [Roy's] head off."[13] Trapped in a body with a truncated life span, however, Roy understands the value of life for its own sake. In a plot twist calculated for its poignancy, Roy saves Deckard because the former needs a witness to the intensity of the desire for more life. The fact that "Roy Batty takes the humane route," Scott continues, proves that "the character is almost more human than human" (Kolb 169). Roy's exploits are so moving they prompted one critic to write that during his "struggle to gain more life, [Roy's] 'human' traits [not only] flower [but] touch grandeur."[14]

The film's technique of humanization by idealization also derives from the tradition of African American slave narratives, whether factual or fictional. Through the figure of George Harris, a Kentucky slave in the prime of his young life, *Uncle Tom's Cabin* shows the reader that some black slaves are at least as talented as, if not more talented than, most of the white master race. Early in the novel, George's master contracts him out to do factory work. Off the plantation, George's natural gifts flower. He invents a hemp cleaning machine that displays "as much mechanical genius as Whitney's cotton-gin." As a result of his "adroitness and ingenuity" he rises to the position of "first hand in the place" (16). But when George's master becomes threatened, he abruptly pulls him from his factory position. George had always impressed those who made his acquaintance "instantly with the idea of something uncommon" (118–19). Back on the plantation, George quickly realizes that he is in numerous ways superior to his master: "I know more about business than he does; I am a better manager than he is; I can read better than he can; I can write a better hand" (20).

As slaves, both George and Roy are subject to the same unjust circumstances. Both men are judged "in the eye of the law not a man but a thing." Both are torn from their families by slavery. George's wife and son, Eliza and Harry, live on a different plantation, the property of a different owner. Roy's twenty-first century family is comprised of the members of the elite Nexus 6 generation of replicants, whom the slave catcher Deckard kills one by one, including Roy's beloved Pris. Both men possess "superior qualifications" but are nevertheless "subject to the control of a vulgar, narrow-minded, tyrannical master" (16). George's master resents his slave's superior qualities so much that he drowns George's only comfort, a puppy given to him by Eliza. His master justifies the gratuitous killing through an appeal to money, claiming that "he couldn't afford to have every nigger keeping his dog [by] feeding him up at his expense" (22). Likewise, the head of the corporation that holds the monopoly on the manufacture and sale of the replicants puts profit and research over any concern about what the replicants may or may not feel, even though replicants pass as humans and possess consciousness. Tyrell has fooled Rachael, his replicant personal assistant, into thinking that she is human by implanting memories into her brain. When Deckard inquires about the emotional cost of the situation to the replicant, Tyrell proclaims, "Commerce is our goal; Rachael is an experiment, nothing more," making clear that he views her as merely the latest test version of the company's primary product.

Viewers who are familiar with the sentimental slave novel may well recognize the family resemblance between Scott's primary cinematic technique for signaling replicant humanity and the cliché of the eye as the window of the soul. The film begins with an extreme close-up of an eye with a light-blue pupil, whose glassy surface reflects the orange bursts of flame of the dark industrial skyline. Presumably it is Leon's eye because, in the next scene, the blade runner Holden examines Leon's eyes to detect whether or not he is a replicant. Because the eye looks human, its effect is ironic. When we first see Leon, we have no idea that he is not human. The very mechanism by which the director emphasizes the slaves' replicant status—giving them glowing red eyes in key moments of the film—has a similar ironic effect. Rachael's eyes glow red when Deckard tests her status as human or replicant—perhaps a sign of her fear of detection. When Pris's eyes do the same in her fight to the death with Deckard, it expresses her passion. Similarly, after Dr. Tyrell tells his "prodigal son" Roy that his life has "burned so very brightly," Roy kills his maker with eyes that burn a defiant red. Likewise, George Harris's "eyes burned" with fury when reproached by his master (21). On such occasions, George was "able to repress every disrespectful word." Yet his "flashing eye [and] gloomy and troubled brow, were part of the natural language that could not be repressed [constituting] indubitable signs [that] showed too plainly that the man could not become a thing" (17).

Both Roy and George serve as living proof that the delineation between master and slave is purely arbitrary. George is a slave because he is black, Roy because he is replicant. *Uncle Tom's Cabin* uses George to give the lie to the notion of inherent white superiority or black inferiority, just as *Blade Runner* sets up the difference between human and replicant to let Roy reveal it to be false. We know that the 1852 novel had the effect of winning northern white readers to the side of abolition, succeeding to such a degree that Lincoln credited the novel with starting the Civil War. But what was the 1982 film's relationship to the racial politics of its time?

Just as George, a black slave, stands out for his light skin, Roy is remarkable for his whiteness. Roy, however, is not just white, but hyperbolically so. Rutger Hauer, the Dutch actor who plays Roy, built a career playing characters that signify northern European masculinity, both Nazi and anti-Nazi. Before *Blade Runner*, he had played Albert Speer in *Inside the Third Reich* (Marvin J. Chomsky, 1982), a television docudrama based on Speer's memoirs, which aired on ABC in 1982. He had also played a WWII Dutch resistance fighter in Paul Verhoeven's 1977 *Soldier of Orange*. The *Blade Runner* cinematographer, Jordan Cronenweth, overexposes Roy's fair body, employing a high-contrast noir style: hard light against a predominantly dark background. His commando physique, platinum blond hair, and blue eyes make him "a poster child for the Aryan Nation," according to Scott Bukatman's British Film Institute volume.[15] In a word, Roy is an *ubermensch*.

In *Inside the Third Reich*, Hauer is a white man playing a member of the master race, Albert Speer. In *Blade Runner*, however, Roy's figure exhibits a tension between the registers of the literal and metaphorical, his actual body and the situation that such a body inhabits. According to Kaja Silverman, Roy is "embodied by a figure that is physically the very embodiment of the Aryan ideal," an ideal that connotes one of the most notoriously racist regimes in history. His status as slave, however, puts him in a category "which our culture still manages, in an attenuated way, to rhyme with negritude." Roy is a bit of a paradox, then: a white body in a black subject position. Thus, Silverman notes, Roy's "hyperbolic 'whiteness' [seems] at first glance deeply problematical" (115).

But even though Roy's Aryan body is associated with racism, Silverman argues that Roy counts as an antiracist figure precisely because of his whiteness. Roy's ultrawhiteness provides the starkest possible contrast to the role "classically occupied by those with dark skin." The contrast "most dramatically denaturalizes the category of 'slave'" by underscoring the point that the mark of slavery does not inhere in the body. Roy proves that the link between black skin and social subordination is "absolutely arbitrary." As a result of the contrast, Roy's whiteness operates as a sort of prompt for "the white spectator" to exercise the golden rule in her or his dealings with black people. His Aryan body obliges white viewers to imagine not only that they could be slaves, too, but to imagine the "absolutely brutal" quality of such a victimized existence (115).

Showing the arbitrariness of the link between one's body and one's place in society does not guarantee a progressive political agenda. *Uncle Tom's Cabin* proves that portraits of abused characters create the possibility of liberalizing popular opinion about an important political issue of the day, such as slavery. But by changing the race of the victim, the same technique of humanizing the victim figure can be used just as easily to serve reactionary as well as progressive politics. For example, D. W. Griffith's 1915 *Birth of a Nation*, the filmic adaptation of Thomas Dixon's 1905 historical romance *The Clansman*, uses the same sentimental tactic as the 1852 *Uncle Tom's Cabin*, but reverses the race of the victim.[16] Instead of a black body in the form of Uncle Tom, *Birth of a Nation* inserts into the position of the victim the white former slaveholder of a recently defeated South. Oppressed by the brutality of blacks newly freed by the Civil War, the white race recaptures the audience's sympathy. *Uncle Tom's Cabin* created widespread guilt among whites for the treatment of blacks held in slavery, which functioned to move whites toward abolition. Following Michael Rogin's important reading of *Birth of a Nation*'s antiblack sentimentalism, "The Sword Became a Flashing Vision," Linda Williams observes that Griffith's film sought to "reverse" these effects some sixty years later, creating sympathy not for the slaves, but for the men who formerly owned them.[17]

Birth of a Nation's relocation of *Uncle Tom's Cabin*'s sentimentality from a black body to a white one helps to explain more contemporary race struggles. Take, for example, the infamous 1993 verdict that acquitted four white LAPD officers charged with the beating of Rodney King. The defense team managed to win the day by convincing the Simi Valley jury that it was the police, not Rodney King, who occupied the position of victim. The LAPD defense strategy counts as a reprise of *Birth of a Nation* because the attorneys exploited the white jury's fears about black men, transforming the white policemen from aggressors into victims. Once identified as victims, the police became the "person[s] best positioned to win moral sympathy," concludes Williams.[18]

Birth of a Nation's sentimentalized version of Northern and Southern whites victimized by black brutality played to the Jim Crow sentiment of its era. In the late twentieth century, *Blade Runner* parallels *Birth of a Nation* in putting its white folk in chains too. In this sense, *Blade Runner* participates in a larger trend of depicting white men as victims. David Savran's 1998 *Taking It Like a Man: White Masculinity, Masochism, and Contemporary American Culture* puts the association between the victim figure and white masculinity into historical perspective. The book notes a shift in the representation of American white masculinity in the late twentieth century. Popular post–civil-rights cultural texts—movies such as the *Rambo* trilogy; several films starring Michael Douglas, including *Fatal Attraction* (Adrian Lyne, 1987), *Falling Down* (Joel Schumacher, 1992), and *Disclosure* (Barry Levinson, 1994); books such as Robert Bly's *Iron John* (1990); and Sam Shepard's plays, such as *Buried Child* (1978)—started to depict "the white male as victim." Savran posits this figure as a response to social movements of the 1960s and 1970s, in particular, a civil rights movement that produced the legal protocol of affirmative action as well as the feminist movement.[19]

The absence of black bodies from *Blade Runner's* Los Angeles is evidence that the film participates in the sentimental logic of casting the white man as victim. The narrative cannot tolerate black bodies on the screen because of the close historical association between "slave" and "black." *Blade Runner* exhibits a paradox with respect to the category of blackness. Metaphorically, it incorporates blackness, yet at the same time, it excludes blackness on the literal level. Any black body or any direct reference to a black body would constitute a rival for the mark of the slave. Any direct references to blackness would constitute competition for the status of the victim and, more importantly, its concomitant moral force. Thus, even though the film needs blackness to do its work, the film's references to it must be indirect, inexplicit, and not literal.

Part of *Blade Runner's* political meaning lies in how the film solves this paradox by cleverly splitting blackness in two. Through this splitting of blackness, coupled with the formula of an Aryan replicant hero victimized by slavery, the film interpolates the viewer as one who is simultaneously for civil rights and for white supremacy. This combination of putting a literal white body into a subject position that rhymes with blackness also allows the film to disguise the way it captures the "undeniable moral power" of the victimized slave figure.[20] In the context of U.S. history, generations of suffering at the hands of white racists and racist institutions make black people signify as the racial victim. The film underwrites Roy's moral appeal with the experience of blacks in America while at the same time eliding the population whose history makes such an appeal possible.[21]

On a note that should alarm any *Blade Runner* fan, at least one political extremist imagines the world according to the same pattern of the enslaved Aryan hero.[22] Consider the following 1995 assertion by Tom Metzger, the leader of a far-right group based in southern California, whose sense of natural superiority is tied to whiteness, the White Aryan Resistance:

> We don't like what is going on now, and we do know we don't have any future. As social power decreases faster and faster, state power increases faster and faster. And we see ourselves, if you will pardon the expression, as the new niggers.[23]

The White Aryan Resistance members view themselves as the new slaves and take such status as an insult to their superiority. Metzger, just like John J. Rambo, feels the strong need to convey the plight of a few good white men overwhelmed by a morally corrupt state.

Metzger's characterization of his own kind as "new niggers" vividly demonstrates that white subject and black subject positions should be understood relationally. According to philosopher Lewis Gordon, "One is white the extent to which one is most distant from black [and] one is black the extent to which one is most distant from white."[24] In Metzger's symbolic world in which white and black signify the onto-logical extremes of human value, "nigger" signifies the lowest grade of blackness, "Aryan" the highest grade of whiteness. His character-ization of his flock as "the new niggers" traces a trajectory wherein white men go from the extreme top to the extreme bottom: "we don't have any future." For a white supremacist like Metzger, there can be no more dramatic narrative trajectory, no more potent scenario of victimization.

Silverman correctly identifies the dramatic contrast of white and black as the engine that generates affect for "the white spectator." But she misreads how that affective action might translate politically because she overlooks the political value of being cast as the victim and ignores the historical context in which Roy's whiteness emerges. The meaning of Roy's body turns on these two points. In light of the sentimental tradition of conferring moral power on the humanized victim and the late twentieth century rhetoric of the victimized white male, Roy can be read as yet another "new nigger." Roy occupies the most abject subject position with a body type that for some sig-nals the highest possible human value.[25] As a result, he garners the highest degree of sympathy. Roy is not only an *ubermensch* but an *uberopfer*.

The other principal white male body in the film—that of Rick Deckard—does not fit the Aryan ideal in the iconography of white supremacy. Yet Deckard's figure does the same work as Roy's. He, too, turns out to be a victim. "I always felt the amusing irony about Harrison's character would be that he was, in fact, a synthetic human," Scott reports. "It's part of the full circle of the initial idea" of what it means to be human; to suggest that Deckard is a replicant "ties it off with a certain elegance" (Sammon 390–1). In the original 1982 version, Scott incorporated clues to suggest that Deckard is replicant rather than human. In one of the kitchen scenes in Deckard's apartment, for example, for a brief moment Deckard's eyes glow red.[26] But for the 1992 director's cut version, Scott guides the viewer to the conclusion narratively rather than symbolically. In both versions of the film, the evil blade runner Gaff (Edward James Olmos) leaves Deckard a calling card, a tiny silver origami unicorn, just before the end of the film when Deckard and Rachael make their escape north. For the director's cut, Scott inserted a scene in which Deckard dreams of a silvery white unicorn. Since, within the timeline of the diegetic world, the unicorn dream scene precedes the one in which Gaff leaves the origami unicorn, the new scene tells the viewer that Gaff must somehow be privy to Deckard's dream life. According to Scott, the origami unicorn counts as Gaff's message through which he says to Deckard, "Listen, pal, I know your innermost thoughts. Therefore you're a replicant. How else would I know this?" (Sammon 391).

The very plausibility of the idea that Deckard is a replicant underscores my reading of Roy as a figure for white supremacy. Following Scott's account, Deckard is the ultimate ironic figure. If Deckard is a replicant, then he is even more of a victim than Roy because he turns out to be the most slavish of all. He is doubly victimized. Deckard is a slave who does not know that he is a slave. He is a replicant manufactured by a corporation that lied to him about his status as replicant so that the corporation could use him for its own purposes—to hunt and kill his own kind. No one else in the film could possibly count as a more poignant victim. While Ford's Deckard may not have a body as Aryan as Hauer's Roy, he has the blackest subject position, especially if he is a replicant. If Deckard is the biggest victim, then he is the figure that most vividly operates to refurbish the image of white masculinity.

The project to refurbish white masculinity requires that Rick Deckard and Roy Batty both appear as victims. Deckard's status as hypervictim, however, puts him at risk of appearing impotent. The film's only sex scene, the rough first kiss between Deckard and Rachael, counters this danger by assuaging any doubts about his male mastery. Set in Deckard's apartment, just after Rachael has saved Deckard from a horrible death at the hands of Leon, the bruised blade runner makes a tender advance with his lips. Instead of responding with a kiss of her own, she turns her head, and then runs to leave the apartment. Deckard catches up to her, angry, blocking the exit with his body. He bangs the door shut with his fist, shoving her hard against the window with both hands. His anger turns into paternal concern as he realizes that he has to teach her how to make love. Just after he kisses her while she's crying, he instructs her, "Now you kiss me." She hesitates. He tries another approach, "Say 'kiss me,'" this time showing her not how to kiss but how to invite him to kiss her. She complies, then proves to be a quick study by offering her own unsolicited solicitation: "Put your hands on me." The scene ends with a shot of the pair in a tight embrace, kissing vigorously, just like any "normal" human couple in the throes of passion.

The "kiss me" scenario confirms Deckard's self-mastery, not to mention his straight status, through sexual domination. Such domination constitutes an important element of Eve Sedgwick's well-known triangulation in which two men strengthen the bonds between themselves through the degradation of a woman, thereby fortifying a male homosocial preeminence in the world.[27] The homosocial bonding in *Blade Runner* both parallels and alters this standard formula. The bonding between the two white principals is mediated through a third term. But *Blade Runner*'s bonding vehicle is not a woman. Because the film gives each man his own heterosexual love object (Deckard gets Rachael, Roy gets Pris) the plot lacks a rivalry between the two male leads over a female character. Instead, the two white warriors bond in the face of an overwhelming Asian presence.

The climactic scene in which Rick Deckard and Roy Batty stalk each other in a fight to the death stages most dramatically *Blade Runner*'s departure from Sedgwick's formula of homosocial bonding. They fight not over a woman, but for life itself; and it is a false fight because Roy is programmed to die very soon. By this point, only two men remain. Deckard has killed all the other replicants, including Zhora, the snake charmer, and Pris, Roy's true love. Deckard is broken and at a disadvantage, due to Roy's superior android physicality. Roy, however, is running out of time. His body is close to its expiration date and has begun to malfunction. At one point during the chase, Roy augments his reputation as "more human than human" in a reprisal of the Crucifixion, plunging a large nail into the palm of his hand to keep it from seizing up.

Set high on a rooftop, the scene stages the moment when repulsion becomes attraction between the two men, ending with Roy's teary farewell. The scene starts at night. It is raining hard, and patches of smoke float about the set. In an attempt to get away from the much more powerful Batty, Deckard has jumped from one building to another; but his leap has fallen short, and he hangs off the rooftop cornice, dangling high above the street. Roy, the avenger, has broken two of Deckard's fingers (one for Zhora, the other for Pris) so he cannot hold on for very long. Roy, in pursuit of Deckard, has made the jump easily. After landing on the other side, Roy stands, holding a white dove, wearing white shorts, his body naked from the waist up and glazed with rainwater. A nearby spotlight runs over his body, the light reflecting back to the camera as a bright white spot on the frame. He leans close and over the edge while Deckard hangs on for his life, but does not move in for the kill. From a low angle representing Deckard's point of view, the camera closes in to a tight shot of Roy's face, wet from blood, sweat, and rain, framed by his platinum blond hair. The spotlight swings toward him and illuminates his fair skin and blue eyes. After a relatively long time without dialogue, Roy looks directly into the camera and speaks: "Quite an experience to live in fear, isn't it? That's what it is to be a slave." Sensing that he has no good options, Deckard cannot hang on any longer. He gasps, then lets go of the cornice. But with a display of preternatural quickness and strength, Batty catches Deckard, and then pulls him up to safety. Even though Roy has every reason to kill the blade runner, Roy saves Deckard.

Roy follows this generous gesture with a final display of his humanity. Batty deposits Deckard onto the roof, and Deckard scrambles away, low like a crab, thinking that Batty will kill him yet. Instead of finishing him off, however, Batty takes a seat a few feet away from Deckard, lotus-style, still gripping the white dove. Then Batty, his fair skin glossy from the heavy rain, calmly delivers what amounts to his death speech. The scene is quiet so that the viewer can hear the patter of rain punctuated by Batty's dying gasps:

> I've seen things that you people wouldn't believe. Attack ships on fire off the shoulder of Orion. I watched c-beams glitter in the dark near the Tanhauser Gate. All those moments will be lost in time. Like tears in rain. Time to die.

Batty lowers his head and expires. The close-up of Deckard's weary face confirms the bonding of the former enemies. Bruised and battered, Deckard first shows disbelief, then admiration. Through Roy's angelic coloring and Christ-like actions, the film urges the audience to follow suit. After Batty dies, the dove struggles free from his hand and flies up toward a blue sky. It is the first time that the viewer has been shown a bright day.

If there is no rivalry over a common female figure, what then serves as the homosocial bonding agent for the two white heroes? A consideration of the background sets indicates what the mediating third term might be. An Asian corporate presence marks the film's climax. A large white and red neon sign looms above the pair as a backdrop for the entire rooftop scene, starting with Batty saving Deckard's life to Batty delivering his death oration. It is a bright red and white neon sign for TDK, a Japanese electronics company. From start to finish of Roy's death scene, the faces of the two white buddies reflect the red glare of what the 1982 viewer knows represents a Japanese multinational corporation.

At least one Asian American Studies critic notes the film's deployment of the Asian as a foil for the white characters. "*Blade Runner*'s representation of a third world, largely Asian, invasion of Los Angeles," writes Lisa Lowe, "rearticulates orientalist typographies in order to construct the white citizen against the background of a multicultural dystopia."[28] Kael describes *Blade Runner*'s vision of Los Angeles in 2019 as "hellish [and] claustrophobic…a cross between Newark and old Singapore."[29] "Only a polyglot refuse of humanity remains," *Time* magazine's Richard Corliss remarks. "Los Angeles is a Japanized nighttown of sleaze and silicon, fetid steam and perpetual rain.…The filthy streets are clogged with Third World losers and carnivores."[30] *Blade Runner* signifies a world gone to hell through its representation of the Asian, a warning to the 1980s and 1990s viewer that a yellow peril threat was close at hand.

As with the TDK set, the film embeds Asian-themed corporate signage into the upper reaches of the urban dystopia to convey the sense of a yellow peril invasion. For example, when Deckard enters an abandoned apartment building, the site of the fight scene between himself and Roy, he looks up through a skylight. The camera gives us a medium long shot of the underside of a blimp with two large video panels facing the street. Each screen runs a commercial featuring a "traditional geisha girl" (Sammon 240). One of the geishas entices the viewer with a glass of beer. The other looks as if she is peering right into the building, like a peeping Tom. Her eyes look directly at the camera and meet the viewer's eyes, as if she were a live person looking back at the viewer. The soundtrack is quiet except for an eerie kabuki chant. According to Jordan Cronenweth, the film's cinematographer, the airships were created to float "through the night with enormously powerful beams emerging from their undersides [bathing] the city in constantly swinging lights." The idea was to impart the sense that the lights were "used for both advertising and crime control," Cronenweth continues, "much the way a prison is monitored by moving searchlights," representing a sinister "invasion of privacy by a supervising force, a form of control."[31]

A similar geisha video image dominates the film's numerous panoramic shots of the city's skyline. In a bridging shot repeated several times during the film, the camera shows a tall skyscraper with an enormous multipaneled video screen that occupies the entirety of one of its facades. The screen features a close-up image of yet another geisha, whose giant powder-white face with bright red lipstick dominates the landscape. In the action of the commercial, the geisha holds up a red pill, puts it in her mouth, swallows, and then smiles. Like the geisha on the blimp, she looks straight at the camera. According to the special effects supervisor, David Dryer, Scott wanted to "continue with the oppressive feeling throughout the landscape" by showing "a bunch of phony oriental commercials where geisha girls are doing unhealthy things. Smoking, taking drugs or whatever" (Sammon 241–3). In another shot, the same huge screen shows commercials for various well-known corporations such as Coca-Cola, thus linking the elements of an "oppressive feeling," corporate rule, and the Asian body.

The giant geisha images give the background sets a sense of liveliness. "The environment in the film is almost a protagonist," says

Figure 5.1   Spaceship and "geisha" screen in *Blade Runner*'s cityscape.

David Dryer.[32] Lawrence Paull, the director of set design, nominated for a 1982 Academy Award for best art direction/set decoration for his work on *Blade Runner*, echoed the same sentiment in an interview ten years after the film's initial release:

> The key thing in film design is that the design works within the context of the story and who the characters are....It's very rare that the design of the show becomes one of the stars....It certainly happened in *Blade Runner*. Most of the time the setting would be a supporting player; [it] just enhances whatever goes on storywise. It doesn't say, "Here I am."[33]

Paull claims that the sets function as a leading player, as opposed to merely supporting the action delivered by the actors. He speaks about *Blade Runner*'s sets as if they had a life of their own, capable of announcing their own presence with a human voice. Paull's words ring especially true when considered in relation to the film's representation of the Asian. If the sets say, "Here I am," the quantity and quality of Asian markers embedded in the backgrounds make them say "I am Asian" as well.

The corporate ruling class uses Asian faces to advertise their goods and services. Not all of the film's Asian markers, however, appear as a supervising corporate force from on high. The film emphasizes a second, proletarian or even lumpen-proletarian, type of yellow peril on the city's streets. The viewer's introduction to Deckard is representative of the film's saturation, to the point of absurdity, of Asian markers in its street scenes. First we see a close-up of a blue-and-white neon Chinese dragon with a glowing red tongue darting in and out of its mouth. Then the camera pans down to the street level and into the heavy sidewalk traffic. Seated at a sushi bar, a white man with blond hair pours a cup of tea from a Japanese teapot, surrounded by a crush of Asians. Two of the patrons are Asian men with white hard hats ringed with Korean writing. Near them sits an Asian woman with the word "Japan" stitched on the back of her jacket. It is raining. Many of the Asians on the sidewalk move by the camera holding Japanese paper umbrellas. The film ensures proper racial identification by outfitting their umbrellas with blue neon shafts, enabling the viewer to see their faces as they parade by the camera.

The soundtrack does its part to signal the ubiquitous Asian presence. As Deckard waits for a sushi order, a voice calls out to him. Behind the counter an old Japanese man in a kimono, the "sushi master" (Robert Okazaki), addresses him in Japanese. Deckard wants a double portion of fish, suggesting that he has twice the body to feed than the regular customer. "Two, two, four," shouts Deckard, as he shakes two fingers twice. The master tells him "two is plenty," but gestures to a seat at the bar, "*Dozo.*" As Deckard expertly rubs together two wooden "chopsticks like an Oriental," two policemen approach from behind. One of them, in uniform, addresses Deckard in Korean (Kolb 155; Sammon 112). The second policeman, Gaff (Edward James Olmos), is a fellow blade runner. Gaff taps Deckard on the shoulder and addresses him in a futuristic tongue, "Cityspeak," a mix of several Asian languages, among others. Even though he is literally surrounded by Asian language, both spoken and written, Deckard gestures that he does not understand. The master translates in English with a heavy Japanese accent, "He say you under arrest, Mr. Deckard." "Got the wrong guy, pal," bellows the hard-boiled dick. Frustrated, Gaff responds to Deckard, "*Lofan!*" a Cantonese pejorative for white people. The bar scene ends when the sushi master identifies Deckard's status to the viewer, "He say you brade runner," unable to pronounce the *l* in "blade."

As I mention above, much of the sequence's Asiatic detail comes to the viewer through the pervasiveness of the written word. It is night;

Figure 5.2   Blade runner Rick Deckard (Harrison Ford) with chopsticks.

but the streetscape is crammed with so many neon signs that there is ample ambient light for reading. The signs are written in Asian characters. Just inside the window behind Deckard is a constellation of red neon signs, all in either kanji or kana, one large sign in the shape of a medallion surrounded by an array of smaller ones. Inscribed within the central medallion are two giant characters in kana. Still more Asian writing fills the television screens in the window and promotion cards lining the bottom of the window. The camera cuts through the crowd to reveal Deckard in the midst of all this Orientalia, leaning with his back up against a television storefront window, casually reading a newspaper while he waits for his sushi. The large neon array serves as a backdrop for the camera's close-up of Deckard. His visage is bathed in the red light of the glowing Asian word. "He's the only one you see who reads [so] you know Deckard is a breed apart," writes *The New Yorker's* Pauline Kael. "We get the vague impression that the more prosperous, clean-cut types have gone off-world to some Scarsdale in space" (945).

The film emphasizes Deckard's status as a breed apart not only by overloading the background sets with Asian markers, but also by portraying Asian people as a degraded form of humanity.[34] All Asian characters with speaking parts are old and decrepit, in contrast to the replicants' youth and vigor. They speak English with a heavy Orientalized accent, marking them as foreign. (Did the Americans of Asian ancestry leave in the same rocket ship with the African Americans?) The sushi master is an old Japanese man. Chew is so shrunken from age that he looks like a piece of dried fruit rattling around in the heavy husk of his animal fur suit that protects him from the refrigeration of his work room. The wrinkled "Cambodian lady" (Kimiro Hiroshige, who, judging by the name, is of Japanese ancestry) who identifies a piece of physical evidence for Deckard, communicates with a voice so ancient that it crackles like dry parchment. In a *Film Quarterly* review, Thomas Dempsey describes the city folk of *Blade Runner's* Los Angeles futurescape as "hordes of punk-Oriental-Krishna-humongous-hustler-lowlifes clustering like cockroaches."[35] "The population seems to be almost entirely ethnic," writes Kael, "poor, hustling Asians and assorted foreigners, who are made to seem not quite degenerate, perhaps, but oddly subhuman. They're all selling, dealing, struggling to get along; they never look up—they're intent on what they're involved in, like slot-machine zealots in Vegas" (945). The film presents "those sewer rat people in the city," Kael notes, "as so dehumanized that their life or death hardly matters. . . . Deckard feels no more connection to them than Ridley Scott does," she continues. "They're just part of the film's bluish-gray, heavy-metal chic" (948).

This bluish-gray of the street level sets plays an important role in the film's look, which, on a visual register, degrades the Asian in formal terms. The makeup supervisor, Marvin Westmore, explains how he blended the bodies of the film's numerous Asian extras into the background sets by covering them in blue, literally.

> One of my biggest challenges was coming up with makeup for all the extras they used in the crowd scenes. Many of them were supposed to be Asians, so I came up with something called "Asian *Blade Runner* Blue." That was applied by a crew of about 40 people—the biggest-sized team I had in my makeup department on *BR* at any one time. It was sort of a greasepaint with a light blue cast to it. (Sammon 110)

Why did Westmore choose blue? Exaggerating the look of the night-time light by making the face look as if it reflects moonlight, perhaps he borrowed the blue makeup convention from 1940s film noir.

The blue makeup for the Asian faces matches the general color scheme for the set designs that a *Film Comment* reviewer, like Kael, characterizes as "bluish-smoky exteriors."[36] A consideration of rudimentary color theory shows how *Blade Runner*'s formal aspects ensure that only white bodies benefit from the film's inquiry of what it takes to be human. The set designer Lawrence Paull explains the genesis of what became the film's overall color palette.

> Ridley came into my office, threw a magazine on my set and said, "That's Sebastian's apartment." Here was this blond fashion model that looked like Irving Penn's wife wearing a long white gown, and she's standing next to this blue-gray wall with these huge, heavy moldings on the wall panels, and its all decaying. It looked like someone had gone in and done a sponge painting on a tenement in New York, and the painting is all peeling back. You could almost sense that there were rats running around at her feet. Here was this woman who looked fabulous against this, and that's how the coloration of that set happened.[37]

Sebastian, one of the principal designers of the Nexus 6 replicants, works for Dr. Tyrell, the head of the corporation that manufactures the replicants. Tyrell represents the replicants' last hope, the only person who might be able to prolong their life span. Because Tyrell is heavily guarded, the escaped slaves concoct a plan to befriend Sebastian to gain access to Tyrell. A good portion of the film's action takes place in or on top of Sebastian's building, including the climactic showdown between Deckard and Batty.

The fashion photograph that served as a template for the film's background sets is a mix of contrasting themes. On the one hand, the photograph's sense of decay ("rats" and New York "tenement") conveys Sebastian's degraded status as a human being. He is stricken with "Methuselah's Syndrome," a disease that ages its victims prematurely, so the authorities have forbidden him from migrating with most of the other earthlings to the healthier environments of the off worlds. On the other, Paull's "Irving Penn" refers to haute couture fashion photography, which signifies wealth and glamour. For example, Penn shot, among many other advertisements, the early Clairol hair coloring campaign that first appeared in *Life* magazine in 1956. "Is it true blondes have more fun?" the ads ask. "If I've only one life, let me live it as a blonde!"[38]

The color scheme of the background sets helps to convey the thematic contrast that produces, to use Paull's words, such a fabulous result for the blond in the frame. On a formal level, Paull's description of the fashion photograph reveals a visual pattern of a small patch of bright color set against a large and dark blue-gray background. Like the blond-haired and blue-eyed Rutger Hauer and Darryl Hanna, the fashion model in the foreground is blond, suggesting that her hair and overall skin tone is fair. She wears a long white gown, suggesting that her light-colored attire covers the length of her body. Thus, the model's overall tone is light, if not white. The photograph renders the background in a dark tone. It is safe to assume that the photograph's wall is a dark blue-gray as opposed to a light one because, on the screen, dark shadows and dust shroud Sebastian's apartment. Setting the long white gown, which reflects light, against the mottled and peeling surface of the dark and sponge-painted wall, which absorbs and diffuses it, heightens the visual contrast.

Governing such a visual composition is what color theorists call "the law of simultaneous contrast of colors." The theorist of color Harald Kueppers explains that "under fixed illumination and observation conditions, after the eye has adapted, the same color sample can reveal different hues, depending only upon the colors surrounding it."[39] The Bauhaus designer Johannes Itten specifies the relationship between a color's identity and the color of its background through the idea of contrast. "The eye," Itten writes, functions "only by means of comparisons, [accepting] a line as long when a shorter line is presented for comparison.... The same line is taken as short when the line compared with it is longer." "Color effects," says Itten, "are similarly intensified or weakened by contrast."[40] The appearance of any given color to the human eye depends to a significant extent on its background.

Michel Eugene Chevreul first defined the simultaneous contrast rule in 1854. "In the case where the eye sees at the same time two contiguous colours," Chevreul writes, "they will appear as dissimilar as possible, both in their optical composition and in the height of their tone."[41] The law is "simultaneous" in the sense that the optical effect occurs when looking at two different colors at the same time. "Contrast" refers to the fact that, when juxtaposed, the colors shift away from one another in two ways. The "optical composition" shifts, Itten explains, because "the eye requires any given color to be balanced by the complementary." The eye, he writes, "will spontaneously generate the latter if it is not present" (78). The shift in "the height of their tone" refers to the fact that a dark color will make an adjacent light color appear even lighter and vice versa.

Paull describes how his set design deployed contrasts between light and dark.

> The only thing that was discussed was that everything would be in a great deal of urban decay. I used many warm gray tones and a great deal of natural aging, dust and everything. The only time we saw hot color was in the neon at night. Charles Knode [a costume designer] found most of the clothes for the actors and extras in used clothing stores.... It was literally, "Put it in the washing machine, pour a pound of real strong coffee in, and see what happens." ...everything was very browned over, very heavily aged and crusted over.[42]

The film's color scheme aimed at dark values for the majority of surfaces in the physical environment. Visually, *Blade Runner* is a very dark film, conveying a world that is starved for light. Kael, for instance, announces that the cityscape is so polluted "that it's dark outside, yet, when we're inside, the brightest lights are on the outside, from the giant searchlights scanning the city and shining in" (944). The dialogue calls the viewer's attention to an excess of light only once, when Deckard prepares to give Rachael the replicant test inside Dr. Tyrell's penthouse apartment. In this single instance, Deckard asks the creator of the replicants to close the window shades.

Paull's description mentions one exception to the darkness of the background sets: neon signs glowing hot, like the aforementioned TDK sign, against the black of night. The kitchen scene in which Deckard cleans himself up after a savage fight with the replicant Leon follows Paull's formula for "hot color." The set of Deckard's kitchen is a faded light brown. He submerges his head slowly into the sink water, running his finger over his teeth to see if they're all there. Then the weary and severely bruised Deckard lifts a shot glass to his lips. The liquor is clear and still, like vodka.[43] As soon as his mouth makes contact with the lip of the glass, a bit of his blood suddenly shoots into the drink. The visual effect is startling. Suspended in the transparent contents of the glass, illuminated by an eye light, the blood swirls like a liquid crimson gem in the dimly lit kitchen.

The kitchen scene's visual composition reveals a principle of visual difference called the contrast of extension, which in the film works in tandem with the law of simultaneous contrast. The contrast of extension involves "the relative areas of two or more color patches," according to Itten, "the contrast between much and little, or great and small" (104). Itten expounds on the combined visual effect of small versus large (contrast of extension) and light versus dark (simultaneous contrast).

> The two factors of light value and extent of area turn out to be most intimately related....If other than harmonious proportions are used in a color composition, thus allowing one color to dominate, then the effect obtained is expressive....The minority color, in distress, as it were, reacts defensively to seem relatively more vivid than if it were present in a harmonious amount....If a color present in minute amount is given opportunity, by protracted contemplation, to assert itself in the eye, it is found to become increasingly concentrated and provocative. (104)

By describing the effect as "expressive," Itten refers to the formula's ability to help tell the story. The visual arrangement of the shot draws the viewer's attention to the only bright spot of color in the scene: Deckard's blood. The shot does not have a great deal of physical action or dialogue. The camera holds its focus on Deckard's profile while he stands silently with the drink pressed against his mouth. He stares straight ahead, as if he is unaware of the blood in the glass. Deckard's lack of knowledge about the presence of his own blood in the shot glass signals the possibility that he himself is a replicant, a question that many hard-core fans of the film debate endlessly.[44] Blood, after all, is the most durable metaphor for lineage.

The two laws of contrasting colors and color areas give us the answer as to why the set designer chose a dark blue-gray for the background's main color. If the formal aspects of the shot highlight the redness of Deckard's blood, then the film's visual scheme also benefits the blond quality of his Aryan-looking peers, Roy and Pris. In the literal terms of color theory, the towheaded couple registers in the range of silvery white to yellow. According to the law of simultaneous contrast, contiguous colors move one another toward their complements or opposites on the color wheel. Chevreul observes, for example, that an *"Orange-Yellow* circle" set against a white background "tends to colour the surrounding space *Indigo."*[45] Just as a dull setting makes the pure colors within such a composition "shine like jewels," to use Itten's words, an overwhelmingly dark and blue environment makes *Blade Runner's* blond-haired replicants look fabulous (15).

In the late twentieth century, *Blade Runner* revises the African American slave narrative to recuperate the power of whiteness, now ensured by yellowness. The most obvious expression of this idea comes not in the film in its final form but via the shooting script, dated February 1981, roughly a year before the film's initial release in 1982. In an ending that was cut from the final print, Deckard and his replicant lover Rachael are escaping "north" in a rocket ship. By this time, Deckard is a fugitive too because of his refusal to kill Rachael. When he looks back and discovers that another blade runner is in pursuit, presumably to kill them, Deckard's voice-over cuts in:

> I knew it on the roof that night. *We were brothers, Roy Batty and I!* Combat models of the highest order. We had fought in wars not yet dreamed of... in vast nightmares still unnamed. We were the new people... Roy and me and Rachael! We were made for this world. It was ours! (Fancher 133; ellipses and italics in the original)

The voice-over recounts the story of how two men—one white, one metaphorically black—bond in the face of disaster to become one, a "new people." The film recuperates white power by giving all the new and improved versions of humanity white bodies. Unlike *Birth of a Nation*, however, *Blade Runner* does not demonize blacks. In an era after WWII and the civil rights movement, such a narrative move would seem un-American. Instead, the film omits black bodies to sidestep the long-standing historical tension between white and black in the United States.

The film may avoid evoking the racial tension generated by the black experience in white America by eliding black bodies, but that tension has by no means disappeared. The film transfers the tension to the Asian. The film's rapprochement between white and "black" requires an Asian threat, represented in humanoid form by Gaff, a blade runner in Deckard's former police unit who now chases Deckard and Rachael. According to the film's 1982 press kit, Gaff signifies a racial mix, "a multilingual bureaucrat with Oriental skin, Japanese eyes, and blue irises" (Kolb 156). Edward James Olmos, the Latino actor who plays Gaff, reports, "I asked Marvin Westmore [the film's make-up artist] to make up my skin in yellowish tones" because "despite his mixed blood, Gaff was more Asian than anything else" (Sammon 114). Gaff's yellowish skin and the meticulous origami figures that he makes as calling cards complement each other. In the film, Gaff does appear to be mixed race. The shooting script, however, makes it clear that his identity was originally conceived as unambiguously Asian. Gaff has much more dialogue than remains in the final cut, but not a word of it is in English. All of his lines are in Japanese. In this 1981 version of the script, Gaff is a "short Japanese guy" with "beedy [sic] eyes and lots of energy" (Fancher 7).

In the original version of the film, Deckard sarcastically describes the perpetually angry Gaff as a "charmer," a physically handicapped bureaucrat interested only in "brown-nosing for a promotion." Similarly, Olmos describes him as "an ambitious, slightly shifty character" (Sammon 113). In a word, Gaff is a model minority sycophant who will sacrifice personal integrity to climb the corporate police ladder. He fits very well into the film's dark and rainy setting where hordes of Asian sewer rat people in the streets signify a nasty and brutish world of corporate consumerism. The overwhelming number of Asian markers constructs an ethos that crushes individuality, draining the joy of life from vibrant men like Deckard and Batty. "Sushi, that's what my ex-wife calls me," exclaims Deckard in the 1982 version's voice-over, "cold fish." The origami-wielding Gaff serves as a perfect foil to Deckard and Batty. As I explain in the chapter on *Rising Sun* (Philip Kaufman, 1993), fed by memories of WWII, widespread paranoia of Japan as an economic threat to U.S. sovereignty during the 1980s and 1990s established the context for *Blade Runner*'s vilification of Asians.

Deckard and Batty start out as enemies, based on the perception that they are different in kind. By the film's end, however, Deckard realizes that their similarities run deeper than their differences and that they are in fact the same type of man, "brothers," regardless of any distinction between human and android. Facing a common threat, "vast nightmares still unnamed," the two male figures find common ground on which to forge a new identity, one that leaves behind the outmoded and corrupt distinctions of the past. In *Blade Runner*'s near future of 2019, the nation's nightmares are Asian.

6

"*Domo Arigato*, Mr. Roboto": *The Matrix* (1999) and the Virtual Asian

It's something very special: a big, muscular, "effects" movie that's wildly generous with visual thrills, manages to never quit making sense…and, most important of all, has a good heart.

—William Gibson, *The Matrix:* The Shooting Script[1]

In HBO's production documentary on Andy and Larry Wachowski's spectacularly successful 1999 science fiction film *The Matrix*, the brothers announce a fondness for Asian popular culture. "We like kung fu movies, we like Japanimation, we like John Woo movies."[2] Traces of these influences abound in both the film and its numerous production histories. For example, an astonished Neo (Keanu Reeves) exclaims, "I know kung fu!" when the computer operator Tank (Marcus Chong) downloads a variety of martial arts skills directly into the protagonist's brain as if it were a hard drive. *The Matrix*'s apocalyptic theme of computer tyranny matches that of Japanimation, the Wachowski's term for *anime*, examples of which include *Akira* (Katsuhiro Ôtomo, 1988) and *Ghost in the Shell* (Mamoru Oshii, 1995).[3] Stylistically, anime is inspired by *manga*, Japanese comic books. Accordingly, in the comic book storyboards used to pitch the film to Warner Brothers, the principal illustrator Steve Skroce draws Trinity (Carrie-Ann Moss) as an Asian woman with narrow angular eyes and straight black hair.[4] The showdown between the hero Neo and the villain Agent Smith (Hugo Weaving) repeats a signature move from John Woo, the acclaimed Hong Kong, and later Hollywood, action director. The fight features a dramatic stalemate in which the combatants draw their weapons simultaneously, each holding a gun to the other's head.

Even though the film relies heavily on Asian popular culture, *The Matrix* puts very few members of the Asian population on screen. On the rare occasions when the viewer sees an Asian actor, the appearance is short and silent. For example, even the most astute viewer may miss the several Asian extras in the open-air market that serves as the backdrop for the principal chase scene. The camera pans over them so quickly that they register only as a blur. The Asian body is even absent from the only speaking part intended for an Asian actor. The film's *Shooting Script* describes a scene in which "a young Chinese man" named "Choi" beckons the loner Neo to come out to a party.[5] In the film, however, Marc Gray, an unambiguously Caucasian actor with red hair, displaces the Asian in the small speaking part.

In an earlier chapter, I argue that the 1982 science fiction film *Blade Runner* exhibits a paradox. The film has no black bodies. Yet it relies on themes inextricably linked to the history of African Americans. *Blade Runner* represents blackness not literally but metaphorically. It does not directly signal blackness through the inclusion of black actors. Instead, the film signifies blackness indirectly by narrating the white androids as rebel slaves, a role that carries a strong association with the African American experience. This indirect mode of representing race enables the director to cast the hyperbolically victimized part of the slave with a hyperbolically white male body, helping to reestablish white male hegemony in the post–civil-rights era.

The Matrix fragments the racial other, in this case the Asian, in a similar fashion. The film needs stereotypical Asian tropes such as kung fu fighting and computers to gain authenticity. But the film tends to signify the Asian indirectly through metaphor rather than directly via an Asian body. In the context of *The Matrix*, I call such a figure a "virtual Asian." This virtual or metaphorical mode of conveying race enables the film to overcome two sets of contradictions in a U.S. context for which race is an extremely volatile issue. On the one hand, the virtual Asian enables the film to capitalize on the film history of the Hong Kong kung fu hero while simultaneously including a protagonist with which a mostly white western audience will identify. On the other hand, the film uses the virtual Asian to exploit the history of the stereotypical Asian villain while simultaneously inoculating itself against charges of racism. Ultimately, the film's ability to signify the Asian without any Asian bodies at all manages tension between white and black by enabling the film to scapegoat Asians for the white mistreatment of black people.

This chapter's Orientalist buddy film is set in the wake of an apocalyptic race war, a war not between white and black, but between humans and computers. "In the early twenty-first century," the film tells us, "all of mankind was united in celebration." In "the blinding inebriation of hubris," humanity invented A. I. or Artificial Intelligence, a "singular consciousness" named after the branch of computer science concerned with the capacity of machines to simulate intelligent human behavior. A. I., in turn, "spawned an entire race of machines" that revolted against humanity. By the time the action of the film begins, the war has bifurcated human experience into what the film calls the "dream world" and the "real world." The dream is what you and I think of as our normal, quotidian world. In reality, however, the skies are "scorched." Every city on the planet lies in ruins.

"It is a time when computers rule the world," according to Laurence Fishburne, the African American actor who plays the mentor figure, Morpheus (Oreck, 1999). The machines have "enslaved" humanity, growing them as a "crop." The majority of humans lie asleep in mechanized pods so that the mechanical masters can harvest human body heat as their main source of energy. To maintain the pacification, the computers have written a program called the matrix, described alternatively in the film as "a neural-interactive simulation" and "a computer-generated dream world." The virtual world keeps the sleeping humans "under control" by tricking them into thinking that they are alive and free.[6] The film traces Neo's transformation from "just another guy" suffering the suffocating regimentation of quotidian life in the matrix into the "cybermessiah," "the One" fated to lead the sleeping humans to their freedom in the real world.[7]

The directors use numerous Hong Kong action film references to authenticate *The Matrix* as a martial arts film. For example, the directors employ a host of signature martial arts poses from Bruce Lee, the late Hong Kong actor whose 1970s films, most notably *Enter the Dragon* (1973), helped to popularize the kung fu genre in the United States. The "dojo" sparring match in which the "Zen-calm" Morpheus trains Neo begins with what Skroce calls a "Bruce Lee move."[8] Neo waves his head back and forth with a cocky smile, hopping up and down like a boxer, then flicking his nose with his thumb. Morpheus responds to Neo's swagger with a "Lee move" of his own, what Skroce describes as a "come here motion," a slow extension of an open hand toward his opponent, daring him to advance (Wachowski, 2000, 133). Neo's showdown with Agent Smith includes dueling Lee references as well. Neo repeats the "come here" gesture, marking his mastery not only of kung fu but also of manipulating the rules that govern the computer-driven matrix. Agent Smith responds by slowly curling his fingers into a fist, while the soundtrack amplifies the cracking of his knuckles. Later in the fight, the villain, in a quick movement, tilts his head sideways. Again the soundtrack loudly registers the cracking of his neck bones. Both of these stylistic devices pay homage to Lee's movies.

The film's kung fu references extend to more recent Hong Kong films. Skroce comments that "while working on the dojo sequence," the production team "endlessly" watched "Hong Kong kung fu movies" (Wachowski, 2000, 100–1). It screened "all the classics," he says, "*Meals on Wheels* (Sammo Hung Kam-Bo, 1984), *Iron Monkey* (Yuen Wo Ping, 1993), *The Tai Chi Master* (Yuen Wo Ping, 1993), *Fist of Legend* (Gordon Chan, 1994)" (Wachowski, 2000, 100–1). In particular, the brothers cherish the work of Yuen Wo Ping, the man whom David Edelstein, the film critic for Slate.com, calls "Hong Kong's greatest action choreographer."[9] "Wo Ping rocks," Larry gushes in one interview (Oreck, 1999). Yuen choreographed the fight scenes for Ang Lee's *Crouching Tiger, Hidden Dragon* (2000), the first film to introduce to a U.S. audience the Hong Kong action convention of putting actors into a harness attached to a wire with a pulley. The wire work gives the fighters "a superhuman, supernatural grace" as they "fly around and jump incredibly," according to Larry. "We wanted to do the action differently" from other U.S. action films, he continues. The "balletic" and "very fluid" motion of wire work is "one of the things we love about Hong Kong action," he continues (Oreck, 1999). After *Crouching Tiger*, the highest grossing foreign film in U.S. history, no Hollywood produced kung fu film could market itself as authentic without wire work.

Yuen's most difficult task, however, was not the choreography of the fight scenes. The Wachowskis hired Yuen and his team to transform the four lead actors—Keanu Reeves, Laurence Fishburne, Carrie-Ann Moss, and Hugo Weaving—"into kung fu masters," according to Phil Oosterhouse, assistant to the directors (Wachowski, 2001, 124). Again, authenticity was the primary concern in the minds of the directors. "We're hoping to shoot the kung fu the way that the Hong Kong guys do," says Larry in an interview prior to the shoot, by having "the real actors exchange four, five, six punches, rather than creating it in the editing process."[10] "In Hong Kong we try to use actors who can fight," says Yuen, "that's always easier" (Oreck, 2001). Thus, the goal was to make *The Matrix'* actors "look like they were born with the skills," according to Yuen (Oreck, 1999).

The regimen was very challenging because the four leads began with no martial arts experience. "My kung fu is just no good," says an exasperated Fishburne on the first day of training (Oreck, 2001). "Initially," says Weaving, the actors were "hopeless at kung fu." The actors trained daily for four months, according to Fishburne. Weaving described the training as "extremely exhausting." The producer Joel Silver agrees, calling the process "a tremendous hardship for the actors," but insists that their effort toward making an authentic kung fu film paid off (Oreck, 1999). According to Silver, *The Matrix* registered as "Warner Brothers' highest grossing film ever," earning $171 million for domestic and $270 million for foreign screenings (Oreck, 2001). It was also the first title to sell a million copies in DVD format.[11]

The film may rely on numerous Hong Kong action references to authenticate itself as a kung fu film, and in turn, to garner a bigger take at the box office. But the quest for authenticity through the Asian did not extend to the casting of the film. Despite the saturation of Asian references, *The Matrix* puts very few Asian bodies on the screen. When they do make the rare appearance, they function to mark the matrix as Asian, as in the scene in which Neo waits to meet the Oracle (Gloria Foster), one of the film's key spiritual figures. The camera pans across a roomful of youngsters who exhibit psychokinetic abilities such as levitating wooden blocks, a sign of a special connection to the matrix. Two of them are Asian girls engaging in stereotypical model minority behavior. One plays chess. The other types on a laptop computer. Then the editing gives us a quick medium close-up of a young Asian boy. In spite of the shot's short duration, the composition ensures a proper racial identification by directing the viewer's gaze to the boy's dark almond-shaped eyes that peer out over a book, immediately identifying him as Asian. The book itself is conspicuously Eastern, bright red, set against a neutral background, with Asian writing, large kanji, adorning the cover and spine. The Chinese characters signify missionary or preacher. Based on the kanji, we can conclude that the book is a tome on Asian religion.[12]

The Asian religion theme continues in the rest of the scene. The camera delivers several fast shots of Asians and their paraphernalia, but it is the lone white male of the group who does all the talking. A young boy (Adryn White) in white robes and shaved head sits cross-legged like a yogi in front of a row of metal spoons twisted into knots. According to Skroce, his shaved head and loose white robes make him look like a "little Shaolin monk," a reference to the famed Chinese order of kung fu fighting priests (Wachowski, 2000, 115). The boy holds a spoon up to his gaze, making it bend and droop with his mind as if it was made of rubber. He hands the straightened spoon to Neo. "It is not the spoon that bends," the boy softly intones, "it is only yourself." His puzzling lines and sotto voce delivery resemble Charlie Chan's fortune cookie riddles of the 1920s. This little Buddha, however, is obviously white with blue eyes and an aristocratic British accent.

In addition to Charlie Chan, the film's little Shaolin monk holds a close relationship to the protagonist of the popular ABC television series *Kung Fu* (1972–1975). Like *The Matrix*'s blue-eyed Buddha, a white actor, David Carradine, plays the role of Kwai Chang Cain, the renegade Shaolin monk who wanders the arid landscape of the wild cowboy west.[13] Like *The Matrix*'s minor character Choi, *Kung Fu*'s lead was written originally for an Asian, namely, Bruce Lee, following his sidekick role as Kato in the 1966 *Green Hornet* television series.[14] At the time, most regarded Lee as the premier martial arts actor in the United States. One critic calls him "the Fred Astaire of Kung Fu films."[15] Even though Lee's acting and kung fu abilities made him a likely match for the show's lead, the producers replaced the Asian actor with "the safely white David Carradine" just before the start of filming.[16] The replacement seemed ludicrous, given the centrality of kung fu to the series and given Carradine's lack of kung fu skills. Of the swap, Chuck Norris, one of Lee's costars in *Way of the Dragon* (Bruce Lee, 1972), dryly commented that "Carradine's as good at martial arts as I am at acting."[17]

The network rejected Lee as "too Chinese," according to a 1972 review of the series in *Getting Together*, a California magazine devoted to Asian American politics.[18] Jim Kelly, the African American martial artist who starred with Lee in *Enter the Dragon*, explains Lee's racial handicap in greater detail. "It was hard as hell for Bruce to become an actor" in the United States. "America did not want a Chinese hero," says Kelly, so "the networks did not want to project a Chinese guy as the main hero." Kelly identified with Lee as a fellow nonwhite person, implying an alternate version of the triangle that I describe in another chapter as the Blaxploitation buddy film: black and yellow racial victims versus a white supremacist culture. "I understand what he went through," Kelly remarks, "just by being black in America."[19] Lee's own reaction alludes to racism as the cause of the decision. "They weren't ready for a Hopalong Wong," said Lee.[20] After the rejection by ABC, Lee left the United States to continue his career in Hong Kong. "I am a yellow-faced Chinese," Lee lamented, "I cannot possibly become an idol for Caucasians."[21]

The little Shaolin monk and Kwai Chang Cain share a kinship with a long line of Hollywood villains and heroes that represent the Asian through white bodies in so-called yellowface to ensure audience identification.[22] For example, the Kentucky-born Charles Middleton played Ming the Merciless in all the Flash Gordon movies, including *Flash Gordon Conquers the Universe* (Ford Beebe and Ray Taylor, 1940). The Swedish-born Warner Oland played Fu Manchu in the late 1920s and early 1930s, including *The Mysterious Dr. Fu Manchu* (Rowland V. Lee, 1929) and *Daughter of the Dragon* (Lloyd Corrigan, 1931). The same actor starred as Charlie Chan in the early to late 1930s, including *Charlie Chan Carries On* (Hamilton MacFadden, 1931) and *Charlie Chan on Broadway* (Eugene Forde, 1937). Katharine Hepburn adopted an Oriental accent and taped her eyelids to play Jade, a young Chinese woman who leads her village against Japanese colonization in the filmic version of Pearl S. Buck's *Dragon Seed* (Jack Conway, 1944). Marlon Brando did the same as Sakini, a kimono-clad Japanese interpreter for the U.S. Army in post-WWII Japan in *The Teahouse of the August Moon* (Daniel Mann, 1956).

The Matrix continues the Hollywood pattern of the virtual Asian through its representation of both its villains and heroes. For example, the film uses direct Asian references to authenticate the matrix as a computer construct. The main title shot features a close-up of the computer code that constitutes the matrix. Vertical lines of glowing green code fill the frame, rapidly streaming in columns from top to bottom. The characters run down the screen "faster than we can read," but slowly enough for the viewer to notice that they look Asian (Wachowski, 2001, 1). Stills of the code reveal that Asian writing, specifically, *hiragana*, traditional Japanese characters, and *katakana*, modern Japanese syllabary, form the matrix code. At the end of the shot, the streams of green Japanese characters transform into white capital roman letters to spell the film's title.

The film uses explicit Japanese references to represent the matrix code. The computer graphic designers, however, temper their presentation of the Asian to avoid accusations of racism. By reversing the Japanese characters and adding a few western numbers and keyboard symbols, the filmmakers create a computer language that looks Asian, but at the same time makes it less likely that a Western viewer will be able to link it to an actual Asian language. In other words, the only idea the images must convey is "Asian." For example, on seeing the matrix code on the set for the first time, Reeves reacts, "It's almost Chinese, Sanskrit." For Reeves, the Japanese script stands in for "Asian," but not much else. The matrix code registers as something monolithically "Oriental," but beyond that he cannot make a more specific identification. "It's weird," Keanu concludes in typical "Bill and Ted" fashion (Oreck, 2001).[23]

The film's climactic scene establishes the Japanese computer code as the very fabric of the evil dream world. The scene begins with Neo's miraculous resuscitation that evokes both Jesus Christ and Sleeping Beauty. Agent Smith has shot Neo dead. In the film's real world, Trinity, the hero's love interest, revives him with a kiss. In the virtual world, Neo rises. All three of the villainous agents fire a salvo of bullets at him. Neo raises his hand and stops the bullets in midair, showing his complete command of the rules within the matrix. Agent Smith rushes at him. Neo blocks the blows as if they were in slow motion and then puts one arm behind his back to show his newly found superiority. The audio sounds heavenly and triumphant orchestral music as Neo looks up and sees the matrix world unmasked, a virtual world constituted by machine language. Bright green computer code fills the frame, matching the rushing vertical stream of glowing characters from the main title. The code streams down the contours of every object in the shot, including the three identical agents and the walls of the narrow hallway. In a literal sense, the scene represents the evil computer world, at its hard kernel of irreducible essence, as Asian. Thus, *The Matrix*'s villains fit the same profile of a yellow peril and model minority hybrid as some of the other Orientalist buddy films in this study.

A consideration of the film's historical context of the late twentieth century helps to explain why the directors chose Japanese writing for its realization of the matrix code. It was a time when many assumed a natural link between computers and the Asian. Prior to Japan's major economic recession of the mid-1990s, many U.S. media articles represented Japan as poised to conquer the world through computer technology. Typical of the widespread alarmist buzz, a 1992 *Fortune* magazine article analyzes the possibility of Japan's displacement of the United States as the "world's richest country."[24] "What if Japan Triumphs?" asks the headline. The bullet underneath reads, "It sure won't mean apocalypse now," a reference to Francis Ford Coppola's Vietnam War film,[25] "but a world in which the U.S. economy is no longer No. 1, would pose many new challenges—and more than a few risks." The primary risk refers to what the article perceives as Japan's domination of the international computer industry. The article claims that Japan has "ten times the number of robots on its assembly lines," evidence of how Japan's economy might "outpace" that of the United States. The fearful reporter asks, "Will America become more dependent on Japanese technology?" (60–2).

The *Fortune* article predicts bad times ahead, citing leading economists who describe Japan's business practice as "predatory" and "techno-industrial Prussianism." "In coming years," says the article, "Japanese companies increasingly will invade high-wage, high value added markets that have long been American strongholds." By 2015, Japan "will enjoy a stranglehold over every leading edge technology," the reporter states. The article ends with an ominous prediction. If Japan continues on its path of domination, it "will also have amended its constitution and begun producing nuclear arms," a fantastic detail that matches *The Matrix*'s narrative of computer hegemony leading to nuclear apocalypse (61–3).

Two of the article's photographs portray the Japanese as a robotic society. The first shows seven Japanese schoolgirls in identical uniforms, white shirts and blue shorts, singing the national anthem. Aside from the uniforms, the girls share the same build and haircut. The composition spaces the girls right to left in a neat row underneath a large Japanese flag at equal distances from one another. Each girl stands in the same rigid military pose, arms held straight down at her sides. The photo on the facing page features the same number of Japanese bodies: seven computer workers identically dressed in blue uniforms. The young men all share the same angled pose. Each sits in front of a large computer while looking at the camera. The green text on the computer monitors matches what will later become the basis for the film's matrix code.

The photographs arrange the identical Japanese bodies according to the visual motif of a grid. In the photo of the schoolgirls, the Japanese flag's bright white field set against the dark background of the stage drapery emphasizes its rectangular shape. The flag's placement at the center of the frame creates symmetry between the right and left sides of the photo. The folds of the drapes create vertical lines that run parallel to the schoolchildren's straightened bodies. The girls are the same height. Thus, their heads create a horizontal line across the page that parallels the line of the stage floor. The computer factory photo repeats the grid pattern. The composition places the men at regular intervals, creating a straight line to the horizon point that parallels the linear arrangement of the machinery. Modular computer parts like circuit boards and monitors dominate the photo. The identical appearance of the machinery mirrors the identical look of the computer workers, suggesting that the men are also interchangeable parts of a larger machine.

The photographs' captions make explicit the causal relationship between Japanese discipline and Japanese world domination. "It starts here," the first caption reads, "strikingly well-disciplined elementary school kids sing Japan's national anthem..." The Japanese government, signified by the flag and the school setting, inculcates regimentation in its citizens at a very young age. The ellipsis at the end of the first caption directs the eye to the second, which starts with its own ellipsis, "...and leads to this," then continues, "Fujitsu workers test supercomputers at a modern factory outside Tokyo." The article, of course, trades in familiar stereotypes of the Japanese. Japanese society produces "strikingly well-disciplined" children who grow up to produce superior computers because the people are themselves interchangeable. Through computer technology, Japan may rule the world (62–3; ellipses in original).

The *Fortune* article states directly the relationship between Japanese regimentation and world domination, but only hints at the role that identical Japanese bodies play in this logic. The article alludes to, but does not state explicitly, the common stereotype that all Asians look alike.[26] Because the stereotype surfaces most prominently during times of national friction between the United States and Asia, we can look to two WWII propaganda texts produced in 1945 by the U.S. government for a more direct characterization of Asians as identical. Frank Capra made *Know Your Enemy: Japan* as a segment of the *Why We Fight* series, one segment of which won the 1945 Academy Award for best documentary. The U.S. Navy circulated its 105-page *Guide to Japan*, a "study of Japanese people," to every American soldier in the Pacific theater, presumably to help orient the troops for the occupation.[27] The two propaganda pieces tell the same story about the Japanese. The extreme discipline of Japanese society reduces the Japanese people to interchangeable and therefore identical parts of a national war machine intent on dominating the world. In such a story, identical bodies signal the transformation of a human being into something less than human, a robot or a machine, something that by definition cannot think for itself.

Both tracts emphasize the theme of identical bodies. Capra features a relentless repetition of shots of identically dressed Japanese, moving in unison, training to fight. The narrator describes "typical Japanese soldier[s]" as being "as much alike as photographic prints off the same negative." Likewise, the film tells us that the Japanese educational system aims "to mass produce students who all think alike." The Navy's tract echoes the same theme. "The people are uniform," it states, "the Japanese people differ among themselves less than do the people of any other large nation." They "look amazingly like each other," the *Guide* continues, "even to the expression on their faces" (40).

Both texts link the identical repetition of bodies to the inability to think independently. "Belief in Japan's divine mission to conquer runs through the whole people," states Capra's narrator, making "all of them willing prisoners of an efficient iron clad social structure....A system of regimentation so perfect it made Hitler's mouth water," implying that the Japanese are even more disciplined than the Germans. The Navy's *Guide* claims that the "deliberate policy of their rulers to stamp out all individuality and free thinking [makes] the average Japanese an unquestioning, obedient worker and soldier....Only a favored few at the top of the social order [are] permitted to think for themselves, [destroying] individuality and initiative, [forcing] everybody into a common mold" (40–2).

By contrast, the *Guide* states that, in America, "we tell our youngsters, 'think for yourself,'...to develop initiative and responsibility." The only words that the Japanese "hear from the cradle to the grave," the *Guide* continues, "are 'obey,' 'obey,' 'obey.'" The Navy tract implies that the American predilection for independent thought has its roots in racial diversity. "America is a great mixture of races from all corners of the globe," it states. "There is no such thing as a typical American." Conversely, the piece blames Japan's tendency to blind obedience on an enforced racial purity. "People who live in Japan proper," according to the *Guide*, "are pure Japanese whose ancestors have lived in Japan for 2000 years." In the polar symbolic world of WWII U.S. propaganda, America's multiple but different people represent the human whereas Japan's multiple but identical people represent the less than human or the machine (40, 42).

Both pieces characterize Japan and the Japanese as machines. Capra's documentary features a scene in which a heavy machine press stamps out identical metal parts, like license plates. The narrator exclaims, "The vicious system of political and religious regimentation [in Japan] hammers, kneads and molds the whole population until it becomes an obedient mass with but a single mind." In a variation on the theme, machine begets machine, when the narrator describes Japanese women as "human machines producing rice and soldiers" for the nation. The Navy's study describes the Japanese government as a "giant press" stamping "out of sheet metal thousands and thousands of identical pieces." The *Guide* cites Japan's feudal history as precedent. Says the *Guide*, like its WWII rulers, the "Japanese shoguns stamped out millions of Japanese all alike" (44).

The film reinforces the Asian imprint of the villains by recycling the same racist tropes used in WWII propaganda to represent the Japanese enemy. Like the WWII tracts, *The Matrix* represents its villains as identical. Thus, even though whites play all the film's villains, they are implicitly coded as Asian. The three men who play the agents have the same body type and the same hair color and cut, parted in the same direction. Their faces are frozen into the same humorless expression. They dress the same: mirrored sunglasses, white shirt, dark suit and tie, silver tie bar. They speak with the same slow, deliberate, monotone voice, enunciating every syllable, like robots. The film represents as identical even the nonhumanoid denizens of the dream world. Like the agents, the biomechanical sentinels that perform search-and-destroy missions in the large sewers of the postapocalyptic cities, described as "squidlike kamikazes" by one critic, move in groups of three and look exactly the same.[28]

The sadistic and super tough agents look alike because they think alike. Designed to mimic JFK era secret service agents, a single electronic feed discretely snakes out of their shirt collars and connects to an ear bud.[29] The common feed suggests that they are working from the same script, as if the same central computer were orchestrating their every regimented move. In key moments, they move in unison like a drill team, such as when they fire a salvo of bullets at Neo in the film's climactic scene. They walk in triangle formation. They perform coordinated tasks without speaking to one another. When they talk, they finish each other's sentences. The film represents the agents as multiple but identical manifestations of a single overarching computer mind, who therefore lack the capacity for independent thought.

Such is the fate of the bulk of humanity. Wired to the matrix through a computer jack in the back of the skull, humans spend their lives asleep in a biomechanical cocoon. Within the diegesis, the computers literally turn individually unique human beings into interchangeable and, therefore, identical parts of a single giant machine. "The matrix," says Morpheus to Neo, "is a computer generated dreamworld built to keep us under control in order to change a human being into this," as he holds up a common household battery, a metaphor for the sleeping humans whose body heat runs the machine world. The rebels register their own sense of human degradation by referring to those still wired to the matrix as "Coppertops," a citation of a popular battery brand name. Batteries, of course, are practically identical.

Within the discourse of the Japanese enemy, if one lacks independent thought, one is a machine. *The Matrix* marks the dream world as one ruled by machines through the figure of the grid. "In the matrix," says the cinematographer, Bill Pope, everything was styled to be grid-like, "like a machine would make it." To emphasize his point, he moves his hands at right angles to one another to convey the vertical and horizontal axes of a grid. Owen Patterson, the film's production designer, chose grid patterns to signal visually the machine world's "feeling of artificial control" (Oreck, 2001). The choice of the grid for this purpose is easy to explain. In mathematical and computer jargon, a matrix is a type of grid.

The film's heavy use of the grid figure reinforces the theme of the human imprisoned in a machine. The first shot of the scene in which the agents interrogate Neo fills the frame with multiple but identical images relayed through television monitors arranged in a grid. The camera looks down on Neo sitting at a table in an impersonal bare room with white walls and floor and a standard-issue steel table. For a brief moment, the television tubes' vertical lines appear as green lines of matrix code, a subtle reminder that we are inside a computer construct. Grids formed by the interior's sectioned wall paneling frame the scene's close-ups of Neo. The numbers on the door handle's locking keypad are arranged in a grid. In another scene, the agents track Neo to his job at the software company, where the camera shows the hero hiding in a series of cubicles. "The entire floor," says the *Shooting Script*, "looks like a human honeycomb," evoking the figures of grid and drone (15). The camera shoots from a low angle to give viewers the sense of being trapped in a maze.

The *Shooting Script* represents the enemy world as one that relentlessly forces the individual to conform to the dictates of the group. In one scene, Neo's boss scolds him for chronic tardiness (14). The film describes the boss as "the ultimate company man," yet another iteration of the model minority, given the Asian ascription of the computer world. "This company," he lectures, "is one of the top software companies in the world because every single employee understands that they are part of a whole.... Thus, if an employee has a problem, the company has a problem." In the computer world, the success of the whole is paramount and depends on each employee conforming to a common set of rules. A conversation between Neo and Tank conveys the same idea. After realizing that the agents will inevitably succeed in extracting vital secrets from the captive Morpheus, Neo asks how long Morpheus can withstand the torture. Tank responds, "Eventually his mind will crack and his alpha patterns will change from this to this," pointing to a computer screen monitoring Morpheus's brain waves. On the monitor, Morpheus's "chaotic" brain wave pattern transforms into the "ordered and symmetrical" pattern shared by the bulk of humanity, asleep and enslaved (Wachowski, 2001, 90).

The film tells us that we must resist slavish group conformity to realize our humanity. At the end of the film, Neo addresses the viewers directly, exhorting us to rail against the "boundaries[,] rules and controls" imposed by what most of us take to be the normal world. He says that "if you can free your mind," from the matrix's excessive regimentation, "you can get [to] a different world, [one] of hope, of peace [in which] all things are possible." Then he flies away like the comic book hero Superman, arcing through the frame with "his long black coat billowing like a black leather cape as he flies faster than a speeding bullet" (Wachowski, 2001, 122). The song "Wake Up" by the heavy metal rock band Rage Against the Machine accompanies the action.

Because of the stereotypical link between the computer robot and the Asian, Keanu Reeves's mixed racial ancestry, Caucasian and Asian, makes him the perfect casting choice for a Hollywood hero who learns to beat a race of machines at their own game. One academic piece on the star describes Reeves's father as "half Hawaiian and half Chinese" and mother as "British."[30] According to *Newsweek*'s David Ansen, Reeves issues from "a Chinese-Hawaiian father and an English mother."[31] Despite his mixed race background, Reeves signifies as white.

MTV gave Reeves the Most Desirable Male Award twice for *Point Break* (Kathryn Bigelow, 1992) and *Speed* (Jan de Bont, 1994), never mentioning his nonwhite lineage. Likewise, *People* magazine's entry on Reeves in its 1995 issue of "The 50 Most Beautiful People in the World" makes no mention of his Asian or Hawaiian ancestry. By contrast, Russell Wong's entry highlights his television role as a "Chinese martial arts expert" in the *Vanishing Son* series (1995), as well as Wong's bloodline, his "Chinese father and Dutch-American mother."[32]

All but one of Reeves's leading roles signify as white. He plays a disaffected heavy metal teen and a French aristocrat in *River's Edge* (Tim Hunter, 1986) and *Dangerous Liaisons* (Stephen Frears, 1988), respectively. In preparation for *The Gift* (Sam Raimi, 2000), Reeves spent three weeks in Georgia to learn "how to be a redneck."[33] Says Reeves of his *Point Break* (1992) FBI agent role, "I get to be called Johnny Utah....I love that," he exclaims.[34] Despite its Native American roots, the name *Utah* signifies as one of the whitest states in the Union. Like Johnny Utah, the names of the majority of his characters signify the common white man. In *Bill and Ted's Excellent Adventure* (Stephen Herek, 1989), he plays the classic high school slacker Ted Logan. In *My Own Private Idaho* (Gus Van Sant, 1991), he plays a male hustler named Scott Favor, the downwardly mobile son of the mayor of Portland, Oregon. In *Speed*, he plays a cop named Jack Traven. Reeves throws touchdown passes as Shane Falco, an NFL quarterback in *The Replacements* (Howard Deutch, 2000). He plays a workaholic advertising executive, Nelson Moss, in *Sweet November* (Pat O'Connor, 2001).

Reeves plays a nonwhite lead only once, when he portrays the Indian prince Siddhartha who renounces the material world in favor of spiritual enlightenment in Bernardo Bertolucci's *The Little Buddha* (1993). The exception proves the rule in this case. The actor required so much dark makeup that he strikes the viewer as a white person in yellowface. One review emphasizes the artificiality of the effect by referring to his body makeup as a "fake tan."[35] Reeves notes that his character's "kohl-rimmed eyes" even estrange him from himself in some fundamental way. "I look like Cleopatra," complains Reeves, a reference to Elizabeth Taylor in the monumental 1963 flop (Joseph L. Mankiewicz, 1963) in which she plays the ancient Oriental queen.[36]

Like the majority of his roles, Reeves's character in *The Matrix* signifies as white. For example, the film makes numerous references to the christological element of Neo's character. Early in the movie, Choi, a buyer of Neo's computer-hacking services, rejoices, "Hallelujah! You are my savior," hailing Neo as "my own personal Jesus Christ!" It is hard to imagine the directors casting an actor who signifies as Asian to play a Jesus figure, the quintessential icon of whiteness. In the scene, Choi even comments, "You look a little whiter than usual." After Cypher (Joe Pantoliano) kills Apoc and Switch, the love-spurned turncoat taunts Trinity (Carrie Ann Moss) by making fun of Neo's "big pretty eyes." Historically, narrow eyes, not big round ones, have been the principal markers of the Asian. The film emphasizes Neo's sense of himself as nondescript and therefore as white. The name "John Anderson," Neo's alter ego in the dream world, emphasizes the unspoken racial norm. As the agents chase Neo at his workplace, he wonders out loud, "Why is this happening to me? What did I do? I'm nobody....I'm not the One," Neo tells Trinity as they prepare to rescue Morpheus. "I'm just another guy."

Reeves may signify as white the instances above, but often the press registers his Asian ancestry, rendering his persona as ambiguous. Some of the pieces display a fascination with the foreign. The *New York Times'* Elvis Mitchell describes Reeves' allure as a "pan-Asian exoticism."[37] "Reeves is looking good," the first sentence of *USA Today's* review of *Speed* announces, "perfect cheekbones, the gift of a gene pool that is half Hawaiian and Chinese."[38] *Newsweek's* description sites the source of his appeal in his "dark almond eyes."[39] The *Toronto Star* reports that, in Hawaiian, Reeves's "unusual handle"—Keanu—means "cool breeze over the mountain."[40]

One scholar claims that Reeves's Asiatic attributes—"his 'mysterious' racial appearance"—are the source of this ambiguity. His face is "open to interpretation," possessing the "changeable" or "malleable features out of which directors have seen fit to construct a persona" says the critic.[41] Another scholar uses the term *ambiguous inbetweenness* to describe the mixed-race Reeves.[42] The *Chicago Tribune* reports that Reeves's "enigmatic face suggests a computer generated composite of every known race and gender."[43] "He has a beauty," muses Bertolucci, "that's not Eastern or Western."[44] Bertolucci's description suggests that Reeves's features look both exotic and normal, but not too exotic or too normal.

Reeves himself tends to minimize his Asian blood. In several places on the Internet, Reeves describes himself as "a bourgeois, middle-class white boy."[45] In a reference to the British naval captain who colonized Hawaii in 1778, John Cook, Keanu tells one reporter that "there are Reeves everywhere" on Oahu, the island from which his father, Samuel Reeves, hails. "I'm sure my ancestors were on the boat," Reeves quips.[46] Most accounts list his proportion of white to Asian as half Caucasian, one quarter Hawaiian, and one quarter Chinese.

Reeves's Captain Cook comment, however, implies that his father has Caucasian blood as well his mother, minimizing the ratio of Asian to Caucasian even further than most reports of his genetic profile.

In terms of both his persona and his film roles, Reeves signifies as mainly Caucasian with a trace of Asian. A reporter for the London newspaper, *The Independent*, writes that Reeves is "fashionably ethnic-looking. But," it quickly adds, "not too ethnic-looking."[47] *Newsweek's* David Ansen characterizes his nonwhite element as "the hint of the Asian."[48] Were he to signify as Asian exclusively, he would have found it difficult to win the role of Neo. Historically, the male actor that romances the white female lead cannot be "too ethnic."[49] Such a configuration would threaten the part of the audience that is white, male, and heterosexual. In *The Cheat* (Cecil B. DeMille, 1915), a white mob nearly lynches Sessue Hayakawa for stealing a kiss from Fannie Ward.[50] Other Asian male figures kiss the white female lead but die before the end of the movie. Bruce Lee's Hollywood biography, *Dragon* (Rob Cohen, 1993), *Ballad of Little Jo* (Maggie Greenwald, 1993), and the Australian *Japanese Story* (Sue Brooks, 2003) fit this profile. Sex does not blemish Jet Li's role in *Kiss of the Dragon* (Chris Nahon, 2001, opposite Bridget Fonda); the same holds true for Chow Yun-Fat's roles in *The Replacement Killers* (Antoine Fuqua, 1998, Mira Sorvino) and *Anna and the King* (Andy Tennant, 1999, Jodie Foster). Chow has voiced interest in a "leading-man role" for a "romance" picture, but by 2007 never secured one. "There is a great deal of racism in the country," notes film scholar David Thomson, referring to Fat. "We break down these barriers very slowly," he laments; "I don't think we are doing it quickly enough to encourage an actor like Chow to think he will get away with it."[51]

Denzel Washington's career has followed a similar path. He almost never kisses the female lead. For example, his relationship with Julia Roberts in Alan J. Pakula's *The Pelican Brief* (1993), in which he plays a newspaper reporter, remains strictly platonic, even though the 1994 *MTV Movie Awards* deemed Washington as Most Desirable Male. Compare *Pelican Brief* to another Roberts film, Richard Donner's *Conspiracy Theory* (1997), in which Mel Gibson plays the unlikely paranoid schizophrenic cab driver who successfully woos Roberts's character, a Justice Department lawyer. In *The Bone Collector* (Phillip Noyce, 1999), the script allows Washington to touch the back of Angelina Jolie's hand, an extremely tame show of physical affection. The same holds true for Will Smith in *Men in*

Black (Barry Sonnenfeld, 1997, Linda Fiorentino) and Wesley Snipes in *Murder at 1600* (Dwight H. Little, 1997, Diane Lane). In Tony Scott's 2004 *Man on Fire*, the director pairs Washington with a pre-pubescent white girl, Dakota Fanning, precluding the threat of miscegenation. A Salon.com film reviewer calls this trend "racism, pure and simple."[52] The exceptions in Washington's case prove the rule. In Carl Franklin's 1995 *Devil in a Blue Dress* he has an explicit sex scene with a black actress (Lisa Nicole Carson). In Mira Nair's 1992 *Mississippi Masala*, Washington not only kisses but also marries the South Asian lead played by Sarita Choudhury.

The same racial and sexual politics that bar black actors from white actresses require Reeves to signify as Asian just enough to make him appealingly exotic, but not enough to impair a Western audience's identification with the white hero. In this sense, he is the very embodiment of the virtual Asian, making him the perfect leading man for a Hollywood film that pits heroic (white and black) American kung fu fighters against Asiatic computers. On the one hand, given the stereotypical link between martial arts and the Asian, Reeves's hint of the Asian authenticates Neo as the best kung fu fighter in the film. By the end of the film, Neo beats everyone with

Figure 6.1 *The Matrix*'s computer-generated agents in formation: Mr. Brown (Paul Goddard), Mr. Smith (Hugo Weaving), and Mr. Jones (Robert Taylor).

his kung fu, including the universally feared agents. Morpheus warns Neo that no one has ever fought an agent and lived. Striking a similar tone of dread, Cypher advises Neo, if "you see an Agent, you do what we do, run." In the final fight scene with Smith, Neo looks as if he is bored, at one point turning away from Smith to fight him with one hand. After Neo dispenses with Smith, the other two agents run off in fear.

On the other hand, given the stereotypical link between the Asian and the machine, especially the computer, Reeves's hint of the Asian authenticates Neo as a messiah figure in a world in which computers have enslaved humans. For example, the movie attributes to Neo a natural relationship to the matrix that none of the other characters possess. When the Nebuchadnezzar crew watches Neo fight for the first time, Mouse exclaims, "Jesus Christ, he's fast! Look at his neural-kinetics! They're way above normal!" The "neural-kinetics" comment locates Neo's advantage in his body, suggesting that his quickness is a sign of an essential kinship to the matrix. Likewise, after Neo dodges a full clip of an agent's bullets, Trinity asks, "Neo, how did you do that? You moved like they moved. I've never seen anyone move that fast."

Several details in the film suggest that one must be part computer to defeat a computer. For example, Neo's alter ego, John Anderson, is a computer programmer. Neo himself is a computer hacker. The *Shooting Script* describes him as "a man who knows more about living inside a computer than outside one" (9). When the viewer sees Neo for the first time, he is asleep at his computer desk, surrounded by computer equipment. His pale skin reflects a streaming glow of data from the monitor. During Neo's first downloading session, Morpheus asks Tank about Neo's status. Tank exclaims, "Ten hours straight," while blinking his eyes from long hours of staring at a computer screen, "he's a machine!" The direct reference to the machine implies a special aptitude for the computer training made possible by not only who, but what, Neo is. He is part human and part computer.

The fact that fans view Reeves as partially Asian makes the kinship between Neo and the computer world more believable. A common stereotype tells us that Asians are inscrutable. Thus, it is not surprising that much of the coverage on Reeves characterizes him as difficult to read. "Everything about him is laced with mystery," his *Speed* costar Sandra Bullock remarks. "That's his charm."[53] *People Magazine* calls him "a most excellent enigma," echoing the title of one of his early hits.⁵⁴ *Rolling Stone* brands him as a "riddle."⁵⁵ Like the press accounts of Reeves, the film presents the Japanese-inspired matrix as enigmatic. When Cypher shows Neo an image of what the *Shooting Script* describes as the "bizarre codes and equations" that constitute the matrix, he says, "There's way too much information to decode the matrix" (56). As Neo decides whether or not to be unplugged, Morpheus says, "Unfortunately, no one can be told what the Matrix is." The matrix is so hopelessly unreadable by humans, even the stalwart of the resistance cannot put it into words. "You have to see it for yourself," he tells Neo.

I have argued that *The Matrix*'s hero and principal villain are virtual Asians. The concluding section shows how this mode enables the film to scapegoat Asians for white racism against black people and simultaneously avoid the risk of being labeled as racist. The film makes racism a central attribute of the villain's profile in the sense that the computers hate humanity as a species. During the torture scene, Smith tells Morpheus that the human race lacks discipline. Unlike every other animal on earth that "instinctively develops a natural equilibrium with the surrounding environment," says Smith, humans "multiply until every natural resource is consumed." Smith continues, "The only way [humans] can survive is to spread to another area." He calls humanity "a disease, a cancer of this planet" for which the computers are "the cure," evoking a sense of eradication or ethnic cleansing. "I hate this place," Smith says, "this zoo, this prison, this reality." The "zoo" reference reveals an attitude of machine superiority akin to what the late twentieth century viewer would call racism. In Smith's version of the great chain of being, the rise of the computers demotes humans to the status of mere animals relative to the machines.

The Matrix transfers the mark of racism onto the virtual Asians by suggesting that the agents hate not just humans but black people in particular. The scowling white man runs his fingers over Morpheus's bald head, coating them with the black man's sweat. "It's the smell," Smith says while rubbing his fingers together, "I feel saturated by it." He continues, "I can taste your stink and every time I do, I fear that I've somehow been infected by it." Then, in a particularly perverse gesture, he shoves his fingers into Morpheus' nostrils, making the black man smell his own "stink." "It's repulsive," he asks rhetorically, "isn't it?" as he grabs Morpheus's head with both hands and shakes him with rage and disgust. The torture scene restages what is now familiar to a post civil rights audience, white men brutalizing a black person, which in turn evokes slavery. The agents have Morpheus in chains. He looks badly beaten, sweating, fighting for breath. One of the agents stabs Morpheus in the neck with a large needle, injecting him with a silver liquid that looks like mercury. Electrodes adorn his head and torso.

During the same period, network television enacted the same transfer, transposing the history of white American hatred of black people onto a model minority Asian figure. In November 1997, ABC's popular television series *NYPD Blue* aired an episode called "It Takes a Village" in which the white and Latino lead detectives investigate the slaying of a Korean grocer. Daniel Dae Kim plays the grocer's arrogant and bigoted son who offends the black and Latino crowd at the crime scene. Several of NBC's *ER* episodes in the fall of 2000 featured a subplot in which the young doctor Deb Chen (Ming-Na Wen) becomes pregnant but keeps the father's identity secret. On Thanksgiving, in her elitist parents' posh mansion, she reveals to her mother (Nancy Kwan) that the father is African American. The daughter asks, "Will you love the baby if the father is black?"[56] The mother answers her daughter's question with stony silence. Chen decides to give the child to an adoption agency because of her immigrant parents' racist beliefs. One of *ER*'s main characters, the white doctor John Carter (Noah Wiley), fills the gap left by the racist parents by helping Chen throughout the pregnancy.

Hollywood films participated in driving the same wedge between black and Asian. In *The Family Man* (Brett Ratner, 2000), a reiteration of the Christmas classic *It's a Wonderful Life* (Frank Capra, 1946), a patronizing Asian male deli clerk (Ken Leung) refuses to honor a black patron's lottery ticket because of his racial prejudice. "You get out now!" the young Asian yells in an "Oriental" accent. "You take the ticket somewhere else!" As it turns out, the patron (Don Cheadle) is an angel sent to earth by God to determine who should enter heaven. "He's testing this guy to see if he's racist," says Ratner in the DVD version's commentary. The white lead character, Jack Campbell (Nicholas Cage), intervenes before the incident between yellow and black becomes violent. This single brief appearance of an Asian serves as the occasion for the white and black characters to bond, setting into motion the main plot device wherein the Christmas ghost gives Campbell a glimpse of an alternate fate.

The same representation surfaced in the elite world of the international film festival. *Slam* (Marc Levin), the 1998 film about a talented young African American rapper (Saul Williams) serving his first jail sentence, won that year's Grand Jury Prize and *Camera D'Or* at Sundance and Cannes, respectively. One scene features an Asian American man's fear and loathing of blackness as the two enter the predominantly black male world of the Washington D.C. prison system. "Get me the fuck off this van," the Asian American (Beau Sia) yells. "My name is fucking Jimmy Huang," he shouts during the transfer ride to prison. "You know who my dad is?" Because Huang is the only nonblack man in the van, prisoner and guard alike, his pronouncement of privilege connotes social elitism, if not racial superiority. In contrast to the rest of the inmates, his pressed business attire signals an upper-class background. Continuing the condescension, he lets the black men know that he is wealthy enough to have lived abroad in Europe. "Damn," he whispers, "I miss Italy." The black man next to Jimmy starts to rap softly to himself as a form of self-steadying prayer. "Great," Huang responds sarcastically, "another black rapper," then barks repeatedly, "would you shut the fuck up." As he walks into prison for the first time, he spits on one of the black guards. In the holding tank, he picks a fight with several black inmates.

When considering the fictional antiblack racism of these Asian figures, it is important to remember that, in American history, the people who beat (castrate and lynch) black people happen to be white men, almost exclusively.[57] For example, 1990s news watchers will remember three well-publicized stories of white police abuse of black men. In 1999, white New York City policemen shot and killed Amadou Diallo because they mistook the African immigrant's wallet for a gun. Just two years earlier in 1997, white members of the same force beat and, with a broom handle, sodomized Abner Louima, a Haitian immigrant, in a Brooklyn station house. Most notoriously, in March 1991 a bystander's home-movie camera caught several white LA policemen mercilessly beating Rodney King, creating one of the most enduring images of white men beating a black man.

The Matrix uses the infamous King beating to complete its relocation of racism from white America to the computer people. When the heroes find themselves ambushed by the agents in an abandoned building, they try to escape via the crawl space behind the walls. Before they can get away, Agent Smith catches up with them and grabs Neo. Morpheus dives through the wall, sacrificing himself so that Neo and the others can run. Morpheus and Smith fight in a small dusty bathroom. Morpheus puts up a valiant effort, but

Smith beats him savagely, then leaves him bloody and groaning on the floor. As Smith leaves the cramped bathroom, he tells the black-clad policemen who wait at the door (we know that they are police because they wear jackets marked POLICE), "Take him." The police swarm into the room with their batons swinging. The scene ends with an overhead shot of the black man on his hands and knees, encircled by nine cops who beat him relentlessly, matching the key icon of "a black man beaten by a white" in what Linda Williams calls the long-standing "American melodrama of black and white."[58]

The Matrix debuted in 1999, eight years after television news replayed endlessly George Halliday's minute-long videotape. The visual rhetoric of the film's Morpheus beating mimics the news footage of the King beating. Lisa Nakamura writes that the scene in which the cops "gather in a circle and beat the black Morpheus invokes images of Rodney King, images indelibly coded as being about the oppression of blacks by whites."[59] Halliday's nighttime footage records up to ten white male officers on the side of a highway under the glare of cruiser headlights, circling a prostrate King, savagely kicking and hitting him with metal batons. Like King in Halliday's video, Morpheus in *The Matrix*'s scene lies semiconscious on the ground, moving slowly on his hands and knees, surrounded by black-clad, baton-wielding police officers. Like the King footage, *The Matrix*'s scene is darkly lit. Like Halliday's high-angle shot of King taken from a balcony above the fray, *The Matrix*'s scene conveys the Morpheus beating through an overhead shot.

Set in the historical context of the United States circa 1999, it becomes apparent that the beating scene displaces white American antiblack violence onto an enemy that is virtually Asian. When Morpheus lands on top of Agent Smith in the bathroom scene, they are face to face, "locked in each other's death grip" (Wachowski, 2001, 80). "The great Morpheus," the white man says to the black man, "we meet at last." Morpheus responds defiantly with a question, "And you are?" "Smith," the villain introduces himself, "Agent Smith." "You all look the same to me" Morpheus retorts with sarcasm. The dialogue renders the villains as identical, just like the stereotypical WWII representation of the Japanese enemy.

In April 1992, thousands of LA residents took to the streets after the Simi Valley jury's acquittal of King's white male police attackers. David Palumbo-Liu's analysis of the uprising's news coverage illustrates how *The Matrix*'s beating scene functions as a mechanism to harmonize relations between white and black at the expense of the Asian. Liu argues that the media's portrayal of the "vigilante Korean," a reference to the armed Asian men who defended their neighborhood stores against looting, counts as a reiteration of the model minority stereotype.[60] The coverage constructed an image of "hard-working, persevering" Asian men independent of "state or federal largesse" who, like the whites in old westerns, take up arms and circle their wagons against savage forces (370). In contrast to the image of white police beating a black man, "white America" could "react positively, immediately, and with ethical purity when viewing Asian-Americans defending themselves against black and Latino looters" (374). The "liminal position of Asian Americans" between black and white allows them to act as a sort of heat shield for "an economic system" run by whites "that historically has pitted Asians against blacks and Latinos" (369–70). Representing "the Asian-American as the white surrogate in the battle of capitalism against chaos" hails the Asian as a sort of buffer that protects whites against black and Latino reaction to white racism (369n.8). Thus, the repetition of the immigrant Asian as model minority shifts "the trauma of racial violence onto Asian America" (379).

The Matrix's mode of the virtual Asian enables such a transfer. The film could not have cast Asian actors to play the lead villains. Most post–civil-rights viewers would have recognized the racist representation of nonwhite people as identical. Putting white men in the role of the evil and identical villains, however, inoculates the film against such charges. Representing the villain as a fantastic nonhuman other disavows white racism against black people by creating a crucial disassociation between white guilt on the one hand and the film's scenes of white men torturing a black man on the other. In other words, Smith's nonhumanity permits the film to stage such brutality without inflaming white guilt because the white men in the film look human but are not really human. They are computers.

If the villains resemble any race aside from white, it is Asian, given the film's prodigious use of tropes that line up so exactly with WWII stereotypes of the Japanese enemy. According to Gina Marchetti, the action film's popularity rests on its ability to provide an imaginary space to "work through those social contradictions that the culture needs to come to grips with" but cannot. Often such movies transpose "very real problems," such as repeated racial animus on the part of whites toward blacks, "to the realm of fantasy," where the viewer can have the pleasure of solving them, if only in fictional terms.[61] Thus, the virtual Asian mode enables the film to appeal to white guilt by resignifying the scene of sin and displacing the responsibility for white racism against black people onto a body that is neither white nor black but vaguely Asian. In large part, *The Matrix* employs the category of the Asian to take the blame for the history of white supremacy.

This book starts with Tay Garnett's WWII combat movie *Bataan*, an incipient Orientalist buddy film that conveyed to American audiences in 1943 a new set of rules that corresponded to the new racial order brought on by the war. The film depicts Japan as an enemy that is even more racist to black Americans than white Americans, transferring the mark of racism from white to Asian. I want to conclude with a Hollywood film that debuted around the turn of the century, *The Last Samurai* (Edward Zwick, 2003). When considered in tandem with *Crash* (Paul Haggis, 2005), the film at the beginning of this study, the bookends suggest that the Orientalist buddy film continues to malign various Asian subgroups as the common enemies who bond white and black, with at least one notable exception.

Whereas *Crash* repeats the triangulated formula unchanged for the most part from its initial appearance in the 1950s, *The Last Samurai* elevates a Japanese figure to play the nonwhite buddy, rewriting the Orientalist buddy film to suit yet another shift in America's economy of racial representation. "The Japanese," wrote University of Chicago sociologist Robert Park in 1913, "is condemned to remain among us an abstraction, a symbol, and a symbol not merely of his own race, but of the Orient and of that vague, ill-defined menace we sometimes refer to as the 'yellow peril.'"[1] Park's claim notwithstanding, I want to suggest that even though Japan has served for so many years as the icon for the yellow peril, especially after Pearl Harbor, the United States of the post-9/11 period can no longer afford to alienate such an important ally in the war on terror.

The Last Samurai's portrayal of Japan's internal struggle for national identity during the Meiji era matches nearly all of the parameters of the Orientalist buddy formula. The movie has an interracial dyad.

But rather than a white and black pairing, *The Last Samurai* elevates a Japanese figure to play the nonwhite buddy. Set in 1876, shortly after Commodore Perry's arrival ended Japan's isolationist policy, Tokyo hires the decorated Civil War veteran Captain Nathan Algren (Tom Cruise) to modernize its national army. Ordered to suppress a samurai revolt led by Katsumoto (Ken Watanabe), a rogue warlord, Algren gives chase to the rebels, who take him prisoner. Initially, the buddies hate each other due, in part, to the white man's racist attitudes toward the Japanese, which the film signals by having Algren use a racial epithet. "I'll kill jappos or the enemies of jappos," he exclaims while negotiating his salary under Japanese employ. "For 500 bucks a month, I'll kill whoever you want." During Algren's confinement in Katsumoto's mountain village, he grows to admire samurai culture so much that he decides to fight on the side of his former enemy. The two men seal their bond on the battlefield during their last stand against the Meiji army. When Katsumoto is gravely wounded, Algren holds him in a tight embrace before helping him commit ritual suicide, an honorable death according to samurai custom.

Shortly after the attacks on the World Trade Center and the Pentagon, many American politicians drew parallels between the Japanese assault on Pearl Harbor and the events of 9/11. Less than two weeks after the 2001 attacks, for example, a Japanese government representative visited the New York City Council to present two checks of $5 million each, one for the city and one for the state. Peter Vallone, Council Speaker and candidate for mayor that year, accepted the city's share of Japanese aid with a prediction that, according to one newspaper report, left the chamber's gallery speechless. In future history books, Vallone declared, "December 7, 1941, will be eclipsed by September 11, 2001."[2] "What Peter was getting at," as one Vallone aide later spun what many considered to be a gaffe, "is that it was an awful day." "It's amazing," the aide explained, "how the two countries," enemies during WWII, "now are able to come together in the spirit of cooperation and friendship." Later that year, during a Pearl Harbor commemoration on the deck of the USS Enterprise, George W. Bush echoed Vallone's assessment. "Today," the commander in chief declared, "our navies are working side by side in the fight against terror." "The bitterness of 60 years ago has passed away," he continued. "The struggles of our war in the Pacific now belong to history."[3]

Bush's speech and Vallone's questionable etiquette suggest that the time of the Japanese as yellow peril has "passed away," in the president's words, for the foreseeable future. Just as "December 7" made it unfeasible for Hollywood to represent the African American in unflattering terms, "September 11" rendered it politically unfeasible for popular films to vilify Japan. The United States needed Japan as an ally in the war on terror. During the 1991 Gulf War, for example, Japan pledged $10.7 billion in aid to operation Desert Storm, the largest donation from any nation outside of the Middle East. By comparison, the next largest non-Muslim donor, Germany, pledged $6.6 billion to the effort.[4] After the start of America's 2003 invasion of Iraq, Japan pledged $1.5 billion for reconstruction, nearly double the total annual aid package for its poor neighbors in Asia.[5]

WWII political expediency prompted Hollywood movies such as *Bataan* to represent African American men in a more favorable manner while simultaneously portraying the Japanese as haters of black people. Post-9/11, however, Hollywood will have to avoid such vilification of the Japanese. For example, in 2006 Clint Eastwood produced and directed two movies that dramatize the WWII battle of Iwo Jima: *Flags of Our Fathers* comes from the American perspective, *Letters from Iwo Jima* from the Japanese. By providing a dual perspective, the companion pieces help to forestall criticisms of one-dimensional stereotyping of the enemy.

Assuming that Americans continue to regard racism as a significant problem, we can be sure that the need for a common enemy to facilitate bonding between white and black will not disappear any time soon. In addition to *Crash*, for example, I would designate the 2008 remake of Robert Wise's 1951 science fiction classic, *The Day the Earth Stood Still*, as a post-9/11 Orientalist buddy film. The remake features a white mother (Jennifer Connelly) and her black stepson (Jaden Smith) who bond when aliens, space invaders who speak Chinese with one another (Keanu Reeves and James Hong), invade Earth. Although, since its post-9/11 economic rise, Hollywood has shown a reluctance to offend China, as evidenced by the delayed release of Dan Bradley's *Red Dawn*, a $60-million remake of the 1984 movie directed by John Milius in which Patrick Swayze and Charlie Sheen fight off a surprise invasion by Russian communists. Bradley shot the remake with Chinese communists as the enemy, but since China is such a lucrative market for Hollywood films, the movie's producers decided to delay the debut in order to digitally replace all the Chinese markers on the military props with North Korean ones.[6]

If the options for an East Asian villain dwindle, the stereotype of the Muslim terrorist seems a likely candidate for the scapegoat who is neither white nor black, given the racial reordering in the wake of 9/11.

Fox's hit series, *24*, is a good example. The show's first two seasons (2001–2003) construct a triangle wherein a white and black duo faces a Middle Eastern terrorist. The bonding between white and black occurs during the first season. The white buddy, the show's protagonist, Jack Bauer (Kiefer Sutherland), is an antiterrorism expert. The black buddy, David Palmer (Dennis Haysbert), is a United States senator and a candidate for the White House. Initially, the show sets white and black against one another. A Serbian terrorist cell kidnaps Bauer's wife and daughter in order to compel him to assassinate the politician. Bauer manages to foil the plot, but the attempt makes Palmer believe that Bauer tried to kill him. Eventually, the two reconcile and bond when Bauer tells Palmer about the kidnapping. During the show's second season, the pair prevents a Middle Eastern terrorist, Syed Ali (Francesco Quinn), from detonating a nuclear bomb over Los Angeles.

In whole or in part, several Hollywood movies that dramatize the events of 9/11 fit the Orientalist buddy film profile. A key scene in Oliver Stone's *World Trade Center* (2006) features white and black bonding in the immediate aftermath of the attack. During an emotional encounter in a hospital waiting room, two strangers, both Americans (Maria Bello and Viola Davis), bond. The scene with the "black woman" is, according to the director's comments on the DVD format, "a means by which Donna [the white character] could reach out a little bit more and understand the whole human condition that day, that we are all the same." Paul Greengrass's *United 93* (2006) depicts the events of the flight whose passengers fought their Middle Eastern hijackers, causing the plane to miss its target and crash into a field in Pennsylvania. Resembling the WWII era *Bataan* that I analyze in chapter 1, *United 93* is a "last stand" combat film. To prevent more deaths on the ground, a disparate collection of strangers, white and black, band together in a suicide mission against the common enemy. In Mike Binder's *Reign Over Me* (2007), two estranged friends, Charlie (Adam Sandler) and Alan (Don Cheadle), bond in the wake of the 9/11 attack. After Charlie's wife and children die as passengers on board one of the planes that hit the World Trade Center, Charlie withdraws totally from his successful life as a Manhattan dentist. As Alan pushes Charlie to accept the reality of his loss by facing the difficult memories of that day, the men, one white and one black, rekindle their friendship.

The fact that so many of the 9/11 hijackers hailed from Saudi Arabia (15 of 19) serves as the basis for the initial distrust between the two principal male characters in Peter Berg's *The Kingdom* (2007). An African American FBI agent, Ronald Fleury (Jamie Foxx), leads a squad to Riyadh to investigate an Al Qaeda terrorist bombing of an American compound. Fleury believes Saudi Arabia to be an inconsistent ally to the United States, which makes him doubt the sincerity of his Saudi host, Colonel Faris Al-Ghazi (Ashraf Barhom). Despite the mistrust, the common goal of bringing to justice the lead terrorist, Abu Hamza (Hezi Saddik), motivates the two to transcend their differences and emphasize what they share. When the terrorist Abu Hamza shoots Al-Ghazi, Fleury holds the latter in his arms as he dies, whispering, "stay with me buddy." It is a tableau reminiscent of the final scene in *The Defiant Ones* (1958) in which Sidney Poitier cradles and sings to a wounded Tony Curtis. In *The Kingdom*, Colonel Al-Ghazi stands in for the white buddy of the Orientalist buddy film, reinforcing the bond between America and its Saudi ally through the common threat of an Al Qaeda villain.

If September 11, 2001 has indeed eclipsed December 7, 1941, then post-9/11 Hollywood is free to represent Asian men as American. In the introduction and in chapter 4, I argue that the Orientalist buddy film's Asian villain must be male and non-American, since white and black bond *qua* American men. As evidence, I cite an abundance of foreign Asian male characters in 1980s and 1990s popular film and television whose alien status is signaled by accented English, but a paucity of American ones (not even in bit parts). In contrast to the 1980s and 1990s, however, there has been a minor explosion of male roles that are both Asian and American in the period just after 9/11. The post-9/11 careers of a few, but representative, Asian American male actors illustrate this change. John Cho and Kal Penn play the leads in the popular *Harold & Kumar* movie series: *Harold & Kumar Go to White Castle* (Danny Leiner, 2004), *Harold & Kumar Escape from Guantanamo Bay* (Jon Hurwitz and Hayden Schlossberg, 2008), and *A Very Harold & Kumar 3D Christmas* (Todd Strauss-Schulson, 2011). Daniel Dae Kim plays the policeman Chin Ho Kelly in *Hawaii Five-0* (CBS, 2010–2012) and the antiterrorism expert Tom Baker in *24* (Fox, 2004). B. D. Wong plays the FBI criminal profiler Dr. George Huang in *Law & Order: Special Victims Unit* (NBC, 2001–2011) and the psychotherapist Dr. John Lee in *Awake* (NBC, 2012). Finally, Steven Yeun plays the zombie killer Glenn in *The Walking Dead* (AMC, 2010–2012). Unlike the vast majority of Hollywood's pre-9/11 Asian male characters, these figures speak a form of English that is unambiguously American.

Notes

Introduction

1. Sigmund Freud, *Civilization and Its Discontents*, trans. James Strachey (New York: W. W. Norton, 1961), 61.
2. David Edelstein, "Review of *Crash*," *Fresh Air*, May 6, 2005 <http://www.npr.org/templates/story/story.php?storyId=4632982> (May 6, 2008).
3. Paul Haggis and Brendan Fraser, "Interview by Terry Gross," *Fresh Air*, April 18, 2008 <http://www.npr.org/templates/story/story.php?storyId=4604990> (May 6, 2008).
4. Matt Dillon, "Interview by Terry Gross," *Fresh Air*, August 10, 2006 <http://www.npr.org/templates/story/story.php?storyId=5633495> (May 6, 2008).
5. Aside from the Koreans involved in the slave trade, the film's only other Asian actor (Art Chudabala) plays a bit part as an insurance adjuster who tells the Iranian man that the company will not cover any damage to his store, looted and vandalized by racists. In DVD format's commentary, Don Cheadle asks the director why he cut one of the adjuster's lines, one that expresses the Asian's sympathy to the shopkeeper, in other words, a humane response. Despite Cheadle's direct question, Haggis does not explain the cut, remarking only that the line "just didn't work."
6. See Edward Said's *Orientalism*, which uses "Orientalist" to refer to Western stereotypes of the Middle East (New York: Vintage Books, 1979). I follow other scholars that use the term to signify representations of East Asia. See, for example, Mari Yoshihara, *Embracing the East: White Women and American Orientalism* (New York: Oxford University Press, 2003).
7. Usually, the buddies are male, the unspoken gender norm of the national citizen under patriarchy. Usually, the white male buddy who represents the nation has a female love interest, proving his heterosexuality.
8. René Girard, "Mimesis and Violence," in *The Girard Reader*, ed. James G. Williams (New York: Crossroad, 1996), 12.
9. Eve Sedgwick, *Between Men: English Literature and Male Homosocial Desire* (New York: Columbia University Press, 1985), 160.
10. Robyn Wiegman, *American Anatomies: Theorizing Race and Gender* (Durham, NC: Duke University Press, 1995), 117, 226, 134. All other references will be contained parenthetically in the text. See also Melvin Donalson,

Masculinity in the Interracial Buddy Film (Jefferson, NC: McFarland, 2006).

11. The editors of the groundbreaking *AIIIEEEEE! An Anthology of Asian American Writers* remark, "American culture, protecting the sanctity of its whiteness, still patronizes us as foreigners and refuses to recognize Asian American literature as 'American' literature." "America does not recognize Asian America as a presence," they continue, "though Asian Americans have been here seven generations." Frank Chin et al., eds., Mentor edn. (1974; New York: Penguin, 1991), xiii; the first paragraph of Ronald Takaki's *Strangers from a Different Shore: A History of Asian Americans* echoes the same problem. He relates an autobiographical anecdote about how he was repeatedly mistaken for a "foreign student" at his Midwestern college, despite the fact that he is a third-generation American (New York: Penguin, 1989), 3; "Asians in America," Gary Okihiro observes, "historically and within our time, have been and are rendered perpetual aliens, strangers in the land of their birth and adoption." "Commentary," in *Locating American Studies: The Evolution of a Discipline*, ed. Lucy Maddox (Baltimore, MD: Johns Hopkins University Press, 1999), 441.

12. Lisa Lowe, *Immigrant Acts: On Asian American Cultural Politics* (Durham, NC: Duke University Press, 1996), 5–6. All other references will be contained parenthetically in the text.

13. Robert G. Lee, *Orientals: Asian Americans in Popular Culture* (Philadelphia, PA: Temple University Press, 1999), ix. All other references will be contained parenthetically in the text.

14. Karen Shimakawa, *National Abjection: The Asian American Body Onstage* (Durham, NC: Duke University Press, 2002), 1–2 (emphasis in the original). All other references will be contained parenthetically in the text.

15. Shimakawa's book does make a fleeting reference to a nonwhite and non-Asian agent in the construction of the Asian as indelibly alien. She writes, "I do not intend to...suggest that a uniform, linear process takes place in the psyches of all [white? non-Asian?] 'Americans' who experience and process the 'difference' posed by Asian Americans in order to arrive at a determination of Asian American abjection" (3).

16. Linda Williams, *Playing the Race Card: Melodramas of Black and White from Uncle Tom to O.J. Simpson* (Princeton, NJ: Princeton University Press, 2001), xiii.

17. For more analysis of the Asian American subject in comparative terms, see my "'Top Dog,' 'Black Threat,' and 'Japanese Cats': The Impact of the White-Black Binary on Asian American Identity," *Radical Philosophy Review* 1, no. 2 (1998): 98–125; "Here Comes the Judge: The Dancing Itos and the Televisual Construction of the Enemy Asian Male," in *Living Color: Race and Television in the United States*, ed. Sasha Torres (Durham, NC: Duke University Press, 1998), 239–53.

18. Claire Jean Kim, *Bitter Fruit: The Politics of Black-Korean Conflict in New York City* (New Haven, CT: Yale University Press, 2000), 10. All other references will be contained parenthetically in the text.

19. Like Kim, Angelo N. Ancheta's analysis has a double-pronged structure. One "axis" he calls "white versus black," the other "American versus foreigner." *Race, Rights, and the Asian American Experience* (New Brunswick, NJ: Rutgers University Press, 1998), 64.

20. I use the verb "to govern" deliberately. Michel Foucault writes that the answer to who we are, the question of the subject, depends upon the "power relations" in which we are "placed," in "Subject" (778). By power he does not mean "an institution of power, or group, or elite, or class but rather" something that "applies itself to immediate everyday life which categorizes the individual, marks him [sic] by his own individuality, attaches him to his own identity, imposes a law of truth on him which he must recognize and which others have to recognize in him," in "Subject" (781). Foucault defines "the exercise of power" as the "way in which certain actions may structure the field of other possible actions," in "Subject" (791), synonymous with what he calls "government." Government refers not "only to political structures or to the management of states," but also to "modes of action, more or less considered or calculated...destined to act upon the possibilities of action of other people," in "Subject" (790). Recognizing that "the analysis of power relations within a society cannot be reduced to the study of a series of institutions," in "Subject" (792), in order to "account for the constitution of the subject within a historical framework," in "Truth" (117), he instructs us to examine that framework's "economy of power relations." He means "the word 'economy'" in its "practical sense," in "Subject" (779), "the rules which control a person's mode of living" as the OED defines it. This set of rules that delimits the range of possible options for the subject Foucault calls "discourse," which he characterizes as the "body of anonymous, historical rules, always determined in the time and space that have defined a given period, and for a given social, economic, and geographical, or linguistic area, the conditions of" what can and cannot be said of the subject, the "truth" of the subject, in *Archeology* (117). "The Subject and Power," *Critical Inquiry* 8, no. 4 (1982): 781–92; "Truth and Power," in *Power/Knowledge: Selected Interviews and Other Writings 1972–1977*, ed. Colin Gordon (New York: Pantheon, 1980), 109–33; *The Archeology of Knowledge*, trans. A. M. Sheridan Smith (New York: Pantheon, 1972).

21. Ed Guerrero, *Framing Blackness: The African American Image in Film* (Philadelphia, PA: Temple University Press, 1993), 127. All other references will be contained parenthetically in the text. See also Robin Wood, *Hollywood from Vietnam to Reagan* (New York: Columbia Univbersity Press, 1986), 227–30.

22. Toni Morrison, *Playing in the Dark: Whiteness and the Literary Imagination* (Cambridge, MA: Harvard University Press, 1992), 63; Michael Omi and Howard Winant, *Racial Formation in the United States from the 1960s to the 1990s*, 2nd edn. (New York: Routledge, 1994), 123; Stuart Hall, "The Whites of Their Eyes: Racist Ideologies and the Media," in *Silver Linings: Some Strategies for the Eighties*, eds. George Bridges and Rosalind Brunt (London: Lawrence and Wishart, 1981), 36; Tali Mendelberg, *The Race*

Card: Campaign Strategy, Implicit Messages and the Norm of Equality (Princeton, NJ: Princeton University Press, 2001), 8–12; Kim, Bitter Fruit, 17–20; John Fiske, Media Matters: Everyday Culture and Political Change (Minneapolis, MN: University of Minnesota Press, 1994), 37–8.

23. U.S. Census Bureau, Census 2000 Demographic Profile Highlights <http://www.census.gov> (April 20, 2006).

24. Howard L. Bingham and Max Wallace, Muhammad Ali's Greatest Fight: Cassius Clay vs. The United States of America (New York: M. Evans & Company, 2000), 119.

I   Strange Fruit: *Bataan* (1943)

1. Gunnar Myrdal, An American Dilemma: The Negro Problem and Modern Democracy (New York: McGraw-Hill, 1964; rpt. 1944), 1006.

2. Gina Marchetti, Romance and the "Yellow Peril": Race, Sex, and Discursive Strategies in Hollywood Fiction (Berkeley, CA: University of California Press, 1993), 2.

3. Gary Y. Okihiro, Margins and Mainstreams: Asians in American History and Culture (Seattle, WA: University of Washington Press, 1994), 119–20.

4. Brian J. Woodman, "A Hollywood War of Wills: Cinematic Representation of Vietnamese Super-Soldiers and America's Defeat in the War," Journal of Film and Video 55, nos. 2–3 (2003): 44.

5. Joseph W. Martin, "130,000,000 Free People Working in Unison and without Partisan Lines," Vital Speeches of the Day 8, no. 8 (1942): 247.

6. "President Cites Unity Plea of 1809," New York Times, May 5, 1942, 15.

7. Jeanine Basinger, The World War II Combat Film: Anatomy of a Genre (Middletown, CT: Wesleyan University Press, 2003), 24, 42, 46. All other references will be contained parenthetically in the text.

8. "News of the Screen," New York Times, June 2, 1943, 21.

9. United States Office of War Information (OWI), Bureau of Motion Pictures, Government Information Manual for the Motion Picture Industry (GIMMPI), (Washington, DC: Office of War Information, 1942), "The Issues" <http://www.libraries.iub.edu/index.php?pageId=3301> (November 22, 2004).

10. John Morton Blum, V Was for Victory: Politics and American Culture during World War II (New York: Harcourt Brace Jovanovich, 1976), 207 (ellipsis in original).

11. Clayton R. Koppes and Gregory D. Black, "Blacks, Loyalty, and Motion-Picture Propaganda in World War II," Journal of American History 73, no. 2 (1986): 385.

12. Horace R. Cayton, Long Old Road (New York: Trident, 1965), 275.

13. Richard Polenberg, War and Society: The United States, 1941–1945 (New York: Lippincott, 1972), 101.

14. Franklin D. Roosevelt, "Executive Order on War News," New York Times, June 14, 1942, 31; "President Forms Top News Agency," New York Times, June 14, 1942, 1.

15. OWI, *GIMMPI*, "Introduction."
16. "Movies Must Submit Scenarios to the OWI," *New York Times*, December 19, 1942, 1.
17. "Davis States Films Need Not Fear OWI," *New York Times*, December 24, 1942, 20.
18. Richard R. Lingeman, *Don't You Know There's a War On? The American Home Front, 1941–1945* (New York: G. P. Putnum's Sons, 1970), 192.
19. OWI, *GIMMPI*, "Introduction"; "Discomfort or Defeat"; "Red Cross Blood Donor Service"; "Children's Army."
20. Thomas Cripps, "Racial Ambiguities in American Propaganda Movies," in *Film and Radio Propaganda in World War II*, ed. K. R. M. Short (Knoxville, TN: University of Tennessee Press, 1983), 132.
21. OWI, *GIMMPI*, "Issues"; "United Nations and Peoples."
22. *Proceedings of the Writers' Congress: Los Angeles, 1943* (Berkeley, CA: University of California Press, 1944), 598–9.
23. Philip Dray, *At the Hands of Persons Unknown: The Lynching of Black America* (New York: Random House, 2002), 440.
24. "Negro Is Lynched by Missouri Crowd," *New York Times*, January 26, 1942, 17.
25. "Hitler in Mississippi," *New York Times*, October 21, 1942, 20.
26. Pearl Buck, "The Asiatic Problem: The Colored People Are Still Waiting, Still Watchful," *Vital Speeches of the Day* 8, no. 10 (1942): 304.
27. Walter White, *A Man Called White* (New York: Arno Press, 1969), 166.
28. Garth E. Pauley, *The Modern Presidency and Civil Rights: Rhetoric on Race from Roosevelt to Nixon* (College Station, TX: Texas A&M University Press, 2001), 25.
29. White, *Man Called White*, 169–70.
30. Thomas Patrick Doherty, *Projections of War: Hollywood, American Culture, and World War II* (New York: Columbia University Press, 1993), 205.
31. Harvard Sitkoff, "Racial Militancy and Interracial Violence in the Second World War," *Journal of American History* 58, no. 3 (1971): 662.
32. Langston Hughes, "Is Hollywood Fair to Negroes?" *Negro Digest*, April 1943, 19.
33. Bosley Crowther, "Cleaving the Color Line: A New Attitude toward Negroes Is Apparent in Some Recent Films—Comment on *Cabin in the Sky* and *Bataan*," *New York Times*, June 6, 1943, X3.
34. Daniel J. Leab, *From Sambo to Superspade: The Black Experience in Motion Pictures* (Boston, MA: Houghton Mifflin, 1975), 122.
35. White, *Man Called White*, 201.
36. Leab, *From Sambo to Superspade*, 130.
37. *Sahara* (Zoltan Korda, 1942) includes a sympathetic black figure that is non-American.
38. Dore Schary, *Heyday: An Autobiography* (Boston, MA: Little, Brown, 1979), 127.
39. Lawrence H. Suid, *Guts and Glory: The Making of the American Military Image in Film* (Lexington, KY: University Press of Kentucky, 2002), 45.

40. Joe Morella, Edward Z. Epstein, and John Griggs, *The Films of World War II* (Secaucus, NJ: Citadel Press, 1973), 132.

41. Lewis B. Funke, "Singer into Actor," *New York Times*, June 20, 1943, X3.

42. "News of the Screen," *New York Times*, June 2, 1943, 21.

43. Bosley Crowther, "Review of *Bataan*," *New York Times*, June 4, 1943, 17; "One More Year: The War's Effect Is Noted in the Films of 1942, Including the 'Ten Best,'" *New York Times*, December 27, 1942, 3.

44. OWI, *GIMMPI*, "Home Front."

45. Anne P. Rice, ed., *Witnessing Lynching: American Writers Respond* (New Brunswick, NJ: Rutgers University Press, 2003), 5.

46. Phillip McGuire, ed., *Taps for a Jim Crow Army: Letters from Black Soldiers in World War II* (Lexington, KY: University Press of Kentucky, 1993), 1, 11, 88.

47. *Going Hollywood: The War Years*, dir. Julian Schlossberg, 1987, DVD.

48. OWI, *GIMMPI*, "United Nations and Peoples"; "Work and Production"; "Enemy."

49. OWI, *GIMMPI*, "Issues."

50. For a discussion of how some WWII combat films ward off the specter of homosexuality, see Robert Eberwein, "'As a Mother Cuddles a Child': Sexuality and Masculinity in World War II Combat Films," in *Masculinity: Bodies, Movies, Culture*, ed. Peter Lehman (New York: Routledge, 2001), 149–66.

51. Neil A. Wynn, *The Afro-American and the Second World War*, revised edn. (New York: Holmes and Meier, 1993), 104.

52. Richard Polenberg, *War and Society: The United States, 1941–1945* (New York: Lippincott, 1972), 101.

53. Richard Wright, *Native Son* (New York: Harper and Row, 1940), xiv, xv (emphasis in original).

54. Myrdal, *An American Dilemma*, 1438 f. 3.

55. *Concentration Camps for Japanese, Congressional Record, Appendix* (Washington, DC: United States Government Printing Office, 1942), A768.

56. Howard W. Odum, *Race and Rumors of Race: Challenge to American Crisis* (Chapel Hill, NC: University of North Carolina Press, 1943), 134.

57. Koppes and Black, "Blacks, Loyalty," 385–6.

58. OWI, *GIMMPI*, "Issues."

59. Doherty, *Projections*, 213.

60. Quoted in Thomas Cripps and David Culbert, "The Negro Soldier: Film Propaganda in Black and White," *American Quarterly* 31, no.5 (1979): 626–7.

61. OWI, *GIMMPI*, "Home Front."

62. Crowther, "Review of *Bataan*," 17.

63. *Classical Film Violence: Designing and Regulating Brutality in Hollywood Cinema, 1930–1968* (New Brunswick, NJ: Rutgers University, 2003), 40, 162. All other references will be contained parenthetically in the text.

64. In DVD format, which allows the viewer to slow the picture, one sees that it is definitely a samurai sword.

65. Amy Louise Wood, "Lynching Photography and the 'Black Beast Rapist' in the Southern White Masculine Imagination," in *Masculinity: Bodies, Movies, Culture*, ed. Peter Lehman (New York: Routledge, 2001), 195.

66. Jacquelyn Dowd Hall, "'The Mind That Burns in Each Body': Women, Rape, and Racial Violence," in *Powers of Desire: The Politics of Sexuality*, ed. Ann Snitow (New York: Monthly Press, 1983), 329–31.

67. Walter White, *Rope and Faggot* (New York: Arno Press, 1969), viii.

68. Grace Elizabeth Hale, *Making Whiteness: The Culture of Segregation in the South, 1890–1940* (New York: Pantheon, 1998), 202.

69. Hale, *Making Whiteness*, 204; Wood, "Lynching Photography," 195.

70. Clayton R. Koppes and Gregory D. Black, *Hollywood Goes to War: How Politics, Profits, and Propaganda Shaped World War II Movies* (Berkeley, CA: University of California Press, 1987), 179.

71. OWI, *GIMMPI*, "Enemy."

72. Blum, *V Was for Victory*, 195.

73. Rice, *Witnessing Lynching*, 236.

74. Leon F. Litwack, "Hellhounds" in *Without Sanctuary: Lynching Photography in America*, ed. James Allen (Santa Fe, NM: Twin Palms Publishers, 2000), 14.

75. White, *Rope and Faggot*, 28. Even though White identified as an African American, his light complexion enabled him to pass as white. See also Dray, *At the Hands of Persons*, 246.

76. James Allen, ed., *Without Sanctuary: Lynching Photography in America* (Santa Fe, NM: Twin Palms Publishers, 2000), 174 n. 24.

77. Shawn Michelle Smith, *Photography on the Color Line: W. E. B. Du Bois, Race, and Visual Culture* (Durham, NC: Duke University Press, 2004), 122–5.

78. Dora Apel, *Imagery of Lynching: Black Men, White Women, and the Mob* (New Brunswick, NJ: Rutgers University Press, 2004), 9.

79. Roberta Smith, "An Ugly Legacy Lives on, Its Glare Unsoftened by Age," *New York Times*, January 13, 2000, 8.

80. Dray, *At the Hands of Persons*, 363.

81. Wood, "Lynching Photography," 208.

82. Dray, *At the Hands of Persons*, 354.

2 White and Black to the Brink: *China Gate* (1957), *Pork Chop Hill* (1959), *All the Young Men* (1960)

1. Lawrence H. Suid, *Guts and Glory: The Making of the American Military Image in Film* (Lexington, KY: University Press of Kentucky, 2002), 137, 142.

2. Clemons's "best friend" and a former WWII internee, Ohashi is a figure that calms "the dead who still haunt the present." See Caroline Chung Simpson's excellent *An Absent Presence: Japanese Americans in Postwar American Culture, 1945–1960* (Durham, NC: Duke University Press, 2001), 5.

3. "Johansson Weeps in Film on Korea," *New York Times*, October 12, 1959, 14.

4. "Byrd Says 'Rights' Mean Dictatorship," *New York Times*, February 20, 1948, 3.

5. "Southern Threats to Democrats Rise," *New York Times*, February 5, 1948, 17.

6. William S. White, "Truman Is Shunned in Votes of South," *New York Times*, July 15, 1948, 9.

7. Paula F. Pfeffer, *A. Philip Randolph, Pioneer of the Civil Rights Movement* (Baton Rouge, Louisiana: Louisiana State University Press, 1990), 128.

8. Jay Walz, "Carolinian Sets Talking Record," *New York Times*, August 30, 1957, 1.

9. Howard Zinn, *A People's History of the United States* (New York: Harper & Row, 1980), 440.

10. Robert Fisher, *Let the People Decide: Neighborhood Organizing in America* (Boston, MA: Twayne, 1984), 97.

11. James A. Morone, *Democratic Wish: Popular Participation and the Limits of American Government* (New York: Basic Books, 1990), 204.

12. Pfeffer, *A. Philip Randolph*, 49–50.

13. "Negro Defense View Told," *New York Times*, March 23, 1948, 28.

14. Richard M. Dalfiume, *Desegregation of the U.S. Armed Forces: Fighting on Two Fronts, 1939–1953* (Columbia, MO: University of Missouri Press, 1969), 164, 169.

15. Harry S. Truman, "Texts of the President's Two Executive Orders," *New York Times*, July 27, 1948, 4.

16. For scholarship on the general topic of race (white and black) in American literature and popular culture, see Leslie Fiedler who argues that blackness is integral to white American identity, "Come Back to the Raft Ag'in, Huck Honey!" in *Collected Essays of Leslie Fiedler*, vol. 1 (New York: Stein and Day, 1971), 142–51. Joseph Boone argues that Fiedler fails to register the homoerotic element of the white and black buddy figure, "Male Independence and the American Quest Genre: Hidden Sexual Politics in the All-Male Worlds of Melville, Twain and London," in *Gender Studies: New Directions in Feminist Criticism*, ed. Judith Spector (Bowling Green, OH: Bowling Green University Popular Press, 1986), 187–217. Toni Morrison agrees with Fiedler, but argues that the majority of literary critics continue to ignore the integral role that blackness plays in the formation of American identity, *Playing in the Dark: Whiteness and the Literary Imagination* (Cambridge, MA: Harvard University Press, 1992). Also see Cynthia Fuchs, "The Buddy Politic," in *Screening the Male: Exploring Masculinities in Hollywood*, ed. Steven Cohan (New York: Routledge, 1993), 194–210; Yvonne Tasker, *Spectacular Bodies, Gender, Genre and the Action Cinema* (New York: Routledge, 1993); Sharon Willis, *High Contrast: Race and Gender in Contemporary Hollywood Film* (Durham, NC: Duke University Press, 1997).

17. Ronald Takaki, *A Different Mirror: A History of Multicultural America* (Boston, MA: Little, Brown, 1993), 75–6.

18. Michael Banton, *The Idea of Race* (Boulder, CO: Westview, 1977), 1.

19. Alexis de Tocqueville, *Democracy in America*, ed. J. P. Mayer (New York: Anchor, 1969), 360.

20. William Jefferson Clinton, "Transcript of President Clinton's Second Inaugural Address to the Nation," *New York Times*, January 21, 1997, A14.

21. Thomas C. Schelling, *Arms and Influence* (Westport, CT: Greenwood, 1976), 99, 116, emphasis in original. All other references will be contained parenthetically in the text.

22. James Shepley, "How Dulles Averted War: Three Times, New Disclosures Show, He Brought U.S. Back from the Brink," *Life*, January 16, 1956, 71.

23. Gerard H. Clarfield and William M. Wiecek, *Nuclear America: Military and Civilian Nuclear Power in the United States 1940–1980* (New York: Harper and Row, 1984), 259.

24. Peter Lev, *Transforming the Screen, 1950–1959*, vol. 7, History of the American Cinema (New York: Charles Scribner's Sons, 2003), 218–19.

25. Stanley Kauffman, "Review of *The Defiant Ones*," *New Republic*, September 1, 1958, 22.

26. Kramer also directed a number of other Hollywood films that dealt with the issues of civil rights and racism, such as *Ship of Fools* (1965) and *Guess Who's Coming to Dinner* (1967), the latter starring Poitier. The 1967 film won that year's Academy Awards for Best Actress (Katherine Hepburn) and Best Original Screenplay. Kramer's corpus created for him a reputation as a pro–civil rights and antiracist director.

27. The way the film poses the question has relevance here. Historically, the axis of freedom and slavery run along the poles of North and South. When slavery was alive as a system, going South for a black person meant harsher treatment, a qualitative and quantitative increase of racism. For example, the North-South distinction figures prominently in Harriet Beecher Stowe's 1852 *Uncle Tom's Cabin: Or, Life among the Lowly* (New York: Signet Classic/Penguin, 1998). The Kentucky slave's worst nightmare was to be "sold down the river." Likewise, in the world of *The Defiant Ones*, going north still meant better treatment for a black person and a better chance at winning freedom.

28. "Review of *The Defiant Ones*," *Catholic World*, October 1958, 65.

29. Kauffman, "Review of *The Defiant Ones*," 23. Most reviews describe the love as "brotherly." Why not just "two men in love"?

30. Bosley Crowther, "Review of *The Defiant Ones*," *New York Times*, September 25, 1958, 25.

31. Robert Hatch, "Review of *The Defiant Ones*," *Nation*, October 11, 1958, 219.

32. James Baldwin, "The Uses of the Blues," in *A World Enclosed: Tragedy*, ed. W. T. Jewkes (1963; New York: Harcourt Brace Jovanovich, 1973), 254–5.

3   The Blaxploitation Buddy Film

1. The third film in the *Black Dragon* series, all starring Van Clief, *Way of the Black Dragon* is dubbed in English, produced originally in Hong Kong in Cantonese.

2. Stephane Dunn, *"Bad Bitches" and Sassy Supermamas: Black Power Action Films* (Chicago, IL: University of Illinois Press, 2008), 88; Yvonne D. Sims, *Women of Blaxploitation* (Jefferson, NC: McFarland, 2006), 44.

3. Alexander Walker, *Stardom: The Hollywood Phenomenon* (New York: Stein and Day), 348.

4. Clifford Mason, "Why Does White America Love Sidney Poitier So?" *New York Times*, November 10, 1967 <http://www.nytimes.com/packages/html/movies/bestpictures/heat-ar.html> (February 17, 2009); Larry Neal, "Beware of the Tar Baby," *New York Times*, August 3, 1969.

5. Donald Bogle, *Toms, Coons, Mulattoes, Mammies and Bucks: An Interpretive History of Blacks in American Films* (New York: Viking, 1973), 312.

6. *Baad Asssss Cinema*, dir. Isaac Julien, Independent Film Channel, 2002, DVD.

7. Keith M. Harris, *Boys, Boyz, Bois: An Ethics of Black Masculinity in Film and Popular Media* (New York: Routledge, 2006), 65; Bogle, *Toms*, 314.

8. Ignoring this history, *The New Yorker*'s Pauline Kael suggests that the genre's depiction of whites is simple hypocrisy. "Except when we were at war," she remarks, "there has never been such racism in American films." Quoted in Daniel J. Leab, *From Sambo to Superspade: The Black Experience in Motion Pictures* (Boston, MA: Houghton Mifflin, 1975), 254.

9. William R. Grant, *Post-Soul Black Cinema* (New York: Routledge, 2004), 36; Harris, *Boys, Boyz*, 70.

10. Grant, *Post-Soul*, 38 (emphasis in the original).

11. Julien, *Baad Asssss Cinema*.

12. David J. Londoner, "The Changing Economics of Entertainment," in *The American Film Industry*, ed. Tino Balio, revised edn. (Madison, WI: University of Wisconsin Press, 1985), 606–7; David A. Cook, *Lost Illusions: American Cinema in the Shadow of Watergate and Vietnam, 1970–1979*, vol. 9, History of the American Cinema (Berkeley, CA: University of California Press, 2000), 9.

13. David Desser, "The Kung Fu Craze: Hong Kong Cinema's First American Reception," in *The Cinema of Hong Kong*, eds. Poshek Fu and David Desser (New York: Cambridge University Press, 2000), 19–20, 38.

14. Amy Abugo Ongiri, "'He Wanted to Be Just Like Bruce Lee': African Americans, Kung Fu Theater and Cultural Exchange at the Margins," *Journal of Asian American Studies* 5, no. 1 (2002): 35.

15. Vijay Prashad, *Everybody Was Kung Fu Fighting: Afro-Asian Connections and the Myth of Cultural Purity* (Boston, MA: Beacon, 2001), 130.

16. Malcolm X, *Malcolm X Speaks: Selected Speeches and Statements* (New York: Merit, 1965), 4–5.

17. Prashad, *Everybody Was Kung Fu*, 131, 143–4. Prashad's is one of two recent books that chronicle the history of blacks and Asians forging an alliance on the common ground of racial victimization, oftentimes in the form of colonialism or transnational capitalism or both, by whites. Prashad recounts a wide variety of alliances between African and Asian peoples and movements "through five centuries and around the globe," including black audience identification with Bruce Lee in the 1970s (x). Likewise, Bill V. Mullen illuminates the "alternative historical trajectories" of black nationalists, anticolonialists and Marxists (Marcus Garvey, W. E. B. Dubois, and Richard Wright among them) who have looked to Asia, at various points during the twentieth century, for solidarity in the struggle against the capitalist global imperialism of many white nations. These alternative histories narrate a "logic of equivalence" between black and yellow people founded upon "class-based theories" that "reimagine [them] as hand-holding gravediggers of Western capitalist modernity." *Afro-Orientalism* (Minneapolis, MN: University of Minnesota Press, 2004), xix, xxv. "I have chosen to discuss the peoples who claim the heritage of the continents of Asian and Africa," writes Prashad, "because they have long been pitted against each other as the model versus the undesirable" (x). Mullen aims to "confirm and echo" Prashad by countering the "dominant Western racial discourses that have situated African Americans as the negative shadow of the Asian American model minority myth" (xix, xviii).
18. "My Lai: An American Tragedy," *Time*, December 5, 1969 <http://www.time.com/time/magazine/article/0,9171,901621,00.html> (January 30, 2009).
19. Tim O'Brien, "The Vietnam in Me," *New York Times*, October 2, 1994, sec. 6, 48. A document in the U.S. Army Crimes Records Center archive at Fort Belvoir, Virginia, states that the soldiers raped "approximately twenty Vietnamese women" whose ages ranged from eleven to forty-five years old. Of this number, the "vaginas" of seven "women were ripped." Quoted in James S. Olson and Randy Roberts, eds., *My Lai: A Brief History with Documents* (Boston, MA: Bedford Books, 1997), 99–101.
20. Kendrick Oliver, "Coming to Terms with the Past: My Lai," *History Today* 56, no. 2 (2006): 37–9; Olson and Roberts, *Brief History*, 22–3, 27.
21. O'Brien, "Vietnam in Me," 48.
22. Oliver, "Coming to Terms," 37–9.
23. Seymour M. Hersh, "Lieutenant Accused of Murdering 109 Civilians," *St. Louis Post-Dispatch*, November 13, 1969 <http://www.pierretristam.com/Bobst/library/wf-200.htm> (February 27, 2009).
24. "Miscue on the Massacre," *Time*, December 5, 1969, 75; Seymour M. Hersh, "The My Lai Massacre," in *Reporting Vietnam*, ed. Milton J. Bates (New York: Library of America, 2000), 413–27.
25. "The Clamor over Calley: Who Shares the Guilt?" *Time*, April 12, 1971 <http://www.time.com/time/magazine/article/0,9171,904957-1,00.html> (February 20, 2009).

26. The photographs appeared in Hal Wingo, "Massacre at Mylai," *Life*, December 5, 1969, 36–45. Four are reproduced in Olson and Roberts, *Brief History*, 172–3.
27. The cover of Olson and Roberts, *Brief History*, has a reproduction of the photograph.
28. "My Lai: An American Tragedy."
29. Oliver, "Coming to Terms," 37.
30. Olson and Roberts, *Brief History*, 192.
31. Oliver, "Coming to Terms," 37.
32. "An Average American Boy?" *Time*, December 5, 1969 <http://www.time.com/time/magazine/article/0,9171,901624–2,00.html> (February 25, 2009).
33. *Four Hours in My Lai*, dir. Kevin Sim, Yorkshire Television, 1989, VHS.
34. "The Clamor over Calley: Who Shares the Guilt?" *Time*, April 12, 1971 <http://www.time.com/time/magazine/article/0,9171,904957–1,00.html> (February 20, 2009).
35. "Why Civilians Are War Victims in Vietnam," *Science Digest*, May 1970, 44.
36. "GI's in Battle: The 'Dink' Complex," *Newsweek*, December 1, 1969, 37.
37. "Clamor over Calley."
38. "Indians and Others," *The Nation*, December 22, 1969, 682–3.
39. Gina Marchetti, "Jackie Chan and the Black Connection," in *Keyframes: Popular Cinema and Cultural Studies*, ed. Matthew Tinkcom and Amy Villarejo (New York: Routledge, 2001), 140.
40. "Sijo Steve Muhammad," <http://www.stevemuhammad.org/> (February 21, 2009).

4 The Orientalist Buddy Film in the 1980s and 1990s: *Flash Gordon* (1980), *Lethal Weapon* (1987–1998), *Rising Sun* (1993)

1. James Fallows, *More Like Us: Making America Great Again* (Boston, MA: Houghton Mifflin, 1989). Quoted in Robert B. Reich, "Is Japan Really out to Get Us?" *New York Times Book Review*, 9 February 1992, 25.
2. Lisa Lowe observes that "the racist discourse that constructs Asians as a homogenous group" implies that "Asians are 'all alike' and conform to 'types,' " in *Immigrant Acts* (71)
3. Sax Rohmer, *The Insidious Dr. Fu-Manchu: Being a Somewhat Detailed Account of the Amazing Adventures of Nayland Smith in his Trailing of the Sinister Chinaman* (New York: McKinlay, Stone & Mackenzie, 1913). For a movie version of the character, see Boris Karloff in *The Mask of Fu Manchu* (Charles Brabin, 1932).
4. Okihiro, *Margins*, 142.

5. Nazil Kibria, "The Contested Meanings of 'Asian American': Racial Dilemmas in the Contemporary US," *Ethnic and Racial Studies* 21, no. 5 (1998): 953.

6. Bernard Weinraub, "For Hollywood Villains, It's Cold War II," *New York Times*, August 6, 1997.

7. One of the main differences between the second and third movies seems to be the addition of a female love interest (Rene Russo) for Riggs, reinforcing the heterosexual status of the white partner.

8. Marchetti, *Romance*, 2.

9. Lance Morrow, "Japan in the Mind of America," *Time*, February 10, 1992, 16.

10. Charles Krauthammer, "Do We Really Need a New Enemy?" *Time*, March 23, 1992, 76.

11. "Mr. Gephardt's Irresponsible Economics," *New York Times*, December 22, 1991, 10.

12. Randall Rothenberg, "Ads That Bash the Japanese: Just Jokes or Veiled Racism?" *New York Times*, July 11, 1990, A1.

13. Viet Thanh Nguyen, *Race and Resistance: Literature and Politics in Asian America* (New York: Oxford University Press, 2002), 146.

14. Quoted in Keith Osajima, "Asian Americans as the Model Minority: An Analysis of the Popular Press Image in the 1960s and 1980s," in *Reflections on Shattered Windows: Promises and Prospects for Asian American Studies*, eds. Gary Y. Okihiro et al., (Pullman, WA: Washington State University Press, 1988), 167.

15. Kibria, "Contested Meanings," 953.

16. Nguyen, *Race and Resistance*, 147.

17. René Girard, *The Scapegoat*, trans. Yvonne Freccero (Baltimore, MD: Johns Hopkins University Press, 1986), 18.

18. Girard, "Mimesis and Violence," 11.

19. Girard, *Scapegoat*, 18–9.

20. Slavoj Zizek, "Eastern Europe's *Republics of Gilead*," *New Left Review* 183 (1990): 56–7 (emphasis in the original).

21. "One is white the extent to which one is most distant from black," and "one is black the extent to which one is most distant from white," philosopher Lewis Gordon writes. "Every in between is a whiteness or blackness waiting to emerge" (5). In an American racial discourse dominated by a white and black binary, the Latino/a emerges as a category of blackness, the Asian as a category of whiteness. *Her Majesty's Other Children: Sketches of Racism from a Neocolonial Age* (New York: Rowman & Littlefield, 1997).

22. James A. Morone, *Democratic Wish: Popular Participation and the Limits of American Government* (New York: Basic Books, 1990), 219. All other references will be contained parenthetically in the text.

23. Adam Yarmolinsky, "Beginnings of OEO," in *On Fighting Poverty*, ed. James Sundquist (New York: Basic Books, 1969), 49.

24. S. M. Miller and Martin Rein, "Participation, Poverty and Administration," *Public Administration Review* 29, no. 1 (1969): 17.

25. John Strange, "Citizen Participation in Community Action and Model Cities Programs," *Public Administration Review* 32, Special Issue (1972): 657.

26. Deborah Gee's 1988 documentary, *Slaying the Dragon* (Center for Asian American Media), analyzes stereotypes of Asian and Asian American women in American media, including that of the "Connie Chung" news anchor.

27. Quoted in Michael S. Kimmel, "Masculinity as Homophobia: Fear, Shame and Silence in the Construction of Gender Identity," in *Readings for Diversity and Social Justice: An Anthology on Racism, Sexism, Anti-Semitism, Heterosexism, Classism, and Ableism*, ed. Maurianne Adams (New York: Routledge, 2000), 214.

28. Quoted in James Hannaham, "Dude, Where's My Manhood?" *Salon.com*, September 17, 2008 <http://images-origin.salon.com/books/review/2008/09/17/guyland/index1.html> (March 4, 2009).

29. Chow Yun Fat plays the king in the remake, *Anna and the King* (Andy Tennant, 1999).

30. Alida Becker, " 'To Make America Wake Up,' " *New York Times Book Review*, 9 February 9, 1992, 23.

31. Michael Crichton, *Rising Sun* (New York: Ballantine, 1992), 393.

32. Michael Shapiro, "Is 'Rising Sun' a Detective Story or Jeremiad?" *New York Times*, July 25, 1993, H9.

33. Philip Kaufman, Rising Sun: *Screenplay* (Hollywood, CA: Script City, 1992), 10.

34. Ronald Takaki, *Strangers from a Different Shore: A History of Asian Americans*, updated and revised edn. (1989; Boston, MA: Back Bay Books, 1998), 387. All other references will be contained parenthetically in the text.

35. Caroline Chung Simpson's *An Absent Presence* explains "how the centrality of internment in some discourses 'screens' it from view," calling the collection of such instances "the specter of internment" (4).

36. Shapiro, "Is 'Rising Sun.' "

5   The Orientalist Buddy Film and the "New Niggers": *Blade Runner* (1982, 1992, and 2007)

1. Harriet Beecher Stowe, *Uncle Tom's Cabin: Or, Life among the Lowly* (1852; New York: Signet Classic/Penguin, 1998), 123. All further references will be contained parenthetically in the text.

2. Danny Peary, "Directing *Alien* and *Blade Runner*: An Interview with Ridley Scott," in *Omni's Screen Flights, Screen Fantasies: The Future According to Science Fiction Cinema*, ed. Danny Peary (Garden City, NY: Doubleday, 1984), 299.

3. Michael Dempsey, "Review of *Blade Runner*," *Film Quarterly* 36, no. 2 (1984): 36.

4. Kaja Silverman, "Back to the Future," *Camera Obscura*, no. 27 (1991): 115. All other references will be contained parenthetically in the text.

5. Scott Bukatman, *Blade Runner*, BFI Modern Classics, ed. Rob White (London: British Film Institute, 1997), 74.

6. For example, Lisa Lowe makes an argument to which I am indebted, that is, the film uses non-whites "to construct the white citizen against the background of a multicultural dystopia," in *Immigrant Acts* (84–5). But, curiously, instead of noting the absence of black people, Lowe's description casts black bodies onto the screen where there are none. "The portrait of Los Angeles as a metropolis," she writes, "congested with poor Asian, Latino, African, and Arab immigrants projects the future of the first world *as* the third world" (84, emphasis in the original); "*Blade Runner* produces a dystopic image of a decaying city," she continues, "engulfed and taken over by Asians, Africans, and Latinos" (86).

7. See Mike Davis, *City of Quartz: Excavating the Future in Los Angeles* (New York: Verso, 1990), 88, 104–5, 144; David Harvey, *The Condition of Postmodernity: An Enquiry into the Origins of Cultural Change* (Oxford, United Kingdom: Basil Blackwell, 1989), 310–11; Lee, *Orientals*, 195.

8. See Silverman, "Back to the Future"; Bukatman, *Blade Runner*, 76.

9. Hampton Fancher and David Webb Peoples, Blade Runner: *Screenplay* (Hollywood, CA: Script City, 1981), 94. All other references will be contained parenthetically in the text.

10. The face and voice are reminiscent of Mickey Rooney's portrayal of Mr. Yunioshi, the Japanese pervert in *Breakfast at Tiffany's* (Blake Edwards, 1961).

11. Philip Fisher, *Still the New World: American Literature in a Culture of Creative Destruction* (Cambridge, MA: Harvard University Press, 1999), 100.

12. In the poem, Blake's voice rages for a dismantling of the established order.

13. William M. Kolb, "*Bladerunner* Film Notes," in *Retrofitting Bladerunner: Issues in Ridley Scott's* Bladerunner *and Philip K. Dick's* Do Androids Dream of Electric Sheep? ed. Judith B. Kerman (Bowling Green, OH: Bowling Green State University Popular Press, 1991), 169. All other references will be contained parenthetically in the text.

14. Dempsey, "Review of *Blade Runner*," 35.

15. Bukatman, *Blade Runner*, 76.

16. Thomas Dixon, *The Clansman: An Historical Romance of the Ku Klux Klan* (New York: Grosset & Dunlap, 1905).

17. Michael Rogin, "'The Sword Became a Flashing Vision': D. W. Griffith's *The Birth of a Nation*," *Representations* 9, Winter (1985): 150–95; Linda Williams, "Versions of Uncle Tom: Race and Gender in American Melodrama," in *New Scholarship from BFI Research*, eds. Duncan Petrie and Colin MacCabe (Bloomington, IN: Indiana University Press, 1996), 112.

18. Williams, "Versions of Uncle Tom," 135.

19. David Savran, *Taking It Like a Man: White Masculinity, Masochism, and Contemporary American Culture* (Princeton, NJ: Princeton University Press, 1998), 4, 190–1.

20. Williams, "Versions of Uncle Tom," 135.

21. I contend that the replicants are metaphors for African American slaves. Robert G. Lee's *Orientals*, by contrast, interprets the replicants as metaphors for model minority Asians (194–6).

22. *Blade Runner* started out as a commercial flop in 1982. But since the ten years between its debut and its "Director's Cut" rerelease in 1992, the film enjoyed a remarkable "metamorphosis from theatrical flop to cult film par excellence." Paul Sammon, *Future Noir: The Making of* Blade Runner (New York: Harper Collins, 1996), 322. All other references will be contained parenthetically in the text. Shortly after its release in video format, it "became one of the most rented tapes on the market," in Bukatman (34). According to the film's producer, Michael Deeley, roughly a half-million cassettes were sold in the home video market as of late 1994, in Sammon (323). In 1983, nine years prior to its rerelease, it finished third, behind *Star Wars* (George Lucas, 1977) and *2001: A Space Odyssey* (Stanley Kubrick, 1968), in the "Most Favourite Science Fiction Film of All Time" contest at the World Science Fiction Convention, in Bukatman (36). *American Cinematographer* magazine included the film in its "Best Shot Films: 1950–1997" awards (March 1998, 130–46). Since its initial release in 1982, *Blade Runner* has also become a darling of the academy. Mike Davis' *City of Quartz: Excavating the Future in Los Angeles*, for example, includes *Blade Runner* as an important part of "a *noir* history of Los Angeles's past and future" and describes such *noir* literature and film as "some of the most acute critiques of the culture of late capitalism" (44, 18). According to Davis, *Blade Runner* is "a fantastic convergence of American 'tough-guy' realism, Weimar expressionism, and existentialized Marxism—all focused on unmasking a 'bright, guilty place' [Welles] called Los Angeles" (44, 18). At the Columbia Film Seminar in 1991, one prominent academic film critic was said to have "cited *Blade Runner* as the only current example of a canonical film from the 1980s." Elissa Marder, "*Blade Runner*'s Moving Still," *Camera Obscura*, no. 27 (1991): 106n.2. That same year marked the appearance of the first anthology devoted to the film that was published by an academic press, *Retrofitting Blade Runner: Issues in Ridley Scott's* Blade Runner *and Philip K. Dick's* Do Androids Dream of Electric Sheep? ed. Judith B. Kerman (Bowling Green, OH: Bowling Green State University Popular Press, 1991). Five years after the "Director's Cut" rerelease, a second edition of *Retrofitting* came out in 1997. Also that year, the British Film Institute gave the film a spot in its "Modern Classic" book series (Bukatman). The volume's blurb hails *Blade Runner* as "one of the most enduring and influential films of the 1980s," which "succeeds brilliantly in depicting a world at once uncannily familiar and startlingly new."

23. Raphael S. Ezekiel, *The Racist Mind: Portraits of American Neo-Nazis and Klansmen* (New York: Viking, 1995), 72.

24. Lewis R. Gordon, *Her Majesty's Other Children: Sketches of Racism from a Neocolonial Age* (New York: Rowman & Littlefield, 1997), 5.

25. See Richard Dyer, *White* (New York: Routledge, 1997).

26. Bukatman, *Blade Runner*, 391.

27. Eve Sedgwick, *Between Men: English Literature and Male Homosocial Desire* (New York: Columbia University Press, 1985).

28. Lowe, *Immigrant Acts*, 85.

29. Pauline Kael, "Review of *Blade Runner*," in *For Keeps*, ed. Pauline Kael (1982; New York: Dutton Signet, 1994), 944. All further references will be contained parenthetically in the text.

30. Richard Corliss, "Review of *Blade Runner*," *Time*, July 12, 1982, 68.

31. Herb Lightman and Richard Patterson, "*Blade Runner*: Production Design and Photography," *American Cinematographer* 63, no. 7 (1982): 723.

32. Corliss, "Review of *Blade Runner*," 68.

33. Lawrence G. Paull, "Lawrence G. Paull," in *By Design: Interviews with Film Production Designers*, ed. Vincent LoBrutto (Westport, CT: Praeger, 1992), 168.

34. Chinua Achebe makes a similar point in "An Image of Africa: Racism in Conrad's *Heart of Darkness*," in *Hopes and Impediments: Selected Essays*, 1st American edn. (New York: Doubleday, 1989), 3.

35. Dempsey, "Review of *Blade Runner*," 33.

36. Harlan Kennedy, "21st Century Nervous Breakdown: Interview with Ridley Scott," *Film Comment* 18, no. 4 (1982): 65.

37. Paull, *By Design*, 173.

38. Malcolm Gladwell, "True Colors: Hair Dye and the Hidden History of Postwar America," *The New Yorker*, March 22, 1999, 70–81.

39. Harald Kueppers, *The Basic Law of Color Theory*, trans. Roger Marcinik (1978; Woodbury, NY: Barron's Educational Series, 1982), 21.

40. Johannes Itten, *The Art of Color: The Subjective Experience and Objective Rationale of Color*, trans. Ernst van Haagen (1961; New York: Van Nostrand Reinhold Co., 1973), 35–6. All other references will be contained parenthetically in the text.

41. Michel Eugene Chevreul, *The Principles of Harmony and Contrast of Colors and Their Applications to the Arts* (1854; New York: Reinhold, 1967), 56.

42. Paull, *By Design*, 172.

43. We know that it is some sort of liquor because by that point we have seen Deckard buy the same liquor more than once. But even though the liquor looks like vodka, the film identifies it as "Tsing Tao," a brand of Chinese beer.

44. See "Deckard a Replicant?" in Sammon, *Future Noir*, 359–64; "Is Deckard a Replicant?" in Bukatman, *Blade Runner*, 80–3.

45. Chevreul, *Principles of Harmony*, 67 (emphasis in the original).

6   "*Domo Arigato, Mr. Roboto*": *The Matrix* (1999) and the Virtual Asian

1. Larry Wachowski and Andy Wachowski, The Matrix: *The Shooting Script* (New York: Newmarket Press, 2001), vii. All other references will be contained parenthetically in the text.

2. *Making* The Matrix (Josh Oreck, 1999). All other references will be contained parenthetically in the text. The Japanese part of the chapter's title comes from the Styx 1983 rock song "Mr. Roboto" from the "Kilroy Was Here" album.

3. Devin Gordon, "The Matrix Makers," *Newsweek*, December 30, 2002, 84.

4. Larry Wachowski and Andy Wachowski, *The Art of* The Matrix (New York: Newmarket Press, 2000) 14–15, 36–7. All other references will be contained parenthetically in the text.

5. Larry Wachowski and Andy Wachowski, The Matrix: *The Shooting Script* (New York: Newmarket Press, 2001), 10. All other references will be contained parenthetically in the text.

6. The film leaves a crucial point unexplained. Since most humans lie asleep and imprisoned, the computers have humans under control regardless of whether or not there is a virtual reality program. Why do the machines need to have a matrix in the first place?

7. Stuart Klawans, "Medium Cool," *Nation*, June 9, 2003, 43.

8. Gordon, "Matrix Makers," 82. "Dojo" is a Japanese word whereas kung fu and Bruce Lee are Chinese figures.

9. David Edelstein, "Bullet Time Again: The Wachowskis Reload," *New York Times*, May 11, 2003, 1.

10. The Matrix *Revisited* (Josh Oreck, 2001). All other references will be contained parenthetically in the text.

11. Gordon, "Matrix Makers," 83.

12. I thank Daniel Youd for the translation.

13. In order to maintain continuity, another Caucasian actor, Radames Pera, played the young Chinese monk in the show's flashback sequences. The fair-haired and blue-eyed Chris Potter played Kwai Chang's son, Peter Cain, in the sequel series, *Kung Fu: The Legend Continues* (1993–1997).

14. Meaghan Morris, "Learning from Bruce Lee: Pedagogy and Political Correctness in Martial Arts Cinema," in *Keyframes: Popular Cinema and Cultural Studies*, eds. Matthew Tinkcom and Amy Villarejo (New York: Routledge, 2001), 183. In a 1992 *Black Belt Magazine* interview, Jim Kelly echoes Morris' claim. "The *Kung Fu* series was written for him." Quoted in Prashad, *Everybody Was Kung Fu*, 129.

15. Stuart M. Kaminsky, "Kung Fu Film as Ghetto Myth," in *Movies as Artifacts: Cultural Criticism of Popular Film*, ed. Michael T. Marsden (Chicago, IL: Nelson-Hall, 1982), 138.

16. Morris, "Learning from Bruce Lee," 183.

17. Richard Meyers, *From Bruce Lee to the Ninjas: Martial Arts Movies* (New York: Carol Publishing Group, 1991), 221.

18. "Kung Fu: A Sweet Poison," *Getting Together*, October 22–November 4 (1972): 4. Quoted in Prashad, *Everybody Was Kung Fu*, 128.

19. Prashad, *Everybody Was Kung Fu*, 129.

20. Yvonne Tasker, "Fists of Fury: Discourses of Race and Masculinity in the Martial Arts Cinema," in *Race and the Subject of Masculinities*, eds. Harry

Stecopoulos and Michael Uebel (Durham, NC: Duke University Press, 1997), 324.

21. Hsin Hsin, "Bruce's Opinion on Kung Fu, Movies, Love and Life," in *Words of the Dragon: Interviews, 1958–1973*, ed. John Little (Boston, MA: Charles E. Tuttle, 1997), 128.

22. For a short account of whites in blackface see, Donald Bogle, *Toms, Coons, Mulattoes, Mammies and Bucks: An Interpretive History of Blacks in American Films* (New York: Viking, 1973), 150.

23. The reference is *Bill and Ted's Excellent Adventure* (Stephen Herek, 1989).

24. Richard I. Kirkland, "What If Japan Triumphs?" *Fortune*, May 18, 1992, 61. All other references will be contained parenthetically in the text.

25. In *Apocalypse Now*, Laurence Fishburne plays a young African American soldier killed by Southeast Asian communists.

26. Because they imply that "Asians are 'all alike' and conform to 'types,'" Lisa Lowe characterizes texts that represent "Asians as a homogenous group" as "racist discourse," in *Immigrant Act*s (71).

27. U.S. Pacific Command and U.S. Navy, Pacific Fleet and Pacific Ocean Areas, *Guide to Japan*, Cincpac-Cincpoa Bulletin, no. 209–45 (Washington, DC: Cincpac-Cincpoa, 1945), 40. All other references will be contained parenthetically in the text.

28. Gordon, "Matrix Makers," 84.

29. Ibid.

30. Michael DeAngelis, *Gay Fandom and Crossover Stardom: James Dean, Mel Gibson, and Keanu Reeves* (Durham, NC: Duke University Press, 2001), 199.

31. David Ansen, "Goodbye, Airhead," *Newsweek*, June 13, 1994, 52. Here, "English" means white. The logic of Ansen's characterization, which is typical of the reporting on Reeves, makes a nonwhite British subject impossible.

32. "The 50 Most Beautiful People in the World," *People*, May 8, 1995, 66.

33. Chris Heath, "The Quiet Man: The Riddle of Keanu Reeves," *Rolling Stone*, August 31, 2000, 50.

34. Tom Green, "Keanu Reeves' Artistic Adventures," *USA Today*, July 18, 1991, D1.

35. Angela Holden, "Blissed Out, Switched on Perfect Boy," *Independent*, September 19, 1994, 22.

36. Sheila Johnston, *Keanu* (London: Pan, 1997), 154.

37. Elvis Mitchell, "An Idealized World and a Troubled Hero," *New York Times*, May 14, 2003, E1.

38. Tom Green, "Built for 'Speed': Keanu Reeves, Catching a Bus to the Big Time," *USA Today*, June 9, 1994, D1.

39. David Ansen, "Goodbye, Airhead," 52.

40. Carrie Rickey, "Call It the Cult of Keanu Reeves: Toronto Actor Is Speeding Away from Adolescence at a Record Clip," *Toronto Star*, June 13, 1994, F4.

41. Carmel Giarratana, "The Keanu Effect: Stardom and the Landscape of the Acting Body," in *Stars in Our Eyes: The Star Phenomenon in the*

Contemporary Era, eds. Angela Ndalianis and Charlotte Henry (Westport, CN: Praeger, 2002), 69.

42. DeAngelis, *Gay Fandom*, 200.

43. Carrie Rickey, "The Importance of Being Keanu: The Heartthrob of *Speed* Talks about His Transformation from Airhead to Man of Action," *Chicago Tribune*, June 26, 1994, Arts section, 16.

44. Rickey, "Call It."

45. "Keanu Reeves Home Page" <http://www.sitevip.net/keanu_reeves/home. htm>; "The Biography Channel-Keanu Reeves Biography" <http://www. thebiographychannel.co.uk/biography_quotes/795:485/Keanu_Reeves. htm> (March 7, 2009).

46. Rickey, "Call It."

47. Holden, "Blissed Out," 22.

48. Ansen, "Goodbye, Airhead," 52.

49. See Jeff Adachi's documentary about Asian men in the Hollywood industry, *The Slanted Screen* (2006).

50. See Gina Marchetti's treatment of *The Cheat* in her first-rate *Romance*, 10–27.

51. "Chow Yun-Fat Wants to Take the Lead in U.S. Films," *Reuters News Service*, May 23, 2007 <http://www.reuters.com/article/entertainmentNews/ idUSN1817506520070523> (March 8, 2009).

52. Charles Taylor, "Black and White and Taboo All Over," *Salon.com*, February 14, 2000 <http://dir.salon.com/ent/feature/2000/02/14/interracial_movies/ index.html> (March 8, 2009).

53. David Bassom, *Keanu Reeves: An Illustrated Story* (London: Hamlyn, 1996), 74.

54. Natasha Stoynoff and Karen Brailsford, "A Most Excellent Enigma," *People*, July 11, 1994, 49.

55. Heath, "Quiet Man," 50.

56. The dialogue is from the episode, "Rescue Me," which aired on November 23, 2000.

57. See Jacquelyn Dowd Hall's account of how white men lynched black men to control white women, "'The Mind That Burns in Each Body': Women, Rape, and Racial Violence" in *Powers of Desire: The Politics of Sexuality*, ed. Ann Snitow (New York: Monthly Press, 1983), 328–49.

58. Williams, *Playing*, xiv, 5, 252.

59. Lisa Nakamura, "Race in the Construct, or the Construction of Race: New Media and Old Identities in *The Matrix*," in *Domain Error: Cyberfeminist Practices*, eds. Maria Fernandez, Faith Wilding, and Michelle Wright (New York: Autonomedia, 2002), 66.

60. David Palumbo-Liu, "Los Angeles, Asians, and Perverse Ventriloquisms: On the Functions of Asian America in the Recent American Imaginary," *Public Culture* 6, no. 2 (1994): 365. All other references will be contained parenthetically in the text.

61. Gina Marchetti, "Action Adventure as Ideology," in *Cultural Politics in Contemporary America*, eds. Ian Angus and Sut Jhally (New York: Routledge, 1989), 187.

Epilogue

1. Stanford M. Lyman, "The 'Yellow Peril' Mystique: Origins and Vicissitudes of a Racist Discourse." *International Journal of Politics, Culture and Society* 13, no. 4 (2000): 699.
2. Dan Janison and Curtis L. Taylor, "America's Ordeal: Vallone Cites Pearl Harbor as Japan Presents Check," *Newsday*, September 22, 2001, A35.
3. Quoted in Emily S. Rosenberg, *A Date Which Will Live: Pearl Harbor in American Memory* (Durham, NC: Duke University Press, 2003), 182.
4. David E. Rosenbaum, "U.S. Has Received $50 Billion in Pledges for War," *New York Times*, February 11, 1991, A13.
5. Masahiro Sato, "Govt Hastens Allocations of Aid to Iraq," *Daily Yomiuri*, January 16, 2004, 3.
6. Ben Fritz and John Horn, "Reel China: Hollywood Tries to Stay on China's Good Side," *Los Angeles Times*, March 16, 2011, <http://www.latimes.com/entertainment/news/la-et-china-red-dawn-20110316,0,995726.story> (March 31, 2012).

Selected Bibliography

Ancheta, Angelo N. *Race, Rights, and the Asian American Experience*. New Brunswick, NJ: Rutgers University Press, 1998.

Apel, Dora. *Imagery of Lynching: Black Men, White Women, and the Mob*. New Brunswick, NJ: Rutgers University Press, 2004.

Baldwin, James. "The Uses of the Blues." In *A World Enclosed: Tragedy*, edited by W. T. Jewkes, 244–57. 1963; New York: Harcourt Brace Jovanovich, 1973.

Banton, Michael. *The Idea of Race*. Boulder, CO: Westview, 1977.

Basinger, Jeanine. *The World War II Combat Film: Anatomy of a Genre*. 1986; Middletown, CT: Wesleyan University Press, 2003.

Bingham, Howard L. and Max Wallace. *Muhammad Ali's Greatest Fight: Cassius Clay vs. the United States of America*. New York: M. Evans & Company, 2000.

Blum, John Morton. *V Was for Victory: Politics and American Culture during World War II*. New York: Harcourt Brace Jovanovich, 1976.

Bly, Robert. *Iron John: A Book about Men*. Reading, MA: Addison-Wesley, 1990.

Bogle, Donald. *Toms, Coons, Mulattoes, Mammies and Bucks: An Interpretive History of Blacks in American Films*. New York: Viking, 1973.

Boone, Joseph. "Male Independence and the American Quest Genre: Hidden Sexual Politics in the All-Male Worlds of Melville, Twain, and London." In *Gender Studies: New Directions in Feminist Criticism*, edited by Judith Spector, 187–217. Bowling Green, OH: Bowling Green University Popular Press, 1986.

Bukatman, Scott. *Blade Runner*. BFI Modern Classics. London: British Film Institute, 1997.

Cayton, Horace R. *Long Old Road*. New York: Trident, 1965.

Cheng, Lucie and Philip Q. Yang. "The 'Model Minority' Deconstructed." In *Contemporary Asian America: A Multidisciplinary Reader*, edited by Min Zhou and James V. Gatewood, 459–82. New York: New York University Press, 2000.

Chin, Frank, Jeffery Paul Chan, Lawson Fusao Inada, and Shawn Wong, eds. *Aiiieeeee! An Anthology of Asian American Writers*. New York: Penguin/Mentor, 1991; rpt. 1974.

Clarfield, Gerard H. and William M. Wiecek. *Nuclear America: Military and Civilian Nuclear Power in the United States 1940–1980*. New York: Harper & Row, 1984.

Cook, David A. *Lost Illusions: American Cinema in the Shadow of Watergate and Vietnam, 1970–1979*. History of the American Cinema, vol. 9. Berkeley, CA: University of California Press, 2000.

Crichton, Michael. *Rising Sun*. New York: Ballantine, 1992.

Cripps, Thomas. "Racial Ambiguities in American Propaganda Movies." In *Film and Radio Propaganda in World War II*, edited by K. R. M. Short, 125–45. Knoxville, TN: University of Tennessee Press, 1983.

Cripps, Thomas and David Culbert. "The Negro Soldier: Film Propaganda in Black and White." *American Quarterly* 31, no. 5 (1979): 616–40.

Dalfiume, Richard M. *Desegregation of the U.S. Armed Forces: Fighting on Two Fronts, 1939–1953*. Columbia, MO: University of Missouri Press, 1969.

Davis, Mike. *City of Quartz: Excavating the Future in Los Angeles*. New York: Verso, 1990.

DeAngelis, Michael. *Gay Fandom and Crossover Stardom: James Dean, Mel Gibson, and Keanu Reeves*. Durham, NC: Duke University Press, 2001.

Desser, David. "The Kung Fu Craze: Hong Kong Cinema's First American Reception." In *The Cinema of Hong Kong*, edited by Poshek Fu and David Desser, 19–43. New York: Cambridge University Press, 2000.

Dixon, Thomas. *The Clansman: An Historical Romance of the Ku Klux Klan*. New York: Grosset & Dunlap, 1905.

Doherty, Thomas Patrick. *Projections of War: Hollywood, American Culture, and World War II*. New York: Columbia University Press, 1993.

Donalson, Melvin. *Masculinity in the Interracial Buddy Film*. Jefferson, NC: McFarland, 2006.

Dower, John W. *War without Mercy: Race and Power in the Pacific War*. New York: Pantheon, 1986.

Dray, Philip. *At the Hands of Persons Unknown: The Lynching of Black America*. New York: Random House, 2002.

Dunn, Stephane. *"Bad Bitches" and Sassy Supermamas: Black Power Action Films*. Chicago, IL: University of Illinois Press, 2008.

Dyer, Richard. "The Role of Stereotypes." In *Media Studies: A Reader*, edited by Paul Marris and Sue Thornham, 245–51. New York: New York University Press, 2000.

Eberwein, Robert. " 'As a Mother Cuddles a Child': Sexuality and Masculinity in World War II Combat Films." In *Masculinity: Bodies, Movies, Culture*, edited by Peter Lehman, 149–66. New York: Routledge, 2001.

Ezekiel, Raphael S. *The Racist Mind: Portraits of American Neo-Nazis and Klansmen*. New York: Viking, 1995.

Fallows, James. *More Like Us: Making America Great Again*. Boston, MA: Houghton Mifflin, 1989.

Fancher, Hampton and David Webb Peoples. Blade Runner: *Screenplay*. Hollywood, CA: Script City, 1981.

Fiedler, Leslie. "Come Back to the Raft Ag'in, Huck Honey!" In *Collected Essays of Leslie Fiedler*, vol. 1, 142–51. New York: Stein and Day, 1971.

Fisher, Philip. *Still the New World: American Literature in a Culture of Creative Destruction*. Cambridge, MA: Harvard University Press, 1999.

Fisher, Robert. *Let the People Decide: Neighborhood Organizing in America*. Boston, MA: Twayne, 1984.

Fiske, John. *Media Matters: Everyday Culture and Political Change*. Minneapolis, MN: University of Minnesota Press, 1994.

Foucault, Michel. *The Archeology of Knowledge*. Translated by A. M. Sheridan Smith. New York: Pantheon, 1972.

Foucault, Michel. "The Subject and Power." *Critical Inquiry* 8, no. 4 (1982): 777–95.

Foucault, Michel. "Truth and Power." In *Power/Knowledge: Selected Interviews and Other Writings 1972–1977*, edited by Colin Gordon. New York: Pantheon, 1980.

Fuchs, Cynthia. "The Buddy Politic." In *Screening the Male: Exploring Masculinities in Hollywood*, edited by Steven Cohan, 194–210. New York: Routledge, 1993.

Girard, René. "Mimesis and Violence." In *The Girard Reader*, edited by James G. Williams, 9–19. New York: Crossroad, 1996.

Girard, René. *The Scapegoat*. Translated by Yvonne Freccero. Baltimore, MD: Johns Hopkins University Press, 1986.

Girard, René. *Violence and the Sacred*. Translated by Patrick Gregory. Baltimore, MD: Johns Hopkins University Press, 1977.

Gordon, Lewis R. *Her Majesty's Other Children: Sketches of Racism from a Neocolonial Age*. New York: Rowman & Littlefield, 1997.

Grant, William R. *Post-Soul Black Cinema: Discontinuities, Innovations, and Breakpoints, 1970–1995*. New York: Routledge, 2004.

Guerrero, Edward. *Framing Blackness: The African American Image in Film*. Philadelphia, PA: Temple University Press, 1993.

Hale, Grace Elizabeth. *Making Whiteness: The Culture of Segregation in the South, 1890–1940*. New York: Pantheon, 1998.

Hall, Jacquelyn Dowd. "'The Mind That Burns in Each Body': Women, Rape, and Racial Violence." In *Powers of Desire: The Politics of Sexuality*, edited by Ann Snitow, 328–49. New York: Monthly Press, 1983.

Hall, Stuart. "The Whites of Their Eyes: Racist Ideologies and the Media." In *Silver Linings: Some Strategies for the Eighties*, edited by George Bridges, 28–52. London: Lawrence & Wishart, 1981.

Harrington, Michael. *The Other America: Poverty in the United States*. New York: Macmillan, 1962.

Harris, Keith M. *Boys, Boyz, Bois: An Ethics of Black Masculinity in Film and Popular Media*. New York: Routledge, 2006.

Harvey, David. *The Condition of Postmodernity: An Enquiry into the Origins of Cultural Change*. Oxford, United Kingdom: Basil Blackwell, 1989.

Hsin, Hsin. "Bruce's Opinion on Kung Fu, Movies, Love and Life." In *Words of the Dragon: Interviews, 1958–1973*, edited by John Little, 117–21. Boston, MA: Charles E. Tuttle, 1997.

James, Allen, ed. *Without Sanctuary: Lynching Photography in America*. Santa Fe, NM: Twin Palms Publishers, 2000.

Kaminsky, Stuart M. "Kung Fu Film as Ghetto Myth." In *Movies as Artifacts: Cultural Criticism of Popular Film*, edited by Michael T. Marsden, 137–44. Chicago, IL: Nelson-Hall, 1982.

Kaufman, Philip. Rising Sun: *Screenplay*. Hollywood, CA: Script City, 1992.

Kerman, Judith B., ed. *Retrofitting* Bladerunner: *Issues in Ridley Scott's* Bladerunner *and Philip K. Dick's* Do Androids Dream of Electric Sheep? Bowling Green, OH: Bowling Green State University Popular Press, 1991.

Kibria, Nazil. "The Contested Meanings of 'Asian American': Racial Dilemmas in the Contemporary US." *Ethnic and Racial Studies* 21, no. 5 (1998): 939–58.

Kim, Claire Jean. *Bitter Fruit: The Politics of Black-Korean Conflict in New York City*. New Haven, CT: Yale University Press, 2000.

Kimmel, Michael S. "Masculinity as Homophobia: Fear, Shame, and Silence in the Construction of Gender Identity." In *Readings for Diversity and Social Justice: An Anthology on Racism, Sexism, Anti-Semitism, Heterosexism, Classism, and Ableism*, edited by Maurianne Adams, 213–19. New York: Routledge, 2000.

Koppes, Clayton R. and Gregory D. Black. "Blacks, Loyalty, and Motion-Picture Propaganda in World War II." *Journal of American History* 73, no. 2 (1986): 383–406.

Koppes, Clayton R. and Gregory D. Black. *Hollywood Goes to War: How Politics, Profits, and Propaganda Shaped World War II Movies*. Berkeley, CA: University of California Press, 1987.

Leab, Daniel J. *From Sambo to Superspade: The Black Experience in Motion Pictures*. Boston, MA: Houghton Mifflin, 1975.

Lee, Robert G. *Orientals: Asian Americans in Popular Culture*. Philadelphia, PA: Temple University Press, 1999.

Lee, Stacey J. *Unraveling The "Model Minority" Stereotype: Listening to Asian American Youth*. New York: Teachers College Press, 1996.

Lev, Peter. *Transforming the Screen, 1950–1959*. Edited by Charles Harpole. History of the American Cinema, vol. 7. New York: Charles Scribner's Sons, 2003.

Lévi-Strauss, Claude. *The Elementary Structures of Kinship*. Revised edn. Boston, MA: Beacon Press, 1969.

Lightman, Herb. "*Blade Runner*: Special Photographic Effects, Excerpts from an Interview with David Dryer." *American Cinematographer* 63, no. 7 (1982): 692–3, 725–32.

Lightman, Herb and Richard Patterson. "*Blade Runner*: Production Design and Photography." *American Cinematographer* 63, no. 7 (1982): 684–91, 715–25.

Lingeman, Richard R. *Don't You Know There's a War On? The American Home Front, 1941–1945*. New York: G. P. Putnam's Sons, 1970.

Locke, Brian. "Here Comes the Judge: The Dancing Itos and the Televisual Construction of the Enemy Asian Male." In *Living Color: Race and Television in the United States*, edited by Sasha Torres, 239–53. Durham, NC: Duke University Press, 1998.

Locke, Brian. "'Top Dog,' 'Black Threat,' and 'Japanese Cats': The Impact of the White-Black Binary on Asian American Identity." *Radical Philosophy Review* 1, no. 2 (1998): 98–125.

Londoner, David J. "The Changing Economics of Entertainment." In *The American Film Industry*, edited by Tino Balio, 603–30. Madison, WI: University of Wisconsin Press, 1985.

Lowe, Lisa. *Immigrant Acts: On Asian American Cultural Politics*. Durham, NC: Duke University Press, 1996.

Major, Wade. "Hollywood's Asian Strategy." *Transpacific*, March 1997, 24–35.

Marchetti, Gina. "Action Adventure as Ideology." In *Cultural Politics in Contemporary America*, edited by Ian Angus and Sut Jhally, 182–97. New York: Routledge, 1989.

Marchetti, Gina. "Jackie Chan and the Black Connection." In *Keyframes: Popular Cinema and Cultural Studies*, edited by Matthew Tinkcom and Amy Villarejo, 137–58. New York: Routledge, 2001.

Marchetti, Gina. *Romance and the "Yellow Peril": Race, Sex, and Discursive Strategies in Hollywood Fiction*. Berkeley, CA: University of California Press, 1993.

Mason, Clifford. "Why Does White America Love Sidney Poitier So?" *New York Times*, November 10, 1967.

McGuire, Phillip, ed. *Taps for a Jim Crow Army: Letters from Black Soldiers in World War II*. Lexington, KY: University Press of Kentucky, 1993.

Mendelberg, Tali. *The Race Card: Campaign Strategy, Implicit Messages, and the Norm of Equality*. Princeton, NJ: Princeton University Press, 2001.

Meyers, Richard. *From Bruce Lee to the Ninjas: Martial Arts Movies*. New York: Carol Publishing Group, 1991.

Miller, S. M. and Martin Rein. "Participation, Poverty and Administration." *Public Administration Review* 29, no. 1 (1969): 15–25.

Morella, Joe, Edward Z. Epstein, and John Griggs. *The Films of World War II*. Secaucus, NJ: Citadel Press, 1973.

Morone, James A. *Democratic Wish: Popular Participation and the Limits of American Government*. New York: Basic Books, 1990.

Morris, Meaghan. "Learning from Bruce Lee: Pedagogy and Political Correctness in Martial Arts Cinema." In *Keyframes: Popular Cinema and Cultural Studies*, edited by Matthew Tinkcom and Amy Villarejo, 171–86. New York: Routledge, 2001.

Morrison, Toni. *Playing in the Dark: Whiteness and the Literary Imagination*. Cambridge, MA: Harvard University Press, 1992.

Mullen, Bill V. *Afro-Orientalism*. Minneaplois, MN: University of Minnesota Press, 2004.

Myrdal, Gunnar. *An American Dilemma: The Negro Problem and Modern Democracy*. New York: McGraw-Hill, 1964; rpt. 1944.

Nakamura, Lisa. "Race in the Construct, or the Construction of Race: New Media and Old Identities in *The Matrix*." In *Domain Error: Cyberfeminist Practices*, edited by Maria Fernandez, Faith Wilding, and Michelle Wright, 63–78. New York: Autonomedia, 2002.

Neal, Larry. "Beware of the Tar Baby." *New York Times*, August 3, 1969.

Nguyen, Viet Thanh. *Race and Resistance: Literature and Politics in Asian America*. New York: Oxford University Press, 2002.

Odum, Howard W. *Race and Rumors of Race: Challenge to American Crisis*. Chapel Hill, NC: University of North Carolina Press, 1943.

Okihiro, Gary Y. "Commentary." In *Locating American Studies: The Evolution of a Discipline*, edited by Lucy Maddox, 440–2. Baltimore, MD: Johns Hopkins University Press, 1999.

Okihiro, Gary Y. *Margins and Mainstreams: Asians in American History and Culture*. Seattle, WA: University of Washington Press, 1994.

Oliver, Kendrick. "Coming to Terms with the Past: My Lai." *History Today* 56, no. 2 (2006): 37–9.

Olson, James S. and Randy Roberts, eds. *My Lai: A Brief History with Documents*. Boston, MA: Bedford Books, 1997.

Omi, Michael and Howard Winant. *Racial Formation in the United States from the 1960s to the 1990s*. 2nd edn. New York: Routledge, 1994.

Ongiri, Amy Abugo. " 'He Wanted to Be Just Like Bruce Lee': African Americans, Kung Fu Theater and Cultural Exchange at the Margins." *Journal of Asian American Studies* 5, no. 1 (2002): 31–40.

Osajima, Keith. "Asian Americans as the Model Minority: An Analysis of the Popular Press Image in the 1960s and 1980s." In *Reflections on Shattered Windows: Promises and Prospects for Asian American Studies*, edited by Gary Y. Okihiro, Shirley Hune, Arthur A. Hansen, and John M. Lui, 165–74. Pullman, WA: Washington State University Press, 1988.

Palumbo-Liu, David. "Los Angeles, Asians, and Perverse Ventriloquisms: On the Functions of Asian America in the Recent American Imaginary." *Public Culture* 6, no. 2 (1994): 365–81

Pauley, Garth E. *The Modern Presidency and Civil Rights: Rhetoric on Race from Roosevelt to Nixon*. College Station, TX: Texas A&M University Press, 2001.

Peary, Danny. "Directing *Alien* and *Blade Runner*: An Interview with Ridley Scott." In *Omni's Screen Flights, Screen Fantasies: The Future according to Science Fiction Cinema*, edited by Danny Peary, 293–302. Garden City, NY: Doubleday, 1984.

Pfeffer, Paula F. *A. Philip Randolph, Pioneer of the Civil Rights Movement*. Baton Rouge, LA: Louisiana State University Press, 1990.

Polenberg, Richard. *War and Society: The United States, 1941–1945*. New York: Lippincott, 1972.

Prashad, Vijay. *Everybody Was Kung Fu Fighting: Afro-Asian Connections and the Myth of Cultural Purity*. Boston, MA: Beacon, 2001.

Prashad, Vijay. *The Karma of Brown Folk*. Minneapolis, MN: University of Minnesota Press, 2000.

Prince, Stephen. *Classical Film Violence: Designing and Regulating Brutality in Hollywood Cinema, 1930–1968*. New Brunswick, NJ: Rutgers University Press, 2003.

Rice, Anne P., ed. *Witnessing Lynching: American Writers Respond*. New Brunswick, NJ: Rutgers University Press, 2003.

Rogin, Michael. "'The Sword Became a Flashing Vision': D. W. Griffith's *The Birth of a Nation*." *Representations* 9, Winter (1985): 150–95.

Rohmer, Sax. *The Insidious Dr. Fu-Manchu: Being a Somewhat Detailed Account of the Amazing Adventures of Nayland Smith in his Trailing of the Sinister Chinaman*. New York: McKinlay, Stone & Mackenzie, 1913.

Rosenberg, Emily S. *A Date Which Will Live: Pearl Harbor in American Memory*. Durham, NC: Duke University Press, 2003.

Said, Edward W. *Orientalism*. New York: Vintage Books, 1979.

Sammon, Paul M. *Future Noir: The Making of* Blade Runner. New York: Harper Collins, 1996.

Savran, David. *Taking It Like a Man: White Masculinity, Masochism, and Contemporary American Culture*. Princeton, NJ: Princeton University Press, 1998.

Schary, Dore. *Heyday: An Autobiography*. Boston, MA: Little, Brown, 1979.

Schelling, Thomas C. *Arms and Influence*. Westport, CT: Greenwood, 1976; rpt. 1966.

Sedgwick, Eve. *Between Men: English Literature and Male Homosocial Desire*. New York: Columbia University Press, 1985.

Shepard, Sam. *Buried Child*. New York: Urizen Books, 1979.

Shim, Doobo. "From Yellow Peril through Model Minority to Renewed Yellow Peril." *Journal of Communication Inquiry* 22, no. 4 (1998): 385–409.

Shimakawa, Karen. *National Abjection: The Asian American Body Onstage*. Durham, NC: Duke University Press, 2002.

Silverman, Kaja. "Back to the Future." *Camera Obscura*, no. 27 (1991): 109–32.

Simpson, Caroline Chung. *An Absent Presence: Japanese Americans in Postwar American Culture, 1945–1960*. Durham, NC: Duke University Press, 2001.

Sims, Yvonne D. *Women of Blaxploitation*. Jefferson, NC: McFarland, 2006.

Sitkoff, Harvard. "Racial Militancy and Interracial Violence in the Second World War." *Journal of American History* 58, no. 3 (1971): 661–81.

Smith, Shawn Michelle. *Photography on the Color Line: W. E. B. Du Bois, Race, and Visual Culture*. Durham, NC: Duke University Press, 2004.

Stowe, Harriet Beecher. *Uncle Tom's Cabin: Or, Life among the Lowly*. New York: Signet Classic/Penguin, 1998; rpt. 1852.

Strange, John. "Citizen Participation in Community Action and Model Cities Programs." *Public Administration Review* 32, Special Issue (1972): 655–69.

Suid, Lawrence H. *Guts and Glory: The Making of the American Military Image in Film*. Lexington, KY: University Press of Kentucky, 2002.

Suzuki, Bob H. "Education and the Socialization of Asian Americans: A Revisionist Analysis of the 'Model Minority' Thesis." *Amerasia Journal* 4, no. 2 (1977): 23–51

Takagi, Dana. *The Retreat from Race: Asian-American Admissions and Racial Politics*. New Brunswick, NJ: Rutgers University Press, 1992.

Takaki, Ronald. *A Different Mirror: A History of Multicultural America*. Boston, MA: Little, Brown, 1993.

Takaki, Ronald. *Strangers from a Different Shore: A History of Asian Americans.* New York: Penguin, 1989.

Tasker, Yvonne. "Fists of Fury: Discourses of Race and Masculinity in the Martial Arts Cinema." In *Race and the Subject of Masculinities*, edited by Harry Stecopoulos and Michael Uebel, 315–36. Durham, NC: Duke University Press, 1997.

Tasker, Yvonne. *Spectacular Bodies, Gender, Genre and the Action Cinema.* New York: Routledge, 1993.

Tocqueville, Alexis de. *Democracy in America.* Edited by J. P. Mayer. New York: Anchor, 1969.

Wachowski, Larry and Andy Wachowski. *The Art of* The Matrix. New York: Newmarket Press, 2000.

Wachowski, Larry and Andy Wachowski. The Matrix: *The Shooting Script.* New York: Newmarket Press, 2001.

Walker, Alexander. *Stardom: The Hollywood Phenomenon.* New York: Stein and Day, 1970.

White, Walter. *A Man Called White.* New York: Arno, 1969.

White, Walter. *Rope and Faggot.* New York: Arno, 1969.

Wiegman, Robyn. *American Anatomies: Theorizing Race and Gender.* Durham, NC: Duke University Press, 1995.

Williams, Linda. *Playing the Race Card: Melodramas of Black and White from Uncle Tom to O.J. Simpson.* Princeton, NJ: Princeton University Press, 2001.

Williams, Linda. "Versions of Uncle Tom: Race and Gender in American Melodrama." In *New Scholarship from BFI Research*, edited by Duncan Petrie and Colin MacCabe, 111–39. Bloomington, IN: Indiana University Press, 1996.

Willis, Sharon. *High Contrast: Race and Gender in Contemporary Hollywood Film.* Durham, NC: Duke University Press, 1997.

Winters, Kari J. *Subjects of Slavery, Agents of Change: Women and Power in Gothic Novels and Slave Narratives, 1790–1865.* Athens, GA: University of Georgia Press, 1992.

Wood, Amy Louise. "Lynching Photography and the 'Black Beast Rapist' in the Southern White Masculine Imagination." In *Masculinity: Bodies, Movies, Culture*, edited by Peter Lehman, 193–211. New York: Routledge, 2001.

Wood, Robin. *Hollywood from Vietnam to Reagan.* New York: Columbia University Press, 1986.

Woodman, Brian J. "A Hollywood War of Wills: Cinematic Representation of Vietnamese Super-Soldiers and America's Defeat in the War." *Journal of Film and Video* 55, no. 2–3 (2003): 44–58.

Wright, Richard. *12 Million Black Voices: A Folk History of the Negro in the United States.* New York: Arno, 1969; rpt. 1941.

Wright, Richard. *Native Son.* New York: Harper & Row, 1940.

Wynn, Neil A. *The Afro-American and the Second World War.* Revised edn. New York: Holmes & Meier, 1993.

X, Malcolm. *Malcolm X Speaks: Selected Speeches and Statements.* New York: Merit, 1965.

Yarmolinsky, Adam. "Beginnings of OEO." In *On Fighting Poverty*, edited by James Sundquist, 34–51. New York: Basic Books, 1969.

Yoshihara, Mari. *Embracing the East: White Women and American Orientalism.* New York: Oxford University Press, 2003.

Zinn, Howard. *A People's History of the United States.* New York: Harper & Row, 1980.

Zizek, Slavoj. "Eastern Europe's *Republics of Gilead*." *New Left Review*, no. 183 (1990): 50–62.

Film and Television Index

24 (Fox, 2001–2010)
48 Hours (Walter Hill, 1982)
2001: A Space Odyssey (Stanley Kubrick, 1968)
A Very Harold & Kumar 3D Christmas (Todd Strauss-Schulson, 2011)
Absolute Power (Clint Eastwood, 1997)
Action in the North Atlantic (Lloyd Bacon, 1943)
Air Force (Howard Hawks, 1943)
Akira (Katsuhiro Ôtomo, 1988)
Alice (Woody Allen, 1990)
All-American Girl (ABC, 1994–1995)
All the Young Men (Hall Bartlett, 1960)
Ally McBeal (Fox, 1997–2002)
Anna and the King (Andy Tennant, 1999)
Awake (NBC, 2012)
Baad Asssss Cinema (Isaac Julien, 2002)
Ballad of Little Jo (Maggie Greenwald, 1993)
Bataan (Tay Garnett, 1943)
Beverly Hills Cop (Martin Brest, 1984)
Bill and Ted's Excellent Adventure (Stephen Herek, 1989)
Birth of a Nation (D. W. Griffith, 1915)
Black Belt Jones (Robert Clouse, 1974)
Black Caesar (Larry Cohen, 1973)
Black Dragon (Chin-Ku Lu, 1974)
Black Dragon's Revenge (Chin-Ku Lu, 1975)
Black Gunn (Robert Hartford-Davis, 1972)
Black Mama, White Mama (Eddie Romero, 1973)
Black Samurai (Al Adamson, 1977)
Black Six (Matt Cimber, 1974)
Blade Runner (Ridley Scott, 1982, 1992, and 2007)
Bone Collector, The (Phillip Noyce, 1999)
Breakfast at Tiffany's (Blake Edwards, 1961)
Brotherhood of Death (Bill Berry, 1976)
Charlie Chan Carries On (Hamilton MacFadden, 1931)
Charlie Chan on Broadway (Eugene Forde, 1937)
Cheat, The (Cecil B. DeMille, 1915)

General Index